THE GREAT IRISH

THE GREAT IRISH REBELLION OF 1798

Edited by
CATHAL PÓIRTÉIR

THE THOMAS DAVIS LECTURE SERIES
General Editor: Michael Littleton

Published in association with
RADIO TELEFÍS ÉIREANN

ᗰERCIER PRESS

IRISH AMERICAN BOOK COMPANY (IABC)
BOULDER, COLORADO

MERCIER PRESS
PO Box 5, 5 French Church Street, Cork
16 Hume Street, Dublin 2

Trade enquiries to CMD DISTRIBUTION,
55a Spruce Avenue, Stillorgan Industrial Park, Blackrock, Dublin

Published in the US and Canada by the
IRISH AMERICAN BOOK COMPANY
6309 Monarch Park Place, Niwot, Colorado, 80503
Tel: (303) 652 2710, (800) 452-7115
Fax: (303) 652 2689, (800) 401-9705

ISBN 185635 226 9

10 9 8 7 6 5 4 3 2 1

Printed in Ireland by Colour Books Ltd.

CONTENTS

PREFACE

THE TWO HUNDREDTH ANNIVERSARY of the 1798 Rebellion in Ireland affords us an opportunity to revisit events which have left a mark on Irish history at national and local levels. Many changes flowed from that failed rebellion and the reaction to it. The words of Theobald Wolfe Tone still echo in Irish republican rhetoric.

The focus of this series of Thomas Davis Lectures is primarily concerned with the events which led up to the rebellion and with what happened in the course of that bloody summer. The thirteen lectures are an attempt to bring together established authorities whose already published work on aspects of the period is highly regarded and to afford an opportunity to newer voices who are engaged in fresh research on other elements of 1798.

The tributaries to the damburst of disaffection which was the 1798 rebellion were complex, depending on a confluence of local, national and international factors. The American War of Independence and the French Revolution carried various resonances for people in Ireland in the late eighteenth-century. The fashionable Francophile intelligentsia and the northern Presbyterians found they could row in behind the philosophy and sentiments of the Enlightenment and international republican idealism through their opposition to the privileged systems of Ireland's own ancient regime.

A separate stream of discontent was already flowing through the Catholic population where it was evidenced by acts of agrarian violence in the peasant community and among the middle classes by a campaign for full emancipation. None of these disparate groups had a stake in the maintenance of an established order which held an aristocratic monopoly on land and political power in Ireland.

The grievances of the time were an unstable mixture of economic, constitutional, religious and political elements. Occasionally public opinion and extra-parliamentary agitation appeared to be on the point of reshaping Irish political life and many were radicalised and swept along in enthusiastic reform movements. The established order saw these building pressures as threats and dealt with them as such, sometimes by political or constitutional manoeuvring or by the threat and use of military might.

Recurring crises all played their parts in the evolution of political instability and polarisation in Ireland. Debates on Enlightenment philosophy, republican radicalism, Irish parliamentary reform, Catholic emancipation and constitutional nationalism gradually became more extreme and violent in their language and organisation as attempts at constitutional reform lost momentum and radical reaction grew against government refusal to concede adequate reforms or reacted against the methods used to stamp out conspiracy. The combination of current thought on local, national and international circumstances gradually drifted towards a temporary union of the discontented. The power of the 'Irish Cabinet', the spectre of union, the limits of constitutional nationalism finally came together and the energies originally channelled towards parliamentary reform became transformed and ended up as anti-English radicalism and republican nationalist separatism. The consequent armed rebellion and its suppression became the bloody summer of 1798 in Ireland.

In this series of Thomas Davis Lectures we have attempted to focus on some of the important philosophies, personalities and events of the rebellion.

Dr David Dickson sketches the deeper Irish background to the events in his contribution 'The State of Ireland before 1798' which examines many of the sources of discontent which were welling up throughout the century independently of events and philosophies outside Ireland. He draws our attention to a cluster of social and economic changes which helped to destabilise Irish society over two generations. Sudden population growth and consequent pressure on land, inflation, urbanisation, increased literacy, political debate and a jostling for position in the swelling bourgeoisie were all parts of a combustible mixture waiting for a spark to set them of, according to David Dickson's evaluation of the state of the country on the eve of the United Irish rebellion.

Dr Kevin Whelan examines the wider intellectual and historical factors which helped create the emotional atmosphere necessary for the final explosion of rebellion. In 'Three Revolutions and a Failure' he puts in context the major political revolutions of the period beginning with the English Revolution of 1688 and followed, much closer to 1798, by the American Revolution of 1776 and the French Revolution of 1789. From these events he traces the growth of the Protestant ascendancy in Ireland, the weakening and abandonment of monarchy, a growth in democratic politics and a rolling back of sectarianism. Whelan depicts the American Revolution as boosting Irish radicalism and providing an opportunity to rebalance the constitutional relationship between Britain and Ireland. The relevance of American developments to Ulster Presbyterians is highlighted as is the more general influence on Protestant nationalism in Ireland. The reform and volunteer movements eventually stalled, sectarian and agrarian tensions grew and the radical stream appeared to have stagnated. Whelan looks at the ways in which the French Revolution reoxygenated the pool of political possibility in Ireland. The expansion of political horizons presented a new vision of non-sectarian and democratic politics to Irish radicals and the war between England and France created the opportunity which carried them towards the threshold of attaining their vision.

Underlining the importance of Gallic involvement on many levels 'France and the 1798 Rebellion' is the focus of Dr Hugh Gough's lecture. In it he interprets the nature of the French Revolution and its relations with the rest of Europe. In the case of Ireland he emphasises that not only the inspiration of France but the promise of military assistance were necessary for the rising of 1798. He points out that early French willingness to export revolutionary principles to the rest of Europe was grasped at by the United Irishmen in Ireland but after the failure of the Bantry Bay expedition of 1796 Ireland fell in the list of French priorities and by 1798 lack of French commitment was one of the major factors in the failure of the rebellion.

The importance of Wolfe Tone as a leader of the United Irishmen at home and as an ambassador for them in France is one of the main planks in the argument presented by Professor Marianne Elliott in 'Wolfe Tone and the Republican Ideal'. Prof. Elliott also examines Tone's continuing place as the main icon of Irish republican idealism to the present day. Her essay on the politics and personality of the man most associated with the birth of Irish republican nationalism challenges militant republican interpretations of Tone and looks at his career, his humanity and his contribution to Irish history. She argues that his abiding philosophy was to end religious dissension in Ireland and the injustice of excluding Catholics from the political life of the nation and eventually to achieve a society of United Irishmen. The article traces the grown of Tone's political philosophy and his importance in the practical and intellectual development of Irish Republicanism. Prof. Elliott also argues that militant separatism was a late addition to Tone's basic philosophy while still allowing that his experiences at home and abroad prompted him to identify English rule as the main source of Ireland's problems.

Five of the contributors have focused on the events of the rebellion on the ground in particular parts of the country. Tommy Graham reviews 'Dublin's role in the 1798 Rebellion'. He carefully examines the reasons why a plausible military strategy and an impressive organisation on paper failed to rise in Dublin city and how events in the capital affected the course of the rebellion in the surrounding counties. He lists a series of disasters in Dublin which prevented any major rising there and how that failure impacted on the rebel armies outside the city who were waiting for the expected rising in Dublin.

Dr. A. T. Q. Stewart revisits the rebellion in the north-east in '1798 in Antrim and Down'. He takes a detailed look at a baffling aspect of that bloody summer – why this cradle of the United Irishmen, the birthplace of republicanism in Ireland, was slow to rise in '98. In doing so he traces the growth of the United Irishmen in Ulster out of the Volunteer movement during a period which saw the rise of sectarian animosities, changing perceptions of the French revolution and the crackdown against the United Irishmen in the north. The pattern and path of insurrection in Antrim and Down are outlined and the Presbyterian character of the rising in both counties is highlighted.

Breandán Mac Suibhne's investigations also centre on Ulster but this time on 'Up not out: Why was there no rising in north-west Ulster'. He notes that the concentration on the high drama of rebellion by many historians has obscured the real depth of United Irish support in areas where they failed to rise, many of which were, nonetheless, areas of United Irish sedition with large numbers of sworn members. He draws our attention to the large numbers of Presbyterians in the north-west of Ulster which helped provide a radical presence in the area. Indeed early croppie activities included the murder of the Revd William Hamilton in Co. Donegal which led to General Lake's instructions to disarm Ulster. MacSuibhne argues that early rebel activity did not lead to rebellion in the north-west in 1798 for a number of reasons including class-based divisions which emerged within the United Irishmen on the issue of rising without French support and the intensification of counter-insurgency activity in 1798 which made local rebellion unlikely.

If the events in the north-west are rarely prominent in descriptions of 1798, the opposite is true of the south-east. 'Wexford in 1798: A Republic Before Its Time' is the theme of Brian Cleary's reassessment of events there. Unlike other counties the Wexford campaign began with victory after victory and saw the establishment of the short-lived Wexford Republic which Cleary examines in detail. He gives us a picture of the first meeting of the Wexford senate and how it attempted to direct the affairs of the people of Wexford by setting up its own committees for civil and military administration in the period of consolidation before the fortunes of war turned decisively against the rebel forces. He stresses that it is no longer tenable that events in Wexford could have taken place without a strong political framework which had grown out of an eighteenth-century Wexford influenced by a radical press and a forward-looking Protestant establishment. He opposes interpretations which see Wexford as being a maelstrom of uncontrollable insurrectionary or sectarian impulses by explaining the political basis for the rebellion in the area and by arguing that the dismantlement of a sectarian state could not avoid having a sectarian dimension to it, once that dismantlement was opposed.

While the awaited French military aid failed to materialise anywhere else, the landing of over a thousand French troops in Mayo in late summer saw 'General Humbert's Campaign in the west'. Military historian Dr Harman Murtagh surveys this campaign, its successes and eventual failure. He gives a detailed military analysis of the reason for Humbert's famous victory at Castlebar and his later defeat at Ballinamuck. In particular, he draws our attention to the involvement of the local leaders of the United Irishmen, the part played by the local peasantry and their final bloody fate after the failure of the rising in the west. He concluded that for the people of Mayo in 1798, their month of 'liberty was a futile tragedy and that the failure to co-ordinate military planning between France and Ireland left a legacy which was bloody, destructive and divisive'.

The military apparatus and repressive laws which the crown forces brought into play against the threat of the United Irishmen was greatly influenced by the political and military intelligence networks set up by Dublin Castle. To encapsulate the workings of one of these Prof. Thomas Bartlett scrutinises 'The Prime Informant: the life and times of "The Sham Squire" Francis Higgins'. The extensive use of spies and agents, informers and informants was widely used to discover, disrupt and defeat the plans of the United Irishmen. This extensive and often successful network took many years to build up and recruited a wide range of people privy to various levels of intelligence.

Bartlett paints a picture of an extraordinary individual who became one of the castle's leading informants who in turn procured and ran a number of his own agents whose information dealt severe blows to the United Irishmen in Dublin and Kildare. His colourful and chequered early life paved the path to his becoming editor of the *Freeman's Journal* and placed him in a position where information and influence came his way. He used his position to develop his own intelligence gathering operation and, despite his most valuable assistance to Dublin Castle's counter insurgency activities, his life as an informant remained a secret until after his death almost fifty years after the rebellion.

Dr Dáire Keogh turns his attention to unravelling the complex story of the role of the clergy in 1798. In 'Scoundrels All – Priests and Prelates in '98' he examines the image of '98 as a priest-led rebellion in the south-east and finds that it masks the real significance of the rebellion's political inspiration and execution. The survival of such images he sees as being the result of post-rebellion propaganda aimed at masking the political significance of the events and argues that such a simplistic analysis hides the true nature of clerical participation in the radical politics of the 1790s. By examining the sources Keogh discovers a more complex story of Catholic involvement which he compares with the well documented actions of Presbyterian clergy and a more problematic assessment of the Anglican clergy at the time. The picture which he paints in a complex one, with portraits of exceptional individuals which come to the foreground against a backdrop of a majority of clergy who avoided taking sides in the rebellion.

Dr Mary Cullen looks at 'Partners in Struggles: The women of 1798'. It seems clear to her that women were more active participants in political debate than has usually been recognised and she argues that women as well as men were active in all aspects of 1798 and examines a number of individual women's contributions as radical thinkers, political activists and recruiters for the United Irishmen. Dr Cullen also puts forward the opinion that the same factors which fostered United Irish republicanism also stimulated feminist assertion and that Enlightenment and republican thinking encouraged challenges to women's traditional roles and saw them become members of oath-bound Societies of United Irishwomen. Dr Cullen also draws our attention to the contrast between United Irish ideology of the women's role, which saw them in a symbolic or supportive role, and popular memory as recorded in story and ballad which sometimes remembers women as having been actual combatants.

Our final look at the legacy of that period is from the folklorists' point of view. Tom Munnelly lends an ear to '1798 and the Balladmakers'. He deals with the idea of '98 as perceived by the people on the ground and as evidenced by the songs of the ballad makers which used 1798 as a main source of inspiration for more than a century. Some songs of the period entered the oral traditions and are sung until the present day. Munnelly examines the genres of song which survived and looks at some interesting aspects of the relationships between ballads, history and the workings of tradition.

These lectures do not try to be a complete history or overview of 1798 in Ireland but I hope that the variety of subject matter and treatment given to the thirteen themes included in this volume has successfully covered not only the complex background and the main events of the 1798 Rebellion, but also many other intriguing elements of this complex picture which may have been underplayed or analysed in other ways until now.

As editor of this volume I take this opportunity to thank all the contributors who gave of their time in a very busy commemorative year, Michael Littleton, General Editor of the Thomas Davis Lectures for allowing me the opportunity to edit this series of lectures on RTÉ Radio 1 and Mary Feehan of Mercier Press for her work in helping me make the series available in book form where we all hope it will be of assistance in understanding the 1798 Rebellion. I would like to thank RTÉ for a special bursary at the Tyrone Guthrie Centre Annaghmakerrig to complete this work.

CATHAL PÓIRTÉIR
TYRONE GUTHRIE CENTRE
ANNAGHMAKERRIG
JULY 1998

THE STATE OF IRELAND
BEFORE 1798

David Dickson

SOME YEARS AGO THE National Gallery of Ireland purchased a striking topographical painting by William Ashford which depicts the formal opening of the Grand Canal Dock at Ringsend close to the mouth of the Liffey, an event that took place on St George's Day, 23 April 1796. Large crowds line the quayside, a few uniformed red-coats hover around the marquees and give a mildly military atmosphere, and in the foreground is the vice-regal yacht of the lord lieutenant, the Earl of Camden. The moment captured by Ashford represents an entirely positive image of eighteenth-century Ireland: popular acclamation of the king's representative as he inaugurates the last segment in the man-made waterway linking the River Shannon with the Liffey, a forty-year project which had been designed to open up the midlands and to reduce Dublin's dependence on imported coal and food; the civil engineer completing the scheme, John Macartney, receiving a knighthood, an act exemplifying the permeability of the class structure, and the opportunities, at least for some, of upward social mobility.[1]

That scene of Canaletto-like tranquillity gives no hint of the coming turmoil, of the United Irish revolution being planned in the same city, or of the civil war which two years later was to cost perhaps 30,000 lives. Yet the deceptive calm of Ashford's painting is not entirely an illusion, for the Ireland of 1796 was in many respects an advanced country by the standards of pre-industrial Europe: to those who thought they knew the country well it seemed that 'improvement', that catch-all eighteenth-century term that embraced material and cultural development, was carrying Irish society towards a fuller state of liberty and civilisation. It had appeared after all to be an enlightened age, and to the many optimistic commentators it seemed that Ireland, whether viewed as kingdom in a dual monarchy or imperial province in a resilient British empire, was now ready to play its part on a wider stage.

Such optimism may have been wearing a little thin by April 1796 – the great war with revolutionary France was now three years old – and it was not at all clear that Britain and its allies were destined for outright military victory. For Ireland it was still very much a war beyond the horizon, and its effects on prices (inflationary) and on employment (generally positive) meant that people had at that stage mixed views about the war and its significance. But for most who cared to consider such things, it was a conventional wisdom that the recent pace of the country's 'improvement' and the incontrovertible fact that Ireland had enjoyed half a century of economic expansion were some guarantee that the country would now be in a stronger position to ride out a time of troubles, whether trouble was from below or without.

In retrospect, we may see things a little differently. We can at least pose the question as to whether there may have been some kind of connection between the cluster of social and economic changes that contemporaries saw as 'improvement' on the one hand, and the political eruption of 1798 on the other. In other words, was an armed challenge from below to the Anglo-Irish government in Dublin Castle a likely event even before Britain and France went to war in 1793, a possible event even before the fall of the Bastille four summers before that?

There are indeed several grounds for linking the structural changes which had taken place in Irish society over the previous two generations with the destabilisation so evident in the course of the 1790s. The historian Jack Goldstone has argued recently from an international comparison of early modern societies which experienced sharp state breakdown at some point in their evolution (Jacobean England, Ottoman Turkey and Ming China in the seventeenth-century, Bourbon France in the late eighteenth) that there were a number of common underlying trends that seem to have predisposed those societies to revolution – to a fundamental re-ordering of governance and power (even if only temporarily).[2] The presence of most or all of such trends in late eighteenth-century Ireland would be at least suggestive of the combustibility of the country before the momentous events of 1796-98.

What might these elements be? Firstly, a long-term growth of population which, all things equal, would have had an inflationary impact, notably on food prices and on land, and in time would have weakened real wages, i.e., the purchasing power of labour. The Irish evidence, poor as it is, makes it quite apparent that between the famine-torn 1740s and the 1790s population expansion was occurring in every county; in aggregate, Ireland's population rose from less than 2,000,000 in the late 1740s to close on 5,000,000 by 1798. It was probably the most pronounced dash in Irish population history, achieved it seems through a combination of improved child survival rates, and of higher fertility rates brought about by younger female age of marriage.

The unprecedented populousness of the island was creating new problems by the 1790s: the position of those at the bottom of the social pyramid, precarious at any time in the eighteenth-century, was getting demonstrably worse – insofar as the earning power of un-skilled labour, male and female, was slipping and the amount of sub-sistence land that the rural poor could afford to rent, and of room space that the urban poor could occupy, were contracting. Those several rungs up the hierarchy of labour were also beginning to feel their living standards under pressure by the 1790s; this was made all the more galling for such people when they could see some of their social near-equals with land and capital – solid family farmers, small-town dealers, petty manufacturers – who by contrast were now part of a rising tide, a tide that was selective in the boats that it was raising. The prices of land, food, craft goods and services were all moving up-wards on a steepening curve by 1796. Some of this inflation was im-ported, but local demographic growth was a powerful motor of in-flation and of greater social inequality and stratification – in both rural and urban Ireland. Eighteenth-century commentators viewing things from above had regarded Irish population growth as an essentially positive development; the poor were perhaps ahead of Thomas Malt-hus in seeing it differently.

What further combustible elements can be detected in late eight-eenth-century Ireland? Rapid urbanisation of pre-industrial societies has been identified by Goldstone as another destabilising factor. Ire-land's two largest cities had roughly trebled in size in the course of the eighteenth century, with Dublin remaining the second largest city in the English-speaking world throughout that era. By the 1790s there were about a dozen large towns of some sophistication and close on 10% of the population of Ireland lived by then in a city or large town. Urbanisation created a predominantly literate and English-speaking social environment, a world of newspapers and ballads, pamphlets and the stirrings of interest in 'public affairs'. Many citizens, particularly the unskilled, were still only a step or two away from the countryside; for them town was in every sense a learning experience.

Large towns were by their nature nurseries of popular politics, and where the right to vote in parliamentary elections was shared by several thousand inhabitants, as in Dublin, the exposure to formal political debate, to the language and issues that exercised parliament, was by now widely and deeply rooted. The trickle-down of an interest in politics from the 'middling sorts' to the unenfranchised craftsmen, and from them to their apprentices, was evident before the 1790s, but became much more visible during the decade. So we can see in the qualitative growth in Irish urbanisation, in the political culture of the big towns and in the growing economic stresses of urban wage-earners, another warning sign.

Urban growth necessarily brought a commensurate expansion of the middling sorts, the stratum that would soon be labelled simply as 'the middle class'; bourgeoisies have been an expanding element of most developing societies in the last millennium, so the growth of a middle class in eighteenth-century Ireland cannot of itself be construed as an ominous development. However the fact that in every large town apart from Belfast some or most of the bourgeoisie were Catholic and therefore outside the political process (prior to the relief act of 1793) implied a dangerous tension between wealth and power in Irish society.

The affluence of this Catholic element was perhaps somewhat exaggerated, certainly in the case of Dublin, although Catholic merchants and doctors in the capital had played a crucial role in the long campaign for relaxation of the penal laws. International comparisons of societies poised on the edge of revolution point to the potency not of a swollen bourgeoisie, disaffected or otherwise, but of tensions higher up. The suggestion is that where rivalries intensify among elite groups for access to state patronage and to other high-status sources of income, then trouble lies ahead: many factors including higher survival rates among the children of the wealthy may generate such rivalry. In such a situation of elite congestion, disaffected elements within that world may exploit social discontent for their own ends and use novel methods of mass political arousal in so doing. It is tempting to seize on one obvious Irish example: the aristocratic Jacobean, Lord Edward Fitzgerald; his father, the first duke of Leinster, was one of twelve children, and Lord Edward was one of eighteen, at least nine of whom survived to adulthood; as twelfth child he had first sought his reputation by means of an army career.[3] Such large families were less typical of the Irish gentry as a whole, but for most landowning families there was growing pressure on the non-inheriting children to carve out new careers for themselves.

There remains the possibility that the pronounced growth in higher education in the late eighteenth-century, at Trinity College Dublin, Oxford, Cambridge, the Inns of Court in London, Glasgow University and beyond, may reflect such pressure.[4] Archibald Hamilton Rowan, founder member of the Dublin Society of United Irishmen, was a Cambridge graduate, but a remarkably high number of United Irish leaders had been through Trinity, had socialised and been politicised there. The numbers entering the Dublin college had trebled between mid-century and the early 1790s. Some students like the Emmets were from a decidedly well-to-do background; others like Wolfe Tone were not; and for quite a few of the most intelligent, the social experience of higher education marked the beginning of a passion for politics. However the wider point is that this surge in college entrants can be seen as a jostling for position and place, a pressure only relieved in the next generation by the huge expansion in the commissioned ranks of army and navy.

THE MATERIAL CIRCUMSTANCES OF life for Irish people in the 1790s was therefore substantially different from those of their grandparents. For many it was a more affluent, wider world, but for the rootless and the near landless a more precarious one. The new tensions that lay beneath the surface of society had created at least the possibility of a forest fire. Two related developments provided sparks aplenty.

The first was the exemplary effects of the bewildering events in France as they unfolded from the summer of 1789. The toppling of the government structures of one of the two world powers of the eighteenth-century was at first received with delight by both Irish political reformers and by conservative Franophobes. But when Edmund Burke's extraordinary tirade against the French Revolution was published in the autumn of 1790, the political classes in Ireland and Britain divided on the issue of whether the French example was a terrible political warning of what happened when men started to redesign the principles and structures of government from scratch, and those who saw the revolutionary transformation as an event of epochal significance marking a new age in the liberation of man.

In domestic Irish terms, the French Revolution re-energised the dormant reform movement: middle class Dublin critics of aristocratic government joined once again with the more advanced wing of Ulster Presbyterianism and together they founded the societies of United Irishmen in Dublin and Belfast. Most of the founding members were young, highly educated, politically well-informed enthusiasts for the business of politics, advocates of popular sovereignty and democracy who recognised in the pro-French writings of Tom Paine a gospel of explosive potential. Paine's *Rights of Man,* published first as a riposte to Burke in the spring of 1791, was recycled by the Dublin reformers, reprinted, serialised and abridged by them, and circulated in Irish town and countryside with remarkable industry: no other part of the English-speaking world can have been as saturated as Ireland with what was the key radical text in the English language.[5]

The goals of reformers who innocently printed off reams of Paine's pamphlet in 1791 were to be redefined over the next four years – from their early desire to purge the Irish parliament and create thereby an accountable 'national government', to later plans for a more fundamental reconstruction of the institutions of Irish civil society within the framework of an independent self-governing state or republic.[6] And so of course were the means for achieving such goals to be redefined – from the mobilisation of public opinion in a non-violent crusade in the early 1790s to the secret organisation of a conspiratorial mass movement that would rise up in concert with a French invasion to overthrow the irreformable regime in Dublin Castle. In the process many would-be reformers faded out of the picture, and it is through the writings of those who journeyed to extreme conclusions that we tend to see the whole process. In particular the autobiographical writings of Tone and his intimate friend, Thomas Russell, revolutionary figures by any definition, reveal the length of the political road that even they had to travel between 1790 and 1796.[7]

Tone's first claim to fame was as author of the *Argument on behalf of the Catholics of Ireland* which by its timing and content had a critical role in reassuring northern Presbyterians of the common interest they shared with their Catholic fellow-countrymen in securing constitutional liberty, an advocacy which it seems directly prepared the way for the founding of the first Belfast Society of United Irishmen. Tone's essay had the plainness of language and the rhetorical vigour of Tom Paine, and it was partly on the strength of this that he was appointed to be in effect executive secretary of the Catholic Committee.

The shattering of the privileged position of the Catholic Church in France from the earliest months of the Revolution – with the declaration of religious freedom, the confiscation of Church property, and the sweeping away of tithes, later followed by the abolition of the religious orders – acted as a catalyst for the revival of Catholic political activity in Ireland. Less menacing in international terms, the Catholic Church in Ireland could now be represented as a potential guarantor of peace and stability if it was accommodated within the constitution. In practical terms, the aim of all Catholic spokesmen at the beginning of the 1790s was to secure further statutory relaxation of the penal laws, building on what had been conceded during the American war.

But once again there were inner tensions between conservative Catholic gentry, backed by the bishops, and the predominantly Dublin-based mercantile politicians whose instincts were to use public opinion to advance Catholic political demands. Association with Painite United Irishmen, and with Tone in particular, introduced the language of rights into Catholic statements and thereby widened the implications of Catholic political claims. The assertion of popular majoritarian rights over chartered and otherwise inherited privileges could be seen as a fundamental challenge to the whole basis of the rule of law and the structure of property in eighteenth-century Ireland. In other words the example of France helped embolden the more radical group of Catholic lobbyists, and greatly raised the stakes in the debate over Catholic relief. The Catholic Committee's decision in 1792 to organise a representative national convention, county by county, was carried through in the teeth of government disapproval. The Catholic convention helped raise popular Catholic expectations, and allowed the public airing of Catholic frustration and anger in a way that would have been inconceivable a few years before: 'Loyalty is stupidity and vice where there is no protection from government, and gratuitous because it is not paid for ...', John Sweetman of Dublin was reported as saying; he added that '[The] King [has] no right to our loyalty, unless we are protected'.[8]

Borrowing from the language of the anti-slavery movement, the convention asserted their aim – emancipation. And this kind of language, once used, could not be put back into the bottle. The 1793 concessions to Catholics, successfully negotiated by the convention delegates in London (the franchise, the right to bear firearms, and the opening up of membership of guilds and corporations), were substantial gains, but the legislation lacked any machinery for enforcement. Thus a broad front of Catholic men of wealth, mercantile and landed, continued to see themselves denied civic equality with their Protestant peers: late in 1794, the prospect of a viceroy with strong sympathies in favour of emancipation rekindled Catholic excitement. However Earl Fitzwilliam's vice-royalty in 1795 was sensationally foreshortened, and his abrupt recall turned Catholic activists, some to despair, some on the road to covert subversive activity. 'We the Catholics of Ireland are at this moment as inflamed as any body so numerous can be ...' wrote Patrick Byrne, the Grafton Street bookseller, to his confidante in Philadelphia; 'the rights of citizenship as I may call it was promised ... the administration that promised it are recalled and the old jobbers are to be reinstated and the same system of corruption and oppression pursued'.[9] Angry private words, reflecting new values and newer disappointments.

Every category of political reformer in the 1790s was thus affected by the political force field centred on Paris. But so were the forces of conservatism: at government level 'the jobbers', the three permanent strong men, Speaker Foster, John Fitzgibbon (now lord chancellor and Earl of Clare), and John Beresford, had become profoundly out of sympathy with reform, political or religious, and their collective influence dominated government policy, particularly in the security area. Their rebuff by Fitzwilliam in 1795 was momentary, and they went on to shape the cluster of statutes in 1796 which markedly restricted civilian liberties, and indeed they encouraged the development of the army's para-policing role thereafter. They had the majority of Irish MPs with them in their tough and often provocative strategy of demonising the opposition, and of suppressing popular political activity with a new ruthlessness.

The challenge of radicalism and of Catholic emancipation had led to a new doctrine in defence of the constitutional status quo, one which spelt out the necessity of maintaining the monopoly of Protestant power within the constitution, both for practical and principled reasons. This doctrine of 'Protestant Ascendancy' was not a socially exclusive policy – indeed its first explicit elaboration was not as might be expected by conservative gentry but rather in a declaration by Dublin corporation (in 1792). The social inclusivity of the concept of 'Protestant Ascendancy' found new expression in the emergence in 1795 of a masonic-style rural organisation in south Ulster, the Orange Order. Their loyalism was socially integrative, but absolute in its exclusion of Catholic participation in its affairs. And even though Orangeism had its progenitors in the linen-country faction-fights of the 1780s and the rough-house behaviour of the Peep-of-Day Boys, it was the far more charged atmosphere of the 1790s which shaped its character and its geographical spread southwards as far as Cork. Not unconnected with the birth of Orangeism was a wave of 'ethnic cleansing' in south Ulster in 1795–6; that activity led to the forced migration of some thousands of disaffected Catholic weaving families into north Connacht.

Nothing contributed to the rapid sharpening of sectarian consciousness so successfully as rumours of such excesses. Many Catholic communities across south Ulster and north Leinster had since the beginning of the 1790s been incorporated into the Defender association, another loose fraternal federation; it was governed by oaths and initiation rituals that combined visceral anti-Protestantism with somewhat garbled Jacobean sentiments and symbols. The interconnections between the urban-centred Catholic Committee and the Defender network were real but shadowy. And the subsequent alliance between the United Irish organisation and the Defenders is also very hard to read and evaluate, Catholic Church leaders were entirely out of sympathy and embarrassed by Defenderism's raw sectarianism, but the anti-clericalist record of revolutionary governments in France made the United Irish enterprise almost as distasteful to senior Catholic Churchmen.

The other spark that completed the destabilisation of the country was the war itself. For, independent of the ideological and material contribution that revolutionary France was making, the coming of hostilities in the wake of wretched harvests dramatically heightened inflation and caused massive urban unemployment in 1793. There was indeed recovery in the mid-1790s before an even graver economic collapse in 1797.

In the early stages of the war the level of both local county rates and excise taxes grew sharply as the Irish exchequer struggled first to fund the Irish militia, raised in 1793, and then to cope with the widening defence budget. A sharp fall in agricultural prices in 1797 coincided with government cancellation of agricultural subsidies, a huge increase in the import duties on salt (one of the few commodities that nearly every household purchased), and with turbulence in the banking system as the convertibility of Bank of Ireland notes into gold was suspended.[10] Business confidence was gravely shaken at least six months before Vinegar Hill.

From the early 1790s the United Irishmen had exploited social and economic grievance. Samuel Neilson, pivotal figure in Belfast radical politics, in reporting in 1792 on the beginnings of the United Irish organisation in rural Ulster, noted that 'the universal question throughout this country is, "when do we begin? do we refuse hearth money, or tithes first?"'[11] The burden of taxes became visibly heavier,

24

and United propaganda attacked the cruel war and its effects on the poor; as their social policies developed they put increasing emphasis on promises to abolish tithes and taxes insofar as these touched the poor. Hostile critics made much of the success that United men were achieving in 1797 in exploiting economic grievance as the secret organisation became a military mass movement. 'Many who seemed well affected last winter,' one Cork land agent reported in June 1797, comparing the domestic calm at the time the French had appeared in Bantry Bay, 'are now very much to the contrary ... the taking off the bounty [i.e., the subsidy] on land carriage [of flour] to Dublin and the late duty on salt have been a great means of perverting the minds of the lower order ...'[12]

THE EMPHASIS HERE HAS BEEN on the interaction of long-term Irish social trends and the external, indeed globally significant, events of the 1790s as an important backdrop to the exploration of the specific issues of 1798 and the rebellion itself. We should at this point just notice that the actual theatres of rebellion – south and east Leinster, east Ulster – were economically among the most advanced, outward-looking districts in the country, areas most affected by the economic development of the previous half century. Many factors, some quite accidental, explain the particular geography of the rising, but we cannot hope to understand the motivations of the rebel participants if we fail to recognise that they were by the standards of the country as a whole notably literate, numerate, and conscious of the world beyond their county horizons.

THREE REVOLUTIONS AND A FAILURE

Kevin Whelan

THE THREE KEY REVOLUTIONS of the early-modern period – the English Revolution in 1688, the American Revolution of 1776 and the French Revolution in 1789 – underpin the political structures and beliefs of the modern world. Each had influential echoes in Ireland. The English Revolution (as in the Battle of the Boyne) inflicted a decisive defeat on Catholic and Stuart Ireland, permitting the establishment of a sectarian state founded on Protestant ascendancy, with its constitutional perimeters patrolled by the penal laws against Catholics.

In a broader sense, we could say that each of these revolutions represented a weakening of the traditional basis of politics – the idea of the monarch as the earthly incarnation of divine power. England forced the monarchy to become answerable to parliament; America jettisoned it entirely; France opted for the sovereignty of the people. The specifically religious element in political structures decreased throughout each of these revolutions. America and France universalised the Protestant idea of liberty and thereby made possible the concept of a democratic politics untainted by sectarian exclusions.

In an Irish context this rolling back of sectarianism caused a great deal of heart-searching. Some continued to promote the old solution. For example in the 1780s, the leading reformer, Henry Flood, made explicit his Protestant version of liberty in his analysis of Irish history:

> Ninety years ago the question was, whether Popery and arbitrary power should be established in the person of King James, or freedom and the Protestant religion in the person of King William – four-fifths of the inhabitants of Ireland adhered to the cause of King James; they were defeated, and I rejoice in their defeat. The laws that followed this event were not laws of persecution, but of political necessity.

The great philosopher, John Toland, himself originating in the Catholic community in Inishowen, argued the absolute necessity of maintaining the sectarian divide in Ireland:

> Nothing should be attempted that might bring about the possibility of a union of civil interests between the Protestants and Papists of Ireland, whose antipathies and animosities all sound politicians will ever labour to keep alive.

So matters stood until the 1770s. The American War of Independence was eagerly followed in Ireland. George Washington quickly became the icon of the emerging American Republic, the modern incarnation of the classical citizen – soldier – statesman. Ireland and America shared a common political language of liberty, corruption, rights, and civic virtue. From the mid eighteenth-century onwards, they also shared an awareness of a more exclusionary trend with an intensifying British nationalism (metropolitan, militant, Protestant) and an expanding empire. Britishness defined itself in an exclusive rather than inclusive way. The shock of rejection as colonial inferiors rather than freeborn Britons humiliated and haunted the colonial elite in both Ireland and America. Their self-identification as Irish or American emerged from their hurt reaction to this British projection of difference. In both Ireland and America, Washington symbolised this refusal of second-class status as perennially juvenile partners in empire. In 1783, the great man rejoiced in Ireland's political progress: 'I would facilitate the Kingdom of Ireland on their emancipation from British control'.

The American Revolution provided a boost to Irish radicalism. As Henry Flood expressed it: 'A voice from America has shouted to liberty, the echo of it caught your people as it passed along the Atlantic and they re-echoed the voice till it reverberated here'. Most of the influential leaders of the United Irishmen were born in the 1760s and were literally as well as politically children of the American Revolution. Archibald Hamilton Rowan, in America during the Revolution, and a friend of Benjamin Franklin, concluded; 'I regretted not being an American; I made up my mind that if I ever could, I would play the same role in Ireland'.

The American crisis allowed Irish politicians to take advantage of an imperial crisis to rebalance the constitutional relationships between Ireland and Britain. In America and Ireland, increasing British pretensions galvanised the colonial elite in both countries into action.

A typical response was to sharpen their identification as American or Irish. Benjamin Franklin could observe: 'The cause of America was the cause of Ireland. The cause of Ireland was the cause of America.' Precisely because of this shared identity problem, the American Revolution impacted enormously on Ireland. The Volunteers, established as a citizen army in 1778, were self-consciously Irish and resolutely distanced from government control. Overwhelmingly Protestant and middle-class, they quickly developed a national organisation as a paramilitary pressure group.

The Volunteers gave Irish patriot opinion a focus and a forum. Astutely used by Henry Grattan, and facing a weak and divided English cabinet, the Volunteers authored the achievement of the 'Constitution of 1782' and the establishment of 'Grattan's Parliament'. These patriots suggested that Ireland might indeed follow the Americans in their search for independence.

The American developments had a particular relevance in east Ulster, the Irish Presbyterian heartland. Their kinsfolk, mostly recent emigrants, were very active in the war, which was extensively reported back in Ireland. Revd William Campbell, moderator of their synod, commented: 'Presbyterians went in thousands to America. And if ships had been found, thousands more would have sought asylum in that land of liberty – a happy refuge from the despotism of England – far removed from the violence of her satellites and legal assassins.' He also noted that:

> The Presbyterians of Ulster condemned this war as unjust, cruel and detestable. They beheld it with anguish and with horror, as the most wanton, unprovoked despotism. Their friends and relations abounded in the different provinces of America, and they heard with pride that they comprised the flower of Washington's army, being carried on by a native love of liberty, to encounter every danger for the sake of their adopted country.

The United Irishman, William Sampson, praised the religious freedom of America: 'Every citizen here is in his own country. To the Protestants, it is a Protestant country; to the Catholic, a Catholic country and the Jew, if he pleases, may establish in it his own Jerusalem'. Presbyterians were keenly aware of the great victory achieved by American dissenters in establishing the separation of church and state in the American constitution. This was a tremendous victory for them over the Anglicans, and in one point of view, the American War of Independence can be viewed as a civil war between Anglicans and Presbyterians – decisively won by the former. By contrast, Irish Presbyterians still smarted under penal restrictions: the 1774 Vestry Act, which excluded Presbyterians from voting rights, was seen as a particularly insulting example of taxation without representation. Fired by the example of America, some Presbyterians now began to seriously contemplate similar changes in Ireland.

The American Revolution also closed the gap between the abstract and idealised ancient world and the realities of modern contemporary society. It renovated the concept of republican virtue and encouraged Irish Protestants (as mobilised in the Volunteers) to assert a renewed degree of parliamentary independence from Britain. The Volunteers saw themselves as representing armed virtue, grafting the eternal verities of classical antiquity onto modern Ireland. However, this emerging Protestant nationalism was still couched within the Whig version of liberty, which resolutely excluded the possibility of extending citizenship to Catholics.

Despite its enormous later reputation, 'Grattan's Parliament', achieved in 1782, quickly proved a major disappointment. Having traumatically lost its American colonies, Britain subsequently gave more sustained attention to the increasingly anomalous situation of Ireland – no longer one of fourteen Atlantic colonies, but a single and newly lonely colony. Precisely because it had greater power, 'Grattan's Parliament' was in fact more rigorously controlled than ever before – using the time honoured method of patronage (or 'corruption' as radicals termed it). William Pitt stated his aim on Anglo-Irish relations in 1785 to be: 'To preserve from further dismemberment and diminution, to unite and connect what remained of our reduced and shattered empire, of which Great Britain and Ireland were now the only considerable members.'

English strategists were worried about the unworkability and volatility of the new relationship. Unable to push through their preferences for a union, they sought throughout the 1780s to assert control by cultivating a new group of political handlers, notably John Foster, John Fitzgibbon and John Beresford.

Foster, Fitzgibbon and Beresford – known dismissively to radicals as 'The Three Jacks' – were all ambitious, skilful politicians, resolutely Anglophile. All were new men, recruited from outside the traditional networks of Irish power politics. They became the crucial managers of the Irish parliament in the English interest. For the radicals, these men were the epitome of Irish corruption, who cynically promoted English policy in Ireland to advance their own careers.

In the mid 1780s, the Volunteer movement stalled, incapable of maintaining its radical momentum, because it split on the issue of admitting Catholics to the citizenship. This in turn paralysed the parliamentary reform movement, whose success would have been necessary to make the parliament more representative and less amenable to London string-pulling.

The much vaunted settlement of 1782 therefore turned out to be a hollow victory. Without reform, which raised the vexed and divisive issue of Catholic rights, the Irish parliament remained vulnerable to a controlling English interest. Parliamentary reformers divided acrimoniously over the Catholics. The heady enthusiasm of the early 1780s sobered into a sullen sectarian stalemate by the end of the decade. The Irish parliament remained gridlocked. The necessary reform could only be achieved by admitting Catholics and it was a fundamental principle of the English version of liberty that Catholics were incapable of exercising democratic responsibilities. The imposition of penal laws and the establishment of a sectarian state was the inevitable result. So was the maintenance of a three tier society, with the Anglicans as first class, the Presbyterians as second class and the Catholic majority as third class members.

Theobald Wolfe Tone fulminated on the failure of the 1782 settlement:

> The revolution of 1782 was a revolution which enabled Irishmen to set at a much higher price their honour, their integrity, and the interests of their country; it was a revolution, which, while at one stroke it doubled the value of every borough monger in the kingdom, left three-fourths of our countrymen slaves as it found them, and the government of

Ireland in the base and wicked and contemptible hands, who had spent their lives in degrading and plundering her;... The power remained in the hands of our enemies, again to be exerted for our ruin, with this difference, that formerly we had our distresses, our injuries, and our insults gratis, at the hands of England; but now we pay very dearly to receive the same with aggravation, through the hands of Irishmen; – yet this we boast of, and call a revolution.

By the end of the 1780s, then, the settlement of 1782 had increased rather than decreased Irish-English tensions. The sectarian temperature was rising in the Ulster countryside, signalled by the Peep-O-Day Boy-Defender clashes. The Munster countryside was once more convulsed by agrarian secret societies – in this case the Rightboys. A strident paper war had emerged over the issue of Protestant Ascendancy. Irish radicalism seemed hopelessly marooned in a sectarian cul-de-sac.

The impact of the French Revolution on Ireland was to release this sectarian stalemate. The leading Catholic power in Europe had – astonishingly – produced a revolution more radical than the much vaunted Glorious (and Protestant) Revolution of 1688. The reception of the French Revolution in Ireland was as a Catholic effort at liberty. This was especially important to the Presbyterians, steeped in the Bible and the Book of Revelations, who were inclined to see the revolution as a millennial event, signifying the long-awaited destruction of popery. The fall of the Bastille quickly became the accepted symbol of the revolution, and the occasion was enthusiastically celebrated at Belfast in the early 1790s. The emphasis on 14 July also conveniently underplayed the divisive 12 July celebrations, as the Williamite tradition increasingly became conservative and staunchly Protestant in the 1790s. For Irish radicals, the French Revolution suggested that hope and history might now indeed rhyme in an Irish context.

Theobald Wolfe Tone became the main interpreter of the French Revolution for an Irish audience with his enormously successful pamphlet *Argument on behalf of the Catholics of Ireland*. Tone argued that the old equation between Catholicism and despotism had been rendered obsolete by the Revolution and that Irish Catholics would demonstrate the same political maturity as their French counterparts.

Once Catholics could be accepted as citizens, the parliamentary reform movement could at last achieve its aims. It was in this sense that Tone described the Revolution as 'the morning star of liberty' in Ireland. The French Revolution, by universalising the narrowly Protestant concept of liberty, and by occurring within a Catholic state, released sectarian gridlock. It also represented an enormous expansion of human sensibility and vision – the largest expansion of the horizons of political possibility in recorded history.

The French Revolution made buoyant the weight of history, the dead hand of the dead generations, weighing like a nightmare on the brains of the living, where the political world appeared as an immutable force, pressing down relentlessly on the self. The revolution released frozen political desire into the living stream of history. Its promotion of human rights offered an alternative path to the idea of political community. The universality of the republican principles of *liberté, egalité, fraternité* furnished a neutral language with which to consider the characteristics of a just state. The republican project supplied an alternative basis for uniting disparate peoples, generating the possibility of a common political home, based on transparent compliance with ethical rather than ethnic principles, on justice, not 'history'.

A window of opportunity was opened in Ireland by the impact of the American and French Revolutions: the moment was brilliantly seized by the United Irishmen, who imaginatively created a vision of non-sectarian, democratic and inclusive politics, which could attract and sustain Irish people in all their inherited complexities. Rather than seeing religious, ethnic and political diversity as a paralysing problem, the United Irishmen saw it as a challenge to construct a wider, more tolerant vision of Irish identity. Rather than clinging grimly to a divided and divisive past, a stifling sepulchre of precedents, the United Irishmen sought to create a shared future, a cradle of possibilities. By facing into the future rather than the past, they wished to heal the hurts of Irish history in a brotherhood of affection, a fellowship of freedom. In their first declaration of principle, they stated in words which echo across the chasm of centuries:

We have thought much about our posterity, little about our ancestors.

Are we forever to walk like beasts of prey over the fields our ancestors stained in blood?

The United Irishmen also understood that they were the heirs to the three previous revolutions. But while the United Irishmen knew they were the heirs, they were not merely copycat importers. As they themselves stated, in their address to the Scottish radicals in 1793:

> We will not buy nor borrow liberty from America nor from France, but we will manufacture it ourselves and work it up with those materials which the hearts of Irishmen furnish them with at home.

There were three novel elements to the United Irish project.

CATHOLICS AS CITIZENS

As articulated by Theobald Wolfe Tone, the United Irishmen audaciously expanded the doctrinaire Whig version of liberty to include Catholics. They thus secularised liberty, in a way free of the sectarian exclusions of the English Revolution and of the atheistic and anti-traditional thrust of the French Revolution. This expansion of the polity to include Catholics exposed the limits of Britishness, which proved imaginatively and ideologically incapable of absorbing it. In this startling rupture, the United Irishmen broke with the sedimented anti-popery of the English Whigs, and thereby shattered the sectarian moulds of the Irish eighteenth-century.

SEPARATISM

A second innovation in United Irish thinking was its espousal of separatism. They believed that the sectarian Irish state (symbolised by its unreformed parliament) was underpinned by the British connection. Remove this connection and it would collapse. Tone wrote that:

> The influence of England was the radical vice of our government and consequently Ireland would never be free, prosperous or happy until she was independent. And that independence was unattainable while the connection with England existed.

By contrast, and illustrating the novelty of the Irish Enlightenment, the Scottish Enlightenment was conceived and developed as a unionist project which increased the integration between Scotland and England in a shared Britishness. Just as it proved incapable of absorbing Catholicism, Britishness proved equally incapable of ingesting Irishness (as it absorbed Welshness and Scottishness). By offering a political analysis of this failure, the United Irishmen explicitly brought separatism onto the Irish political agenda for the first time.

VERNACULAR VISION

In terms of cultural politics, the United Irishmen disputed the standard Enlightenment espousal of universalism and rejection of regional cultures as inevitably doomed to obsolescence. The United Irishmen argued instead for an equal weighting of cultures, signified in the Irish case by giving proper weight to the Gaelic (indigenous) elements. By retrieving and then returning the native to the high cultural ground, the United Irishmen espoused an exemplary cultural pluralism of a radical rather than liberal kind. They sought to deepen the timeline of Irish history to include the despised pre-colonial past, but not to claim that past as the exclusive preserve of the indigenous Irish, but as a shared and valued birthright of all Irish people. By imagining this inclusive Irish past, the United Irishmen also jettisoned the exclusive British past in Ireland as a divisive colonial hangover. The United Irishmen were therefore bearers of an alternative Enlightenment, which respected cultural specificity and which balanced the rights of man (individual and inalienable) with the rights of cultures, however small, to respect and self-determination. In this sense, the United Irishmen were not cultural but republican nationalists.

The celebrated Belfast Harp Festival of 1792 was literally a staging of this politics of culture, a public expression of this new determination to give equal weight to the Gaelic as well as the English component in Irish culture. The harp restrung would harmonise and amplify the Irish acoustic. The United Irishmen, notably Sampson, Russell and MacNeven, identified the need to balance the particularity of national culture alongside the universal and cosmopolitan political ideas of the Enlightenment. The Harp Festival was a public gesture in this direction. Just as in the religious sphere, the United Irishmen sought to transcend the disabling binaries of 'colonial' and 'native' and to assert the shared ownership of a rich Irish past by all the traditions of Ireland.

The United Irishmen miscellany *Bolg an tSolair* (1795) was a similar assertion of cultural appropriation, as was their adoption of the slogan *Éireann go brách* (Ireland forever), their use of popular Gaelic tunes for their political ballads and their encouragement of the cult of Carolan as the national bard. These initiatives deepened the politics of culture which emerged in the 1780s, most notably in the innovative volumes of Charlotte Brooke and Joseph Cooper Walker and in the embryonic nationalism of the Volunteer movement.

By the early 1790s, it was becoming increasingly clear that the French Revolution would unleash a titanic European struggle between 'democracy' and 'aristocracy', between republicanism and monarchy, between *'liberté, egalité and fraternité'* and the *ancien régime*. Burke's emotional tirade *Reflections on the Revolution in France* and Paine's caustic response *The Rights of Man* established the battlefield as one of ideas. As France and Great Britain moved inexorably towards conflict, it became apparent that this would be the first modern war, a new war of principle and ideology rather than an old war of tactical and dynastic advantage. The French mass mobilisation of highly-motivated citizen soldiers as opposed to reliance on a small professional standing army redefined the very nature of the warfare. The number of combatants and casualties escalated to unprecedented proportions and the theatre of war aggressively expanded to embrace all Europe.

In these circumstances, once war finally broke out in 1793, the United Irishmen, grudgingly tolerated in peacetime, were immediately banned as a potentially (if not actually) treasonable organisation. Concessions to Catholics, granted both to keep them from the clutches of the United Irishmen and to trade relief for recruits, stopped. An increasingly rigid conservative regime under William Pitt took over in Britain, a regime which instinctively sided with the *Ancien Régime* in France, thereby demonstrating the shallowness of the democratic credentials of the Glorious Revolution.

The 1790s was the pivotal decade in modern European history.

England and France locked horns in an international battle for domination, in the first great war in which modernity confronted tradition. In Ireland, the United Irishmen – and with them political modernity – were to be its casualties.

The United Irish project was defeated by the London and Dublin governments, who deliberately injected sectarianism as an antidote to them. This period marked the first deployment of raw sectarianism as a counter-revolutionary measure by the state. As a direct consequence, revived sectarian animosity infected a desolate political landscape that came to look increasingly anachronistic and increasingly 'Irish'. The only way the Irish could be accommodated safely within the union was to be demodernised politically and then have these anachronisms ascribed to their native backwardness, rather than to a toxic policy of sectarianism, military coercion and cultural regression. Ireland was to be returned, at a cost of 30,000 lives, to the sectarian moulds from which the United Irishmen had tried to rescue it. A key British policy maker, Lord Redesdale, observed after the Act of Union was passed:

> Neither can I agree with some who think it immaterial to England whether the principal people here are Protestant or Catholics, or whether the whole nation was Catholic. For, though the maxim, divide and govern, has been often reprobated, it is nevertheless true that the division facilitates the governing of the country.

FRANCE AND THE 1798 REBELLION

Hugh Gough

1798 WAS A DRAMATIC year for much of western and Mediterranean Europe. Revolutionary France had already annexed Belgium, Savoy and Nice, and occupied the German Rhineland. She had set up dependent satellite republics in Holland (the Batavian Republic) and northern Italy (the Cisalpine Republic). In December 1797 she was to invade Switzerland and establish the Helvetian Republic during the following spring. In February 1798 it was the turn of the Papal states where a French invasion removed the pope and led to the establishment of a Roman Republic. Malta was annexed in June, Egypt invaded in the following month, and Naples invaded in December. Every time the diplomats of Europe dusted off their maps the boundaries and names had changed. Yet so too had the political complexion, for everywhere that French armies went, revolutionary institutions and legislation followed in the form of written constitutions, centralised administrations, social reform and legal change. Ireland is, of course, an exception to this development. The rebellion of 1798 was certainly a product of the French Revolution and would never have happened without the promise of French military assistance or without the inspiration that events in France provided. Yet the rebellion failed, and French invasion attempts over the summer of 1798 failed too. For the diplomats of Europe, neither the map of Ireland nor its political complexion changed. So why did France become involved in 1798, what were its aims, and why did it fail?

To understand French involvement we need first to understand the nature of its revolution and its impact on Europe. By the late 1790s the revolution was almost nine years old and the innocent optimism that had surrounded its outbreak in the summer of 1789 had long since faded. The constitution painstakingly put together by the first National Assembly between 1789 and 1791 had collapsed in the summer of 1792 under the pressure of an Austrian invasion. The monarchy was abolished, Louis XVI guillotined six months later and thousands more political suspects decapitated by the guillotine during 1793–4, as the

Committee of Public Safety used terror and political centralisation to crush counter-revolution and fight the war. After the fall of Robespierre the pendulum moved back towards political moderation and, in the following autumn, the Directory was established. Its constitution gave executive power to five Directors, elected by the two houses of the legislature – the Council of Five Hundred and the Council of Elders – whose deputies were in turn elected on a suffrage that gave most adult males the vote. In comparison with the rest of Europe – Britain and Ireland included – it was a radical regime that embodied many of the revolution's political gains. Yet it was also a weak regime, crippled by corruption and the political divisions that inevitably resulted from the upheavals that had rocked the country since 1789.[1] On the right, royalists wanted to bring back the monarchy; on the left, radical Jacobins wanted a democratic dictatorship. In the centre even the Directory's own supporters were divided between a moderate right, which wanted a conservative republic, and a moderate left which wanted a reforming republic. The system was made more unstable by the fact that one Director was replaced every year, which meant that the power balance within the executive could change unpredictably. One-third of the deputies in the Council of Five Hundred were replaced by annual elections too, with similar results. After two years of instability a *coup d'état* in September 1797, the so-called *fructidor* coup, ousted the moderate right from power and began a habit of military intervention that was to end with Napoleon Bonaparte's seizure of power in 1799.

This instability reflected the pressure of war. In 1790 the National Assembly had renounced war, stating that France intended to live at peace with its European neighbours. War was claimed to be the work of kings and aristocrats, a vice of the *ancien régime* that France had broken free from in 1789. Free people would now live in peace with one another. But peace did not last for long. Less than two years later, convinced that counter-revolution was being supported by the queen's brother-in-law, the emperor of Austria Leopold II, France declared war on Austria. Convinced that 'oppressed peoples' throughout Europe would support French armies because of the ideals of the revolution, deputies of the Girondin group quickly turned the war into a political campaign to export revolutionary principles to the rest of Europe. They promised to come to the assistance of revolutionary minorities and to revolutionise the countries that they conquered. This was an ideological crusade and the result was a predictable catastrophe, for very few so-called 'oppressed peoples' welcomed French troops when they appeared over the horizon, while governments united to resist French aggression.[2] France was rapidly faced with a hostile First Coalition, made up of major European states except Russia, and it took the iron grip of the Committee of Public Safety during the terror of 1793–4 to re-organise her armies and roll back the tide. In the summer of 1795, the coalition began to fall apart as first Prussia, then Spain, made peace. Two years later, in the summer of 1797, Austria signed the preliminary peace of Léoben after Bonaparte's stunning victories in northern Italy.[3]

By then France dominated much of western Europe, with the annexation of Belgium, Savoy and Nice, the occupation of the Rhineland and the establishment of satellite republics in Holland and northern Italy.[4] But victory was not complete while Britain remained at war, and Britain did so, less because of any opposition to the revolution in principle, than because of the fact that French expansion had destroyed the European balance of power. How permanent could any European peace be with such a major shift in French strength? The answer to that depended on the precise extent of French intentions and they were by no means clear, for political opinion in Paris was divided. Conservative republicans, including Lazare Carnot who supported Tone in the ill-fated Bantry Bay expedition of 1796, wanted a swift end to the war and were willing to bargain off some of the territorial gains to get a general settlement. But they were ousted from power in the *fructidor* coup of 1797 by the republican left, which wanted to retain the so-called 'natural frontiers' of the Alps, the Pyrenees, and Rhine. That involved retaining Belgium and the German Rhineland. Jean-François Reubell was the Director most closely associated with this policy. He recognised that such a major extension of French power would require a trade off with Austria by abandoning Napoleon's gains in northern Italy to Vienna in exchange for the Rhineland.[5] But there was a Corsican fly in that particular ointment, for Napoleon was a shrewd and ruthless political animal with his own personal ambitions. He had negotiated the Treaty of Léoben with Austria over the Directors heads in the spring of 1797, set up the Cisalpine Republic on his own initiative and even conducted a cynical carve-up of the Venetian Republic with Austria. He certainly had no real interest in the natural frontiers.[6] Instead, as a true Corsican, his ambitions were Mediterranean and he aimed to establish French influence there.

It was against this background that the events of 1798 in Ireland took place. In the short term both Bonaparte and the Directors could agree that their major problem was Britain and that the British government was the major obstacle to French control of Europe – whatever the exact shape of that control would eventually be. Public opinion in Britain was war weary, and in both 1796 and 1797 the Prime Minister, William Pitt, had opened peace negotiations. But on both occasions the talks had broken down. War therefore continued, but the difficulty from France's point of view was that Britain was an island with a powerful navy that had blockaded French ports since 1793 and annihilated her colonial trade. The French navy, for its part, had been badly affected by the revolution. Most naval officers had been noble, and had either resigned because of their hostility to the revolution or been replaced because of their aristocratic origins. Their replacements were political appointees with little naval experience, and indiscipline had rapidly spread among the ranks. The revolution had solved its military problems on land by appointing new generals and increasing the size of its armies, but that would not work in the navy. Maritime experience was important there, and even increasing the number of sailors was impossible without increasing the number of ships. That could not be done overnight. The failure of Hoche's expedition to Bantry Bay in the winter of 1796 was largely due to naval incompetence and had resulted in substantial losses. By the end of 1797 Britain had 120 ships of the line: France only 57. Britain had 387 frigates and light vessels; France a mere 65. And, although Britain had experienced naval mutinies in the summer of 1797, the skill and experience of her sailors far out-classed that of the French.[7]

Britain could therefore only be defeated by an invasion, and in October 1797 the Directory ordered the formation of an army of England under Bonaparte's command, which was to be ferried across the channel for an invasion in the spring of 1798. 36,000 troops were withdrawn from Italy in December and the final plans drawn up in the following month envisaged a total invasion force of some 56,000 men. Yet by late February both the naval and military preparations had fallen well behind schedule. Bonaparte lost interest and, after a quick tour of the ports in February, advised the Directory to abandon the project. Instead he suggested an attack on England through Hanover, or through Egypt.[8] Hanover was ruled out because it would offend Prussia, so Egypt was chosen instead, on the grounds that it would enable France to advance towards India and throttle Britain's crucial trade routes there. So, on 19 May 1798 – just days before the United Irish rising in Dublin – Bonaparte left Toulon with 36,000 troops on his ill-fated Egyptian expedition.

The Egyptian expedition took many of France's best troops and ships away from Europe and it is significant that Ireland was not chosen as the alternative to a direct attack on Britain. The reasons are straightforward: Napoleon regarded an Irish expedition as too risky, while the Directory, ever since the failure of Hoche's expedition to Bantry Bay, had lost interest in a direct invasion.[9] Instead it expected the Irish to stage their own rising first, and undertook only to send troops and assistance when that happened. As a result it kept several divisions raised for the Bantry Bay expedition near the port of Brest and, in the summer of 1797, encouraged its military ally, the Batavian Republic, to mount an Irish expedition from its naval base at Texel. But there was no serious attempt to organise a direct invasion and after Hoche died in September 1797 Ireland dropped further down the French priority list. The position was made clear in an official statement in the summer of 1797:

> ... the state of fermentation in Ireland offers us ... the most favourable opportunity of defeating England; but we cannot immediately send the projected expedition. The fate of the continent must first be decided ... We want the Irish to proclaim the independence of their island and we will help in this laudable enterprise, but with no formal guarantee on our part. Our conduct towards them must follow the same lines as that adopted for the people of Italy who declared themselves independent. We protected their liberty, but we made no agreement to sustain their

41

new political status for fear of jeopardising the re-establishment of peace.[10]

Ireland was no longer a top priority. England now was and, as a result, when the rebellion finally broke out in Dublin in late May, the Directory was poorly placed to respond. Its best troops were cruising south in the Mediterranean towards Malta, while over 100,000 others were stationed in defensive positions along the Rhine, or in Holland, Italy and Switzerland. Its reaction was therefore improvised, ineffective, and late. Four members of the United Irishmen in Paris – Lowry, Hamilton, Bartholomew Teeling and Joseph Orr appealed to the Directory on 16 June to send 1,000 men and 5,000 guns to the north or the north-west of Ireland to help the revolt. Their letter reinforced the French belief that the revolt was powerful enough to succeed with just a modicum of French support:

> In requesting such small forces you can see that we are certain that Ireland will end by ridding itself of the British yoke. It will only be after seeing the most precious blood of its children being spilt and its territory devastated. Nevertheless we are convinced that these forces, however small they may be, can render important services to the cause of liberty.

Three days later the Directory gave a positive answer, ordering four vessels to leave Brest as soon as possible with 1,200 soldiers and substantial supplies of arms on board. By early July an overall plan provided for ships to sail from Dunkirk, Calais and Boulogne, carrying arms, ammunition and United Irish exiles. The French commander in Holland, Joubert, was to persuade the Dutch to prepare ships for a small Franco-Dutch army of some 300 men to leave from Texel with substantial supplies of arms. From France itself a major invasion force of 4,000 men and a field train of artillery under General Hardy was to sail from Brest, and General Humbert was to sail from Rochefort in 3 frigates (the *Concorde*, the *Médée* and the *Surveillante*) with just over 1,000 troops made up of an infantry battalion and a half company of artillery.[11]

All these expeditions were designed to land in the north-west because the United Irish exiles in Paris were adamant that it was an area with little military cover but a number of excellent landing places:

The part of the coast that we are referring to is not guarded in any way; there are many safe landing places; there are little or no soldiers in the area of the north-west; the people there are unusually brave and more used to handling arms than in any other part of the island; yet they have all been disarmed a year ago after the proclamation of General Lake.[12]

Once they had landed the orders given to Hardy, the general in charge, were quite specific. He was to land, contact local United Irishmen and distribute proclamations announcing the French arrival, confirm their intention of supporting the revolt and make contact with United Irish activists:

As soon as you can it will be valuable to gather around you a number of the leaders of the patriot party and organise with them a provisional government for the whole country, on behalf of the United Irishmen, if there is not already one established. Ensure that places are given to men who are noted for their virtues, their love for liberty, and let the government become the central point for the giving of orders and for the receiving of accounts and reports. In every town and canton you should equally set up civil or military administrators, depending on the circumstances, who will correspond with the provisional government, and carry out all acts of the superior authority.[13]

This was classic French invasion procedure, as practised in Belgium, the Rhineland and Lombardy: first the victories and then the appointment of local revolutionaries to administrative posts within a hierarchical system under French control. The French were confident that the system would work, because of repeated assurances from United Irish exile that local revolutionaries would be happy to co-operate. Hardy himself assured his men that:

The Irish will welcome you with joy. They will fulfil all the duties of hospitality towards you; their solicitude and mine will see to all your needs, and they will supplement your wages with their money. They will do more than that, for they will throw themselves into your ranks to hasten the destruction of the tyrants which have for too long oppressed them with impunity.[14]

However, everything then went tragically wrong. In late June and early July delay followed delay.[15] The Directors became concerned that Austria was about to resume hostilities because of the invasion of

43

Egypt and was unwilling to commit itself too heavily. There was conflict between Schérer, the minister of war, who was personally opposed to the project, and the minister of the navy, Bruix, who was in charge of it. Financial problems arose over the money needed to purchase ships' supplies, and troops refused to embark until they had been paid in advance. To make matters worse the initial commander of the expedition, Chérin, fell ill, then fell out with the minister of war and finally resigned in late August, leaving General Hardy in charge. In the middle of the chaos General Humbert was the first to leave, sailing from Rochefort on 5 August with 1,019 men and over 2,000 rifles. He landed in Killala Bay in north Mayo two weeks later, having failed to make it to Killybegs, his initial destination. Jean-Joseph Amable Humbert was a courageous soldier who had joined the army as a volunteer in 1792 and quickly climbed through the ranks. Having served in the civil war in the Vendée under Hoche, he had also been in the Bantry expedition. Yet he was no Hoche, and certainly no Bonaparte, lacking both political acumen and anything more than basic tactical sense.[16] Several of his officers were mediocre too – many of them noted more for their drinking records than for their military ability and suffering from debilitating war wounds. Most of the troops were young and experienced but much of that experience had been gained in guerrilla activity in the Vendée against counter-revolutionaries, and not in the kind of pitched battles that faced them in Ireland.[17] In the event the tiny French army took Killala easily and support flowed in from the neighbouring areas as local peasants rushed to join up and wear French uniforms. The French were delighted by the enthusiasm, though somewhat bemused by the appearance of scapulas and crucifixes, which they had last seen carried by their counter-revolutionary enemies in the Vendée. They were also bewildered by the apparent belief that they had come in the name of the Virgin Mary rather than of the French Republic. Nevertheless Humbert advanced from Killala to take Castlebar on 26 August. Then, despite explicit instructions that he was to move north to await the arrival of the main forces due to come from Brest under General Hardy, instead set off for Dublin. The army led by General Cornwallis closed in and on 8 September Humbert's 900 troops, along with the Irish volunteers that had joined him were defeated at Ballinamuck. Many of the volunteers were slaughtered but Humbert and his officers were taken to Dublin before being repatriated to France.[18]

The fate of the other elements of the invasion force was no better. Napper Tandy sailed from Dunkirk to arrive in Donegal on 17 September, accompanied by a little over 100 United Irish exiles and 80 French officers. He quickly learnt that the revolt had failed and decided that there was nothing to be gained by staying. Hardy meanwhile was blockaded in Brest and when the admiral in charge of the expedition, Bompard, did manage to get out on 16 September, with ten ships holding some 3,000 men on board, British frigates tracked them to Donegal. They moved in off Lough Swilly on 12 October to capture a ship of the line and three frigates. Wolfe Tone was among the prisoners taken. Two back-up expeditions in October were planned, but cancelled when Bompard's defeat was known. Two Dutch frigates that sailed out of Texel at the end of August, had been captured by the British next morning.

The failure of the 1798 expeditions was due to three factors: the over-confidence of the United Irishmen, the power of the British navy and the multiple commitments of the French Directory. The United Irish leaders in Paris had been confident that the insurrection would be a success, and, had they been correct, there would have been a good base for French operations when Humbert landed in the summer of 1798. Instead the rising was over by the end of June, well before Humbert arrived. The power of the British navy, however, ensured that even this late assistance was difficult to deliver. The British blockades of Brest and Texel could never be wholly secure, as had been shown in 1796 when Hoche's expedition had been able to slip out of Brest and cruise round the south-west of Ireland untouched and unsuspected. Yet those blockades were effective in 1798 and prevented Hardy's forces from arriving at the same time as Humbert's. If that had happened, then the French military campaign would have been stronger and better led. Finally, the commitments of the Directory ensured that its response to the appeal from Ireland was slow and fragmented. The best French troops were in the middle east, many of the others were stationed on the Rhine frontier, and the 10,000 or so that were mobilised for the Irish expeditions took a painful amount of time to get into position.

Does that mean that 1798 was a fatal lost opportunity for Ireland? If the French had come in time, and in sufficient numbers, would an Irish Republic have been established and the history of Ireland taken a totally different direction? Any attempt to answer this involves moving from history to speculation, yet it is an important question because of the significance of 1798 in the development of Irish nationalism. It therefore calls for a balanced assessment of the Irish situation and French intentions. The Irish situation is examined by other historians in this book, and needs no further analysis here. For the French intentions, an initial approach is to examine the orders given to Hardy and Humbert cited above. They were quite clear: French troops were to assist the insurrection, help to organise an adequate command structure and ensure an independent Ireland. In a general address to his soldiers (who never landed), Hardy claimed that the Irish deserved freedom and that they should be treated not as enemies but as 'born friends of the French republic'. Their property, customs, persons and religion were to be respected.[19] There is no doubt, therefore, that the Directory and its generals had the best of intentions and that if things had worked out according to plan an Irish republic would have come about. However, the experience of French military occupation elsewhere in Europe suggests that good intentions were rarely translated into practice. Material and religious problems lay at the heart of the problem. In Belgium and the Rhineland, as in the satellite republics in Holland or Italy, the costs of French intervention were high in terms of taxation, requisitions and confiscations. French rule, whether in annexed territories or satellite republics, tended to rest on the support of small middle class minorities, with the mass of the population either apathetic or outraged by high taxes and military indiscipline.[20] It is difficult to believe that Ireland would have been different, if only because much of the information that the French had been given in Paris by United Irish exiles had been overly optimistic. Once captured at Ballinamuck, French officers expressed their surprise at the poverty they had met in the west of Ireland, which they attributed to the ignorance, superstition and idleness of the population. They were also surprised not to have received support from the middle and upper classes, or from Protestants, as many of the United Irishmen in Paris had assured them that they would. The religious problem would also have led to serious difficulties, for the virulent anti-clericalism of French soldiers had already offended large swathes of the population of other conquered countries such as Belgium, the Rhineland and Italy.[21] The generals were well aware of the problem and, like Hardy, urged their troops to respect Catholic practice, but for many of the men in the ranks the connection between Catholicism and counter-revolution was so deeply embedded in their experience that attacks on churches, priests and religious objects had already been a frequent occurrence. Most of Humbert's troops had spent a long period in the Vendée pitted against Catholic guerrilla counter-revolutionaries. Their anti-clerical susceptibilities, and those of their fellow troops who failed to land, would certainly have been political dynamite in an Ireland where religion and identity were as closely linked as they had been in the counter-revolutionary Vendée.

Even if French armies had maintained discipline, it is doubtful if their small numbers would have been enough to take control of the whole island. Here again the optimism of the exiles in Paris was problematic, for they had encouraged the belief that token forces were all that was needed. But the reality was very different. In the event, the French troops committed to Ireland would not have been enough to ensure a rapid victory and a prolonged military conflict – or even stalemate – would probably have resulted, even if Hardy had been able to land successfully. The death toll in Wexford would have paled in comparison with the casualties from a prolonged civil war. And for what purpose? Probably not an independent republic, for there is absolutely no indication either that the French intended to garrison Ireland, or that the United Irishmen expected a prolonged occupation. The most likely scenario is that France, if victorious, would have used Ireland in negotiations with Britain to end the war and that the country would have been returned to Britain as part of a general European settlement. Certainly neither the Directory nor Napoleon had any special commitment to Ireland's independence except insofar as it secured French power. The problem with assessing the 1798 rebellion has always been the question of what might have happened if the French had arrived in time or in sufficient numbers. Much of the available evidence suggests that, however revolutionary and noble the ideology that Tone and the United Irish had developed over the previous eight years, what would have happened would have been a bloody civil war followed by a negotiated settlement and a draconian version of the Act of Union. The French failure in 1798 was therefore probably not a missed opportunity, but a fortunate escape for all three countries.

WOLFE TONE AND THE
REPUBLICAN IDEAL

Marianne Elliott

WHEN I WROTE MY biography of Wolfe Tone in 1989, I was struck at how the stories and images which had developed around his name had greatly diminished his sheer humanity, even humility. The colossal statue on Stephen's Green has nothing of the light-hearted, incorrigibly optimistic Tone of reality, even if it is in keeping with the stature his name has acquired in Irish nationalist tradition. Tone is hailed (or damned, depending on one's viewpoint) as the founder of Irish republican nationalism. As such, his name, political philosophy, life and early death became powerful political weapons in the hands of later generations of republican nationalists. The annual pilgrimages to his grave at Bodenstown are nearly always the occasions for key political statements by the respective parties. Despite the very large corpus of works of Tone – still readily accessible in print – the one passage (indeed the only one) which is widely known is 'the common name of Irishman' one, written at the height of his mission to revolutionary France in the summer of 1796:

> To subvert the tyranny of our execrable government, to break the connection with England, the never-failing source of all our political evils, to assert the independence of my country – these were my objects. To unite the whole people of Ireland, to abolish the memory of past dissensions, and to substitute the common name of Irishman, in the place of the denominations of Protestant, Catholic and Dissenter – these were my means.

It became – and has remained – central to militant republicanism's claim that Britain is the cause of all Ireland's wrongs. In fact Tone was far too clever and pragmatic ever to have reached such a simplistic conclusion. His real message was that Ireland's abiding evil was her religious dissensions; and he was in a better position than most to realise the consequences, for it was the bigotry that he encountered in Irish society which launched his political career. It is the detail of that career which is as important as the political writings in explaining how this Anglican barrister was to become the icon of later Catholic nationalism.

TONE WAS BORN IN DUBLIN IN 1763 into a middle-class Protestant family. His education – in a private classical school, at Trinity College Dublin and finally at the Inns of Court in London – groomed him as a member of Ireland's Protestant élite, with good prospects of attaining legal and political office. His formative years were those of 'Grattan's Parliament', a period looked back to by constitutional nationalists as one in which Ireland came close to resolving peacefully its anomalous constitutional position. After almost a century of insecurity and grudging acceptance of England's tight colonial control, the Irish Protestants had emerged in the 1780s as confident, improving, deeply influenced by Enlightenment ideas of reason and progress and impatient at the impediments imposed on that progress by England's control of their commerce, government and legislative process. A constitutional opposition had won legislative independence for Ireland in 1782, while retaining the connection with England through the crown and executive.

The reality of that 'independence', however, remained a dead letter. Necessary political reform did not follow because of Protestant fears of restoring political rights to the Catholics. But the rhetoric of reforming pamphleteers in the 1780s had created a novel force in Ireland: that of public opinion. It was on the tail of this rhetorical outpouring that Tone emerged as a leading reformer, and it was his discovery that much of the rhetoric was pure posturing which set him on the road to republicanism of the separatist variety. Analysing why Irish political life remained as corrupt and unrepresentative after 1782 as it had been before, Tone discovered the cause in the disunion of Irishmen. The outcome was his first mature work: *An Argument on behalf of the Catholics of Ireland* (1791). Irritated by the anti-popery even of the most radical Presbyterians in Belfast, Tone adopted their own arguments to highlight the inconsistency of excluding the Catholics from their reform demands. They could hardly complain about the failure of reform or proclaim the rights of man, when they refused to extend them to two-thirds of the nation. For it was their own refusal to admit the Catholics into their reform demands which permitted government to reject them. He confronted all the traditional shibboleths of Protestant imagination: the idea of 'popery' as subversive and intolerant, its adherents incapable of independent thinking and irretrievably backward. These he countered in turn, showing how the nature of international Catholicism had been altered by the French Revolution. If the traditional accusations had ever been true – and he accepted that they had – the Protestants had only themselves to blame:

> We plunge them by law, and continue them by statute, in gross ignorance, and then we make the incapacity we have created an argument for their exclusion from the common rights of man! We plead our crime in justification of itself.

Behind his own lingering Protestant prejudices lay a growing conviction in the fundamental injustice of excluding Catholics from the political life of the nation. It was an argument based on the principle of natural rights and Tone was making it before Paine's *Rights of Man* burst upon the world.

Tone's *Argument* marked the turning point in his own life and indeed in the development of Irish nationalism generally. He was always restless for success and he was not finding it in the legal profession. As a political pamphleteer he was unrivalled. His works addressed controversial issues with force and authority. They were written in plain man's English, and became best-sellers in their time. His *Argument* brought him to the notice of radical Catholic and Protestant leaders. His invitation to Belfast in October 1791 to help found the Society of United Irishmen was the immediate and most famous outcome. But equally important – and arguably more so for his own political development – was his appointment as agent, then secretary to the Catholic Committee, then campaigning for a total repeal of the penal laws.

For the next three years, Tone acted as the chief publicist to both movements. Newspaper articles, letters, pamphlets, propositions and petitions flowed from his pen, bringing him the kind of fame he had always craved. Expectations of full emancipation for the Catholics and an extension of political and civil rights generally ran high, and some, Tone included, spoke privately of the eventual possibility of a negotiated independence from England – though before 1795, this was never a serious public proposition, even for Tone.

However, war erupted between England and revolutionary France in 1793. The executions of Louis XVI, Marie Antoinette and the French nobles, sent a tremor through the existing social and political establishments of Europe. French subversion abroad made governments nervous of radical movements at home, and demands considered constitutional before 1793, became positively subversive after it. In Ireland war-induced panic produced a series of coercive measures which startled even Whitehall by their severity. The United Irishmen were banned, demands for Catholic emancipation and political reform rejected, and the sudden clamp down when hopes had been running so high left reformers of all hues stunned. The arrival of a secret French agent just at this time, with offers of military assistance, forced a decision about the future direction of radicalism. Because of his reputation as the most talented of the United Irishmen's political writers, Tone was asked by the agent to draw up a statement on the current political state of Ireland. Although his co-operation had been somewhat half-hearted, Tone was now implicated in treason, because the agent was discovered, arrested and tried.

This does not mean that Tone was an avowed militant separatist by 1794 – quite the contrary. Having laid low for the best part of a year, he expected to be rehabilitated under the new pro-Catholic regime of Earl Fitzwilliam in early 1795. But he was to be rudely disillusioned. To the Whigs and many other pro-emancipationist constitutional politicians, he was now considered as much a traitor as by the government party, and so he was treated. Their message to him was clear: if you do not leave the country, you may be tried for treason. It left him but a few weeks to comply and there is a note of desperation in his final preparations. His journey to Belfast in May 1795, en route to America and then France, is now the stuff of legend. For it was on the Cavehill, overlooking Belfast, that he, along with Thomas Russell, Henry Joy McCracken and a number of other United Irishmen, claimed to have taken an oath to make Ireland independent of England. It is the point at which modern Irish republicanism is said to have started. But Tone's republicanism was still not fully developed. His departure from Ireland has more the character of flight than pre-planned mission and it is unlikely that the ideas for which he is best known would ever have been enunciated had they not now gone through the crucible of American, and more particularly French, republican influences.

His growing recognition that the power of a narrow Protestant élite in Ireland ultimately depended on England, was more finely tuned by his discovery of a similar governing class in America. His disillusionment with the way American independence was developing was the backdrop to his extremely negative comments about American society in his journals. He hated the country's materialism and much else besides and his fanatical allusions to America in his Paris journals so embarrassed his widow two decades later – by which time she was an American resident – that she excised them altogether when putting the journals to press. They did not re-surface until this century.

TONE COMMENCED HIS SECRET MISSION to France in February 1796. By then the French government was hardened to foreign exiles seeking help to effect domestic revolutions. Yet Tone managed to convince the Directory that the Irish were different, that they were a friendly nation with whose assistance England might be defeated. This was no mean achievement and Tone's negotiating skills must have been a good deal more developed than his characteristic self-mockery would have us believe. Certainly he succeeded in turning French plans for a wrecking diversion into a full-scale campaign for Irish liberation and negotiated and sailed on board a major French invasion attempt on Ireland in December 1796. In command was France's most fêted general, Lazare Hoche. Though he was slightly younger than Tone, the two men were remarkably similar in character. Their friendship was a crucial element in Tone's success. For a few months in 1796 Ireland was central to French revolutionary war strategy.

It was during this time – as he awaited orders to leave for Brest to take up his posting on board the expedition – that Tone wrote the document on which much of his future reputation was to be based: his autobiography. His writing of the autobiography came on the heels of a long period of clarification, synthesisation and inevitable propaganda, as he argued Ireland's case with a sceptical French Directory, and its polemical tone is quite out of character with the style of his daily journals. It was to become the gospel of Irish republicanism. The elements of that gospel, stripped of its French terminology, are that the Catholics are the nation proper and Protestant power is based on 'massacre and plunder' and penalisation of the Catholics. In this reading Protestant nationalism does not figure. Indeed Tone overcompensates for his own Protestant background – a common trait in liberal Irish Protestantism through the ages. The northern Presbyterians are spared such blanket condemnation by virtue of their anti-Englishness, anti-Anglicanism and what Tone sees as their natural republicanism. In all he rather glamorises the Presbyterians and never comes to terms with their anti-popery.

In looking back on his own political development, he admits that he did not actively seek a republic, that the pinnacle of his ambition for a while was a seat in the Irish Parliament and that his anti-Englishness was instinct rather than principle. Yet although his journals show a more contained dislike of England, the process of exile – more particularly his months of writing anti-English propaganda for the Directory – had funnelled his own and Ireland's problems to one source: English rule. The atmosphere in France in 1796 in itself would have crystallised such feelings, for Anglo-phobia was all pervasive, and France's tendency to attribute all her own problems to England's evil influence would have provided a ready model. By September 1796, therefore, the emotional propaganda of Tone's French writings had been refined and accepted as his 'theory', a 'theory' which in retrospect he felt had determined his actions since 1791. The outcome was his 'common name of Irishman' statement. It would become the most quoted passage in modern Irish history.

THE IRISH EXPEDITION FINALLY SAILED from Brest on 15 December 1796. It carried 14,500 troops and arms and ammunition for the Irish expected to join the French standard. It was one of the largest expeditions to sail from French shores during the revolutionary wars and neither the British navy nor the Irish defence forces were prepared to meet it. Expectations of success ran high. But things went badly wrong from the outset. One ship foundered just out of Brest, with the loss of all but 45 of the 1,300 men on board. The next day the rest of the fleet was scattered in dense fog and both Hoche and the naval commander were blown far off course, and never re-joined the main fleet. As the reduced fleet entered Bantry Bay on 22 December, the weather deteriorated, damaging and scattering the remaining ships. Seasickness completed for Tone the miserable experience. By the time Hoche's ship finally neared the Irish coast on 30 December, the main fleet had already returned to France. 'England,' Tone wrote in his journal, 'has not had such an escape since the Spanish Armada'.

Over a third of the French force and a quarter of the ships had been lost at sea and French opinion had now turned against another Irish attempt. Tone still found in Hoche an ardent supporter. But Hoche's health had been irretrievably damaged by the Bantry Bay experience and he died of tuberculosis nine months later. Tone was in despair. Not only had he lost a personal friend, but the fate of the Irish mission to France had depended on Hoche's support. Having been unopposed in his efforts for the past year and a half, he now found his reputation and credentials called into doubt by squabbling fellow United Irishmen, who had been arriving in France in increasing numbers to escape the government clamp-down at home. Tone's heightened sense of honour was offended by their accusations. When news of the 1798 rebellion arrived in France, it came as a surprise alike to the Irish exiles and the Ireland-watchers in French government circles and the rush to send help produced little over 4,500 men (less than a third of the forces which had sailed with Hoche).

There had been a disillusionment and distancing of himself from the exiled Irish in Tone's final writings in France. His participation on board the small expedition which left Brest on 26 September had an air of resignation rather than hopefulness. By then the other forces which had sailed from France had already failed, and as his ship neared the Donegal coast on 12 October, it was attacked and captured by the British navy. Tone was arrested and transferred to Dublin. When he left it three years earlier, even many government supporters had thought him badly treated. Now, with his activities in France exposed to the world, they were resentful and angry at having been so duped.

Tone was tried and capitally convicted in the Royal (now Collins') Barracks. As a French officer he had genuinely thought his request for execution by firing squad would have been granted. It is a token of how far he had become a Frenchman in his last months. In his trial speech he seemed not to recognise the Ireland to which he had returned. He distanced himself from the bloodshed and sectarian overtones of the 1798 rebellion:

> I have endeavoured by every means in my power to break [the] connection [with England] ... to create a people in Ireland ... to abolish the infernal spirit of religious persecution by uniting the Catholics and the Dissenters ... for a fair and open war I was prepared; if that has degenerated into a system of assassination, massacre and plunder, I do most sincerely lament it.

For the national glory to which he had aspired, Tone's death may have been timely. Had he been exchanged back to France with the other French officers, it is likely that he would have further distanced himself from militant Irish republicanism as he saw it developing and been content to pursue his career as a French soldier. On the evening of 11 November Tone learnt that he had been sentenced to be publicly hanged the following morning. Shortly afterwards he cut his own throat with a penknife and died a week later on 19 November.

Even today many Irish people find it difficult to accept that Tone died by his own hand. And yet such action was totally in line with Tone's political thought. In the classical tradition in which he was educated, the suicides of figures such as Cato and Socrates were considered part of republican virtue, the dignified assertion of personal control by man. In France it was a common occurrence, particularly among successive waves of deposed politicians. He had talked the matter through with his family before he had sailed from France. In eighteenth-century Enlightenment thinking, Tone's suicide would have been considered the supreme affirmation of his own republicanism.

TO THE UNITED IRISH MOVEMENT, Tone's loss was irreparable. The sectarian divisions which he had so decried, would decimate the movement. The squabbles of the Irish exiles in France would disgust the French officials, once so eager to help. But even by contemporaries who disagreed with his political principles, Tone was considered as completely immune from such pettiness. It was his character as much as his writings which won people over. He was a compulsive writer and talker, and it is the spontaneity, humour and sheer honesty of his journals which are the main reason for their lasting appeal. The tendency to quote simply his more polemical statements misrepresents the man. He was no Pearse. He had no martyr complex. He was too practical, too compassionate to see some kind of victory in unnecessary bloodshed. His republicanism was the product of that age of enlightenment and cosmopolitanism which was only brought to a close by the onset of romanticism at the end of the eighteenth-century. There is a sense in his last days that it was an age which had already disappeared and his own republicanism may not have survived intact had he lived to draw the lessons of 1798.

This talk has been based on my book: *Wolfe Tone. Prophet of Irish Independence* (Yale UP, 1989). For a shorter and very readable survey, see Thomas Bartlett, *Theobald Wolfe Tone* (Dundalgen Press, 1997).

Dublin's role in the 1798 Rebellion

Tommy Graham

DESPITE THE ARREST OF almost the entire Leinster leadership at Oliver Bond's on 12 March 1798, Dublin's United Irishmen continued to prepare for rebellion. Membership continued to expand, from 1,500 in January to almost 10,000 by May, with an additional 9,000 claimed for the county; a plausible military strategy for a rising had been adopted as early as March; officers had been elected; weapons had been procured; and most important of all, the organisation's leadership had not been penetrated by castle spies or informers.

So what did happen in Dublin on the night of 23 May? If there was such an impressive organisation on paper why was there no apparent rising in the city?

On 11 May Camden informed London that a rising was expected in the city – 'Orders have been given, as some of the lower orders who give us intelligence have informed us, that they should provide pikes and be ready if called upon to rise ... in 13 or 14 days time' (i.e., 23 or 24 May).[1] The arrest of Lord Edward Fitzgerald, their intended commander-in-chief, on 19 May, was a shattering blow to the United Irishmen, but not an entirely fatal one. Preparations for a rising continued under Samuel Neilson's direction. On 21 May, Neilson brought the date for the rising forward by a day, to the night of Wednesday, 23 May.[2] The castle's best-placed spy, Samuel Sproule, was still not sure if the rising was to be on Wednesday or Thursday.[3]

Wednesday, 23 May, dawned with the castle still unclear as to the timing, the place or even the form of the rising. That morning Sproule had been dispatched to the militia camp at Loughlinstown, twelve miles south-east of the city, but had little to report – 'their movements are so quick and changes so many that few of themselves know where they will be six hours hence'.[4] Sproule's best source was from Lucan, venue for the co-ordination of Dublin's United Irishmen with the surrounding counties, particularly with Kildare, which was expected to provide the core of the intended rebel advance on the capital. Sproule's source was lieutenant to the local United Irish captain, John McMahon, who acted as liaison between Dublin and the surrounding counties.[5]

A second report from Sproule reached the castle at 4.30pm. McMahon had left instructions with his lieutenant to mobilise their company in half an hour. Two deputies had been dispatched, one each to Kildare and Wicklow, in order to raise them that night. But Sproule was still not sure if Dublin was to rise on the same night or the one following (as the castle expected), after the Kildare and Wicklow rebels had drawn the military out of the city.[6] By 9pm he was still not sure.[7]

Meanwhile at precisely the same time Samuel Neilson assembled fifteen Dublin city and county colonels near Abbey Street, produced a map and assigned each a post to occupy.[8] The main rendezvous points were Smithfield on the northside and Newmarket (beside the Coombe) on the southside. Orders were also given to intercept the mail coaches in order to rouse the rest of the country. However, an hour earlier the crucial information, of a rising in the city at 10pm, had already been communicated to the castle by the spy Thomas Boyle.[9]

According to Jonah Barrington, the yeomanry occupied Smithfield, 'considered as the *probable* point of attack ... as night approached' (about 9pm, the very time when Neilson assembled Dublin's colonels).[10] He described the scene with irreverent hilarity:

> The gradations of their discipline and enthusiasm were, however, extremely amusing; those who had imbibed their full quantum of generous fluids, were the most fierce and enthusiastic; others who had dined on substantial matters were as steady as posts. But those who had paraded before dinner, after standing under arms for some hours, could endure it no longer, and a forced loan of cheese, tongues, and bottled porter, from a Mr. Murray, of Great George's Street, was unanimously decided upon and immediately carried into execution.

He had an equally jaundiced view of the military tactics involved:

> It [Smithfield] ... formed altogether one of the most disagreeable positions in which an immense body of demi-disciplined men and horses

ever were stationed in solid mass, without any other order than, 'if you are attacked, defend yourselves to the last extremity'.

The cavalry and infantry were, in some places, so compactly interwoven, that a dragoon could not wield his sword without cutting down a foot soldier, nor a foot soldier discharge his musket without knocking down a trooper. The cavalry being elevated, could breathe freely in the crowd; but the infantry could scarcely avoid suffocation. A few hundred insurgents, with long pikes, coming on rapidly in the dark, might, without difficulty, have assailed the yeomen at once from five different points.[11]

Barrington's worst fears were never realised. The mere presence of massed ranks of yeomanry at the rendezvous points was sufficient to persuade the small bands of rebels attempting to assemble to return home. According to the loyalist historian Sir Richard Musgrave:

The rebel drums were to have beaten to arms an hour after ours ... if they had preceded us by ever so small a space of time, the fate of the city and its loyal inhabitants would have been decided; for the mass of the people, armed with pikes and other weapons, were lurking in lanes, alleys and bye-places, ready to start forth on the first beat of their drums, and would have occupied all the streets and assassinated the yeomen before they could have reached their respective stations.[12]

Neilson, meanwhile, left the meeting of colonels and headed towards Newgate jail in order to reconnoitre it for an attack to liberate its prisoners (including Lord Edward, Oliver Bond and Henry Jackson). Neilson was recognised by Gregg, the jailer, and arrested after a great struggle.

After this series of disasters it is not surprising that Dublin's rising fell apart before it even started. Not only had the yeomanry occupied Smithfield, Newmarket and other rendezvous points but they had also barricaded the Liffey bridges, seriously impeding rebel communication within the city, and set up checkpoints on the main approach-roads and canal bridges, effectively blocking large-scale rebel infiltration from outside.[13]

Given this unfavourable situation what is remarkable is not so much the absence of rebellion in the city but the degree to which the attempt was made at all. According to the Revd William Bennet, former private secretary to Viceroy Westmorland and later bishop of

Cloyne, there was physical evidence to prove it:

> As the rebels came in detached bodies to parade in the places marked out
> for them, they found them already seized by the king's troops, and after
> sunrise the lanes and alleys to Smithfield and other posts were found
> full of pikes and muskets which they had dropped and thrown away in
> their precipitate retreat.[14]

Meanwhile thousands of rebels attempted to converge on the metropolis from the surrounding county to reinforce their city comrades but were stopped by the yeomanry checkpoints or else stopped short themselves once they realised that the rising had not gone according to plan.[15]

Bennet presents this assessment of the potential threat the rebels represented:

> Neilson was one of the most determined and intelligent of all the rebel
> leaders, and it was entirely owing to his and Lord Edward Fitzgerald
> being apprehended that the night of the 23rd passed over so quietly. The
> columns of the rebels which surrounded the town waited one for the
> other to begin, and had any daring officer been found to lead his men
> under fire, the others from Ringsend, Eccles St, Clontarf and Harold's
> Cross in all which places were large bodies of them, would have probably followed the example, which might have been of the worst consequences as the garrison was so weak, and the troops from Loughlinstown camp did not arrive till two in the morning.[16]

United Irish forces did attempt to effect the plan agreed upon. Rebel armies began to mobilise on the night of 23 May in the surrounding counties – Wicklow, Kildare, Meath and north County Dublin – and by the morning of 24 May held a crescent of positions around the capital. Their task was to deal with local government forces before advancing on the city.

Three mail coaches had been stopped; the Belfast mail at Santry; the Athlone mail at Lucan; and the Cork mail at Naas.[17] Not all had been stopped. The Enniskillen mail coach had managed to dodge the Meath rebels gathering at Dunboyne, while the Cork mail had given Dublin rebels the slip at Clondalkin before it was stopped by a party of Kildare rebels under Michael Reynolds at Naas. Immediately adjacent to the city, meanwhile, on the night of 23 May, rebel bands from the five surrounding baronies advanced into the metropolis to link up with their comrades within. The intended rendezvous never took place, thanks to Boyle's last-minute information, and on the morning of 24 May they hovered hesitantly on the edges of the city. Nevertheless Musgrave claimed that 'it was afterwards discovered that many rebels had passed over the bridges before the troops took post on them'.[18]

The rebel armies in the counties around Dublin waited in vain for the expected rising in the city. To make matters worse, after the arrest of Neilson, there were no leaders of national authority remaining who might have issued fresh instructions in an attempt to retrieve a desperate situation, for example, by ordering an immediate advance on Dublin. None came and by the evening of Saturday 26 May, government forces had scored a major success, with the routing of the Meath rebels gathered at Tara. Despite this victory Camden warned London on 28 May of an imminent provisions crisis in the capital if the rebellion lasted.[19] Fortunately for government, the Kildare rebels, intimidated by the defeat at Tara, attempted to negotiate terms, a process of conciliation ended abruptly by General Duff's massacre of unarmed rebels at the Curragh on Tuesday 29 May. Although Kildare rebels remained in the field for another two months (until Aylmer's surrender at Timahoe on 23 July), they were largely ineffective. Within a week of the outbreak of rebellion, therefore, the rebel blockade of Dublin was lifted and the focus of attention shifted southwards to Wexford.

In the wake of the rebellion's defeat some provincial United Irishmen blamed the Dubliners for failing to rise.[20] In reality the position of Dublin's rebels was an impossible one after the disasters of 23 May. The city was saturated with government troops and remained so for the duration of the rebellion.[21] Wholesale arrests decimated United Irish organisation. A 9pm to 5am curfew was imposed and the yeomanry continued to man checkpoints.[22] Exemplary executions of rebels apprehended within the city or in the skirmishes on its outskirts were carried out at the main city bridges, an exercise in terror that was complemented by the circulation of rumours and reports of the impending massacre and plunder of the city's inhabitants by the

rebels.[23] These reports had their effect, particularly on 'the men of property'. According to McNally, 'the merchants and traders' were increasingly unsympathetic to the rebel cause, and Camden himself
reported approvingly to London on 'the spirit of loyalty shown by all
descriptions of the respectable inhabitants of Dublin'. The point was
demonstrated most cynically by the public declaration of loyalty by
Dublin's leading Catholic merchant and onetime United Irishman,
John Keogh.[24] The loyalty, or at least neutrality, of this middle stratum
was to prove a crucial factor in government's favour. The spymaster
Francis Higgins observed a similar class differentiation lower down the
social scale. While apprentices remained radical, shopmen and clerks
were less enthusiastic.[25] In the face of these severe pressures Dublin's
United Irish leadership collapsed: delegates in the city were 'all astray',
according to Thomas Boyle. There were no meetings planned nor
had orders been issued for two or three days.[26]

In or around 28 May, John Martin, an Augustinian friar from
Drogheda, and its leading United Irishman, slipped into town as an
emissary from the rebels of the surrounding counties, who wished to
ascertain the intentions of their city comrades. Martin's position as a
regular clergyman, unattached to any particular parish, was a perfect
cover for his roving mission. He was already a preacher of some note
not only in his own diocese of Meath but also in neighbouring Dublin before being sworn a United Irishman in Easter 1797. Thereafter
he combined his spiritual with his political role and preached for 'a
levelling of all units ... and the dissolution of all establishments'. He
had been particularly active in the Dunboyne area.[27] He found morale
low after the defeats of the previous days, so low, in fact, that the city
committee was afraid to meet him. He had to settle for a meeting
with a twenty-five-man 'Committee of the District of Thomas Street',
probably the committee of the Workhouse division, headed by James
Moore, a Thomas Street ironmonger. The Workhouse was the only
one of the city's four United Irish divisions which continued to function. According to Sproule 500 of its men gathered at Mill Street in
the Tenters on the night of Thursday 24 May, in anticipation of a
second attempt at insurrection in the city and waited two hours (between 11pm and 1am) before dispersing. It was no isolated effort and

was co-ordinated by the ubiquitous McMahon who was attempting to liase with Wicklow rebels and sympathetic militia in Loughlinstown. It came to nothing because it depended upon word of the north rising.[28]

Martin was dispatched to co-ordinate a renewed effort with rebels outside the city. He returned to Dunboyne but was unsuccessful in promoting a second rising there and headed south to Kilbride in County Wicklow before reporting back to individuals of the Thomas Street committee. The committee itself was afraid to meet him. Morale revived somewhat with news of the successes in Wexford and Martin was again dispatched to try his luck in that quarter. At Rathfarnham he consulted with the local parish priest, Ledwich, uncle of Patrick Ledwich, the rebel captain executed at Queen's Bridge on 26 May. Next he met Joseph Holt in a shebeen nearby before heading off towards Arklow via Roundwood and Rathdrum.

In the meantime all Wexford was aflame. Enniscorthy fell on 28 May, Wexford town on 31 May and on 4 June government fortunes reached their nadir with Walpole's defeat at Ballymore, near Gorey, and the consequent possibility of a rebel advance on the capital. Dublin's United Irishmen could claim some indirect credit for these rebel successes. It was the potential threat they posed which prevented Viceroy Camden from deploying the necessary troops to crush the Wexford rebellion at an early stage.[29] The gravity of the government's situation was well summed up by Bennet:

> Our situation at Dublin was remarkably perilous from the defeat of Walpole on the 4th of June to the defeat of the rebels at Arklow on the 9th, particularly as in the interval the rebellion broke out in the north. There were *four well-organised regiments of rebels in the city* ready to rise at the first approach of their friends.[30]

Neither Bennet's nor Camden's concern was mere paranoia. The revival of rebel fortunes was accompanied by a revival of their activity in Dublin city. Higgins reported that plans for a rising had not been abandoned and that meetings had been resumed. One rebel sergeant in particular had been seen calling at public houses and leaving details of rendezvous, directions and times in anticipation of the expected assault.[31]

On Wednesday 6 June, Fr Michael Murphy, of the north Wexford army, wrote to a confederate in Dublin, Thomas Houston of Thomas Street:

> Great events are ripening ... we shall have an army of brave republicans, one hundred thousand strong, with fourteen pieces of cannon on Tuesday [12 June] before Dublin; your heart will beat high at the news. You will rise with a proportionable force.[32]

McNally also warned the castle of a rising on 12 June.[33] Martin's mission to the south was to co-ordinate an attack on the city on the very same date.

The plan communicated by Martin presumed a rebel victory at Arklow and a consequent advance on Dublin along the coast. Meanwhile a second column, under the command of Wicklow captains, Holt, Nugent and Doyle, was to assemble in the mountains above Rathfarnham.[34] There was no mention of a rising inside the city and the evidence suggests that Dublin rebels were expected to join this latter column in order to draw government forces out of the city and leave it open to a third attack from Kildare and Meath rebels to the west. According to McNally north County Dublin was to rise if the Wicklowmen made their attack.[35] On 9 June Musgrave claimed that a party of rebels was heading towards the Wicklow mountains via Rathfarnham complete with green cockades and flags (suggesting an organised exodus)[36] and on 10 June Higgins reported that

> the fugitives who fled the city as well as members who skulk in their counties are directed by circular letter to join those societies who will detach themselves from the metropolis and pitch a camp at a strong position 4 or 5 miles form Dublin (I believe near Kilgobbin).

Not only that but he also claimed that Neilson was involved and had smuggled a letter out of jail.[37]

Martin was arrested near Rathdrum the day before the intended attack and made a full confession. His apprehension made little difference since the Wexford rebels had already been narrowly defeated at Arklow three days before, thus ending any realistic prospect of a rebel assault on the capital, although Musgrave claimed that as late as 19 June the Wexford rebels might have broken out of their impending encirclement and made a dash for Dublin.[38] Meanwhile, at Ballinahinch, County Down, on the same day (12 June) the Ulster United Irishmen made their last stand. By 15 June the castle was ready for the decisive attack on Wexford, but, ever conscious of the threat in Dublin itself, awaited reinforcements from England, which were delayed for lack of wind due to the unusually fine weather.[39] Within a week the Wexford rebels were encircled and decisively defeated at Vinegar Hill (21 June).

So there was no rebellion in Dublin in 1798 (apart from a few skirmishes in the county). But there were active Dublin rebels. According to Musgrave:

> As the disaffected in the metropolis were disappointed in their experience of raising an insurrection there, numbers of them left it at different times, and displayed their zeal in the cause of the union, by joining rebel encampments in the country.

In particular he observed that

> a great many servants and mechanicks, and other persons of various descriptions, suddenly disappeared in Dublin, and the neighbourhood of Blackrock; and it was observed, that the same thing took place, when the rebels were about to make any great effort in Wexford, Wicklow or Kildare.[40]

The evidence for this phenomenon is overwhelming. After some initial hesitation at the beginning of June, when a rebel advance on the capital still seemed a possibility, report after report reached the castle of bands of Dublin rebels heading towards the Wicklow mountains.[41]

It is more difficult to quantify the extent of Dublin participation in active rebellion. One indication is a list appended to the parliamentary reports of the Committees of Secrecy of 1,064 'persons who have surrendered themselves in the City of Dublin, confessed themselves being engaged in the present rebellion, and the number of arms surrendered, from the 29th of June last to the 9th day of September 1798'.[42] Unfortunately there is no indication of what exactly 'engaged' means. Did it mean United Irishmen who were passive supporters within the city or did it mean those who had returned to the city after active involvement in the rebellion outside?

There are a number of reasons for assuming the latter. In the first place, the dates involved (29 June to 9 September) would have allowed plenty of time for any active Dublin rebels to return to the city. Secondly, mixed in is a significant number of people from outside Dublin who were from counties that saw large-scale combat – Wicklow (eighteen), Wexford (ten), Kildare and Westmeath (six each), Carlow (three) and Meath (one). Thirdly, there was a pronounced southside bias in the figures for both the city and county of Dublin, i.e., in favour of those areas nearest the theatre of operations. For example the two Dublin baronies adjacent to the Wicklow mountains, Uppercross and Rathdown, accounted for three-quarters of the 104 County Dublin names listed, despite making up only 27% of the county's return of men claimed on the eve of the rebellion.[43] Sixteen were from Rathfarnham alone, which crops up again and again in the sources as a staging post for Dublin rebels heading towards the scene of the action in Wicklow and Wexford. The bias was even more pronounced for the 914 names for the city itself. Eighty-three per cent come from south of the river although the two south-side divisions (Workhouse and Green) accounted for only 40% of the returns of men claimed before the rebellion.[44] But why should geographic proximity to the theatre of operations be a factor in a city of limited area? A probable explanation was that the yeomanry checkpoints on the Liffey bridges were effective in preventing northside rebels from crossing the river and joining their comrades in the field to the south. In addition it has already been suggested that the Workhouse division was the only one of the four that continued to function after the outbreak of rebellion which would account for its disproportionately high number of active rebels, and indeed most of those from the neighbouring Green division were from streets adjacent to it.

| | NORTHSIDE | | SOUTHSIDE | | |
	Barrack	Rotunda	Green	Workhouse	TOTAL
Population of	25,000	35,000	65,000	55,000	180,000
Dublin City	14%	20%	36%	30%	100%
Last return of	1,953	3,996	1,540	2,400	9,889
UIM claimed	20%	40%	15%	25%	100%
'Engaged in	86	73	254	501	914
present	9%	8%	28%	55%	100%
rebellion ...'					
Ratio of	1:23	1:55	1:6	1:5	1:11
participation					

A fourth reason for assuming that this was largely a list of active Dublin rebels is its lowly social make-up. Only fifteen feature in the 1797 directory list of 'merchants and traders'.[45] Neither were the bulk of them United Irishmen of particular rank. Only thirty-two can be corroborated as United Irishmen from other sources – spy reports, lists of suspects, etc. – in other words were worthy of previous castle attention as secretaries, treasurers, baronial or divisional committee men, captains, colonels, etc. This is to be expected. Those on the list received protections on surrendering themselves, an option open only to those below the rank of captain or its civil equivalent in United Irish structures. Exceptions were sometimes made, however, and amongst the confirmed United Irishmen was a leavening of eight military men. One was James McAnally, probable colonel for the north Dublin barony of Balrothery. Another was John Toole, referred to as a 'major' in one information, who definitely left town to join the rebels on 4 June.[46] Apart from these exceptions, what we have here is a list of rank-and-file United Irishmen and it is difficult to believe that they would have felt it necessary to surrender themselves unless they were involved in something more than simply passive support for the rebel cause within the city.

One-third were weavers of one sort or another and the proportion rises to half in the Workhouse division – the Liberties, heart of Dublin's textile industry. Of these one-third were silk weavers, easily the most highly represented occupation in the overall sample (10%). This is not surprising: Dublin's textile industry in general was in recession in the late 1790s but silk weaving in particular was very badly hit and unemployment was highest in that sector, a decisive factor, according to Francis Higgins, in inducing men to join the rebels outside the city.[47] They had little to lose. It was also an indication of how adept the United Irishmen were in harnessing social discontent for revolutionary purposes.

How well organised was this exodus? Or to put it another way, to what extent did the Dubliners maintain their command structure in the field? According to Francis Higgins sixteen United Irishmen met in Farrington's pub in Rathmines at six o'clock on the morning of 4 June in order to mobilise small parties to join the rebels to the south. On 13 June he reported on 'field meetings of four committees' in Rathgar for the same purpose. The leading figures at the 4 June meeting were John Toole, a member of the city committee but also referred to as a 'major', and the Rotunda division colonel, Southwell McClune. The battle of New Ross occurred the following day and it is a remarkable fact that 'Colonel McClune, Dublin', appears on a 'list of rebel captains who obtained provisions from Commissary Brennan's book, Ross army and Corbett's Hill'.[48] Amongst the forty 'captains' listed are three from Dublin, one of whom was John Rourke, owner of the 'Golden Bottle' pub in Thomas Street and brother of Felix Rourke of Rathcoole, colonel for the County Dublin barony of Newcastle.[49] By the end of June McClune was a commander in the Wicklow mountains fighting a rearguard action and he sent messages into the city calling on United Irishmen to join him. He later surrendered and obtained a pardon.[50]

Felix Rourke gave an account of his involvement in the fighting in a series of letters to a sweetheart in Dublin, Mary Finaghty of 191 Abbey Street.[51] Because of illness, he laid low in the Donnybrook area until the middle of June, but later joined the retreating Wicklow and Wexford rebels at Whelp Rock near Blessington, 'where they formed a junction with *the county and city of Dublin rebels* under Markam, Rattigan [the Workhouse division colonel] and Rourke'. He went on to describe 'a long fatiguing march without sleep for two nights' into

County Meath and an attack on Clonard on 10 July led by 'the city and county of Dublin troops'. The presence of an organised Dublin contingent in the rump of the Wexford/Wicklow rebel army that eventually disintegrated by the middle of July was confirmed by Higgins who observed that many of their officers were tradesmen from the city.[52]

Those United Irishmen who remained behind were not entirely idle in pursuance of the cause. It was no small task simply to maintain lines of communication with the rebels outside the city and various ingenious methods were devised. For example, one courier, Hoey, a butter dealer from Kevin Street, passed off his frequent trips up and down the mountains as fishing trips![53] More seriously, Higgins claimed that funeral societies were United Irish covers and centres of com-munication.[54] In particular he complained about the pro-rebel propa-ganda disseminated in the city by the 'Humane Committee for the Relief of Prisoners' which met at the Globe Coffee House.[55] There are numerous references to arms and ammunition being smuggled out to the rebels, by women in particular. Of greater significance in the long-run was the traffic in the opposite direction. Throughout the fighting in Wexford wounded rebels were ferried up along the coast and landed at Clontarf, Howth, Rush and Skerries in order to recu-perate in safe houses.[56] They were also brought into the city itself. As rebel fortunes declined able-bodied rebel fugitives added to the in-flux. It was indeed ironic that the safest place for rebels on the run such as Myles Byrne of Wicklow was right under the nose of the castle, amidst the narrow alleys and laneways of Dublin's plebeian neighbourhoods.[57] These fugitive country rebels were to play a promi-nent role in the subsequent re-organisation of the movement and in Robert Emmet's renewed attempt five years later.[58]

Although Dublin's direct contribution to the rebellion was signi-ficant, the irony was that the more significant it became the less likelihood there was of a rising in or around the city itself, the castle's greatest fear. When the rebellion was in full flood in Wexford the more militant Dublin rebels headed south to join it but the corollary was that by July when its tattered remnants made its way northwards and pleaded with Dublin to rise, the more timid elements who had remained behind were the least likely to oblige. On 25 June (a week after the rebel defeat at Vinegar Hill) Under-Secretary Cooke reported to Wyckham in London that 'there are still endeavours to raise the people in the vicinity of Dublin but not with much effect'. By the time the rump of the Wexford/Wicklow army staggered its way northwards into Meath and Louth in the middle of July he reported that 'very few joined them in the vicinity of Dublin where they expected a general insurrection'.[59]

Fear was not the only motivation for rebel inaction. The new Viceroy Cornwallis' more conciliatory approach, made possible by the savage repression that had preceded it, had its effect and many Dublin United Irishmen embraced the amnesty offered.[60] Class antagonism was another factor. Thomas Boyle observed that 'the better sort of people in the county of Dublin have got completely quiet and wish for peace and good order, but the lower orders are as wicked as ever'.[61] The 'lower orders' drew their own conclusions. According to Francis Higgins 'they have declared they were deceived by higher ranks of people and would not be so again'. Likewise McNally reported a similar perception of betrayal by their leaders amongst the 'common people'.[62]

The last large rebel force, mainly Kildare rebels under William Aylmer, surrendered at Timahoe on 23 July. Five days later Cooke reported to London that 'Dublin and the county of Dublin [were] quiet'.[63]

1798 IN ANTRIM AND DOWN

A. T. Q. Stewart

DURING THE LAST, AND most eventful, decade of the eighteenth-century, insurrection was like the legendary tenth wave, towering above Ireland before crashing down on 23 May 1798. Some would say that in the foam and debris of that crash modern Ireland was born; others that it was an unparalleled catastrophe which created most of the problems we have with us today. At the time, however, most observers were baffled by one aspect of it, the fact that the north, the cradle of the United Irish movement, appeared at first to take no part in it. At its fiercest, indeed, the rebellion broke out in the quarter from which it was least expected, County Wexford. 'The quiet of the north,' wrote the under-secretary Edward Cooke, 'is to me unaccountable', a reaction shared to the full by Wolfe Tone, when tidings of the Irish rebellion first reached him in Paris. 'In all this business I do not hear one syllable about the north, which astonishes me more than I can express. Are they afraid? Have they changed their opinions? What can be the cause of their passive submission, at this moment, so little suited to their former zeal and energy?'[1]

Tone's questions have exercised historians ever since. It was, after all, the Presbyterian Dissenters who imported republicanism to Ireland, long before the French Revolution. Making his vice-regal tour of Ireland in 1787, the Duke of Rutland had observed that 'the province of Ulster is filled with Dissenters, who are in general very factious – great levellers and republicans'.[2] The Society of United Irishmen met first in Belfast as the 'secret committee' of the Belfast Volunteers. All the members were Presbyterian, and two of them were sons of the manse. These were the men who invited Wolfe Tone to come to Belfast in October 1791 to help frame their resolutions. One month later a second society was formed in Dublin on a wider religious base.[3]

The original society reflected the Presbyterian ethos, that curious mixture of classical and Calvinist republicanism, a contractual view of kingship, and repudiation of prelacy, combined with an egalitarianism which, however democratic in politics, stopped short at questions of theology. The United Irish Society grew out of the Volunteer movement, and it cannot be properly understood outside that context. The Volunteers of Belfast had placed themselves at the forefront of the popular reform agitation of the 1780s, and had carried it beyond achieving the independence of the Irish parliament, to the more contentious questions of the franchise and Catholic emancipation. Emigration had given them a close cousinage with the American colonists, whose cause they had warmly supported. Thereafter the campaign for reform of the representation had faltered, but the sudden and unexpected success of the French Revolution in 1789 revived both it and the Volunteer movement, the latter now modelled on the French national guard.

These were the events leading to the birth of the United Irish Society, which at first was open and constitutional, but, after France declared war in 1793, went underground. It became a proscribed and clandestine association, organised on military lines in preparation for revolution. In the early years the United Irishmen, who were for the most part urban middle class radicals, had established only a handful of societies outside Belfast and Dublin, but the 'New System' (as it was called) proved very popular, and recruited successfully in almost every part of Ireland, though mainly in the east.[4]

Much had occurred since 1791 to alter sentiment in the north. Although a few of the northern radicals, men like Samuel Neilson and Robert Simms, remained in the movement to the end, others had quietly shifted their position for economic reasons. The Rights of Man had been a fashionable cause when Belfast was rising to economic importance, and they had felt themselves to be under-represented; now they began to see on what side their bread was buttered. Enthusiasm for the French Revolution waned as it degenerated into the Jacobin Terror, and cooled altogether when the French overthrew the constitution of the Dutch Republic and occupied Switzerland. When France threatened war on its former ally, the United States, the disillusion was complete. At the same time there was a downward shift in the personnel of the United Irishmen, accelerated by the re-

73

pressive measures taken by the military, during the period of martial law, against the rural population.

There were, however, discontents of longer standing, which disconcertingly revived at this time. Far from dying down at the end of the eighteenth century, as so many people believe, sectarian animosities flared up again with renewed intensity. A long-smothered conflict in County Armagh between Protestant Peep O'Day Boys and Catholic Defenders burst into flame in 1795, leading to the formation of the Orange Society there.[5] Once established, with its rapidly proliferating system of lodges, imitating freemasonry, it both emphasised the divisions and provided a convenient weapon to be used against the United Irishmen in any rebellion which might occur. This was, indeed, what happened, and the yeomanry, raised first in the north after 1796, contained great numbers of Orangemen. When, in the last phase of their tactical preparations, the United Irishmen set out to forge an alliance with Defenders in south Down, and in Louth, and far beyond, their anti-Orange propaganda not only instilled fear in the Catholic population as far afield as Wexford, but further alienated the majority of their co-religionists.

And yet, as General Lake reported grimly from Belfast in January 1798, the United Irish flame in the north was 'smothered but not extinguished'.[6] Social order was slowly breaking down, a situation which paradoxically alarmed some of the United Irish leaders, who now wished for the French to come quickly before the revolution was completely out of control. Since the disappointment of Bantry Bay at Christmas 1796, the only question had been the timing of the French return. The movement was at its most formidable in the summer of 1797, that 'year of lost opportunity' as Marianne Elliott has called it.[7] The signal was almost given in May. Recruitment was at its zenith; firearms and gunpowder were being stored everywhere and blacksmiths' forges were busy night and day making pike-heads. This was going on simultaneously with what appeared to be a successful disarming of the province. Official returns reported the recovery of more than 10,000 pikes, to say nothing of half a dozen small pieces of artillery from Ballymena and Downpatrick. Later on, four of the five of the volunteer cannon in Belfast were handed over.[8]

In spite of this, some well-informed observers were convinced of an alteration in radical sentiment. 'A wonderful change has taken place among republicans in the north, especially in and near Belfast,' Bishop Percy of Dromore wrote to his wife. 'They now abhor the French as much as they formerly were partial to them, and are grown quite loyal'.[9] He considered that the north was perfectly safe, and the Revd Charles Warburton, who had seen the civil unrest at close quarters in County Armagh, went so far as to predict that the northern Dissenter would now be 'quietly a spectator of that destructive flame which he himself originally kindled up!'[10]

At first it seemed that he would be proved right. For a whole two weeks after the outbreaks in Kildare, Carlow and Wexford, the north remained ominously quiet. Belfast was securely guarded by its large military garrison. A curfew was in force, and the streets were patrolled by the yeomanry, while every house had to display a notice with the names of those residing in it. Then, suddenly, on Thursday 7 June, County Antrim erupted. The truth was that under the surface calm the United Irish leadership had been prey to an agonising indecision. As Dean Warburton had foreseen, the wiser heads realised that no national revolution could be effected without foreign aid, the likelihood of which was fast receding.

After the arrest of sixteen leading United Irishmen in Dublin on 12 March, there was little effective communication with the Supreme Executive. It now consisted very largely of Lord Edward Fitzgerald, who had been in any case an advocate for an immediate rising without French help. When, from his hiding place, he drew up plans for an assault on the capital, it was agreed that the signal to the rest of the country was to be the burning of the mail-coaches on the main routes to the provincial centres. The Belfast mail was intercepted and burned on the evening of 23 May, but Robert Simms, the adjutant-general for County Antrim issued no orders, and his opposite number in County Down, the Revd William Steel Dickson, was still frenetically riding about the county to consult his officers, an activity which he later tried to represent as pastoral visiting.[11]

Simms was resolutely opposed to a premature rising before the French came, and he procrastinated, even putting off vital liaison with

County Down. As the days went by, some of the younger and more hot-headed United Irishmen began to suspect him of treachery. By now they knew that their organisation was infiltrated by government spies, and this was in fact one reason for Simms' enigmatic behaviour. There was also a great deal of concern about the preparedness of the other Ulster counties. A meeting of the provincial directory was held in an inn at Armagh on 29 May, and the leadership was denounced.[12] Simms was meanwhile trying to get a consensus among his colonels. Assembling them in one place was not easy with martial law and curfew operating, and a meeting at Parkgate on 1 June was disturbed as a party of dragoons unwittingly galloped through the village. Reassembling in a straggling manner in Templepatrick, the colonels were stunned when Simms abruptly resigned his command. Three possible candidates to replace him were suggested, and it was agreed that a final decision on action was to be taken two days later. Perhaps not surprisingly, none of the men nominated could be contacted (one was actually Henry Munro who afterwards became the commander in Down). The colonels met again on 3 June, at a desolate spot on Ballyboley Mountain called the Sheep-Ree. A vote was taken and it was decided to postpone insurrection until the French arrived. When news of this decision reached the village of Ballyeaston, where some of the younger officers were anxiously waiting the result, there was uproar in the crowd, and Henry Joy McCracken, a Belfast cottonmaster who had spent a good part of 1797 in Kilmainham Jail, was unanimously elected supreme commander for the whole of Ulster.[13]

McCracken hastily drew up a plan of action. His home town of Belfast was too well defended to be taken by surprise, but he knew that the magistrates of the county were due to meet in Antrim town on 7 June. Antrim, at the north-east corner of Lough Neagh, was situated on the main route from Belfast to Ballymena and Derry. He sent orders secretly to every unit in the county to seize the towns and military bases close to them, and simultaneously to assemble a huge reserve force on Donegore Hill near to Antrim. He himself would lead the men of Belfast and south Antrim in a direct attack on the town, while the local United Irishmen and Defenders were to secure Randalstown. At dawn on the seventh, with a white mist lying on the fields, and the promise of a perfect summer day, McCracken raised the standard of revolt on the old Norman rath at Craigarogan on the road between Glengormley and Templepatrick. As reassuring messages arrived that the county was everywhere in arms, three contingents formed up behind McCracken, and as they marched off in the sumer dawn they began to sing the Marseillaise.[14]

The first shot in the rebellion had been fired in the seaport of Larne as darkness fell on the previous evening. There United Irishmen had clashed with loyalists and the small garrison, and occupied the town before moving out to join the units converging on Donegore.[15] Further north on the coast a large body of insurgents assembled on Bellair Hill at Glenarm, later to be commanded by a Presbyterian minister, the Revd Robert Acheson, 'in a green jacket, faced with yellow, white breeches, black hose and silver-buckled shoes'.[16] At Ballymena, United Men from all the surrounding localities surged into the town and besieged loyalists in the Market House. A day or two later they would be reinforced by the north Antrim men, who had been kept out of Coleraine by Lord Henry Murray and his Manx Fencibles.[17] The epicentre of the revolt, however, was to be found in the valley of the Sixmilewater, the area about Templepatrick, where almost every village produced its quota of insurgents armed with pikes and muskets. This call to arms would long be remembered in County Antrim as 'the Turn-out'.

Unfortunately for McCracken, every detail of his plans was already known to General Nugent (who had succeeded Lake in the northern command) thanks to Nicholas Mageean, a young Catholic farmer from County Down, who was a member of the provincial directory. On 6 June Mageean had sent an urgent warning that the rebellion would take place next day. Nugent's difficulty was not lack of information, but the vital need to hold on to Belfast and keep communications open to Dublin, at a time when his forces were being weakened by detaching to the south. He nevertheless decided to take the risk of dispatching two mixed columns of regulars, dragoons, militia and yeomanry, one from Belfast, the other from Lisburn, to engage McCracken at Antrim, and thus check the rebellion on the first day.[18]

Major Seddon and the small garrison in Antrim, who had been warned by Nugent early in the morning and promised reinforcements, prepared to make a stubborn defence. McCracken, despite his overwhelming superiority in numbers, hesitated far too long before entering the town. By the time he did so, the army columns had made their rendezvous a few miles to the south. Colonel William Lumley, the young Etonian commanding the dragoons, obtained permission to press on ahead and give the rustics a taste of cavalry warfare. Arriving in Antrim he made the now familiar error of leading a cavalry charge against the long pikes, and was badly mauled. Though a long and distinguished military career still lay ahead of him, he was himself lamed for life by a slashed Achilles tendon. When the main force arrived, Colonel Durham bombarded the town for half an hour before unleashing his infantry.

By then things were starting to go badly for McCracken. As the long hot afternoon wore on, confusion overtook the insurgent columns coming in from the east and north, while, on the other side of the town Samuel Orr's column from Randalstown was inexplicably late. Even before the Monaghan Militia advanced into the town a general rout had begun, and many of the people shot by the Monaghans were loyalists venturing out to welcome them.[19] Only the indomitable James Hope and his 'Spartan band' of sharp-shooters held out to the end, and then escaped by a brilliant rearguard action, but the fate of the Antrim insurrection had been decided on the first day. When the news from Antrim reached Donegore Hill, the huge concourse there melted away.

At Ballymena, ten miles farther north, a Committee of Public Safety had been set up, and for three days the town was under a republican form of government.[20] The army advanced slowly towards Ballymena, threatening to burn it down if the insurgents were still found in possession, but Colonel Clavering, acting apparently on his initiative, offered an amnesty if arms were handed in. Some members of the committee, respected local citizens who did not want the town to be destroyed, seem to have acted as mediators with the military, and the amnesty was recommended to the crowds. The United Irishmen who rejected it vowed to continue the resistance elsewhere and left the town, where arms soon piled up in the inn-yards and on the roads leading out into the country. At Glenarm the insurgents also dispersed, and Acheson saved his life by surrendering on terms.[21]

In County Down the pattern of insurrection was different. The arrest of Steel Dickson on 4 June had thrown the United Irish leadership into confusion, and the rising there was not synchronised with that in Antrim. In the next few days the initiative was taken by some of the younger men, including probationers for the Presbyterian ministry, who roused north Down and the Ards peninsula. After an unsuccessful attempt on Newtownards, which was then abandoned by its garrison, the Ards men took the small swivel guns from a ship in Bangor harbour, and moved westwards, 'as a plague of locusts came in Egypt' to join with the bodies of insurgents who were beginning to gather in the centre of the county. On Saturday 9 June a detachment of the Yorkshire Fencibles, commanded by Colonel Chetwynd-Stapylton, with units of yeomanry and loyalist volunteers, was ambushed at Saintfield. Once Stapylton had extricated himself from the narrow road, where the musketeers and pikemen were able to create much havoc, he brought his artillery into play and despite heavy casualties managed to retreat in good order to Comber. He lost three of his officers, one of whom was his own cousin, Captain William Chetwynd.[22] The body of the Revd Robert Mortimer, the chancellor of Down cathedral, was left leaning against a gate.

The United Irishmen were immensely encouraged by this early victory (the only one in the entire rising) but their rapid occupation of large parts of the county was the consequence of Nugent prudently calling in all his isolated garrisons. On 'Pike Sunday', 10 June, the Revd Thomas Leslie Birch of First Saintfield preached to a vast rebel host at the Creevy Rocks on a text from Ezekiel, 'Cause them that have charge over the city to draw near, every man with his destroying weapon in his hand'.[23] On Monday Henry Munro, a Lisburn linen draper, was elected commander for the county. He sent out messengers in all directions to summon support for 'the Liberty war' and moved his army to Ballynahinch, where he set up his camp and headquarters on Ednavady Hill, in the estate of the Earl of Moira at Montalto.

On Tuesday morning Nugent, reassured by the good news pouring in from Antrim, felt sufficiently secure to move against Munro in Down. A large mixed force, accompanied by half a dozen six-pounder field guns, two howitzers and ammunition wagons, wound its way out of Belfast across the Long Bridge and into the Down countryside. Soon its progress was marked by the smoke of burning farmsteads. Finding Saintfield completely deserted, Nugent pressed on to Ballynahinch which he reached as the sun was beginning to set on another perfect summer day. He at once dislodged a body of rebels on Windmill Hill and established his headquarters there, facing Mont-alto across the town. He threw out a screen of infantry and drew up the Fifeshire Fencibles and Militia to protect his flank. Then he began the bombardment of Ednavady Hill.

The artillery fire had a demoralising effect, as cannon balls scythed through the trees and undergrowth, and considerable numbers of the insurgents slipped away under the cover of darkness. Later there were suggestions that a whole detachment of Defenders from south Down had withdrawn after a disagreement with the Presbyterians over tactics. Some of Munro's officers had certainly argued for a night attack while the Monaghan Militia, who had occupied and looted the town, were incapacitated from drink and exhaustion, but they had been over-ruled. Instead Munro attacked at dawn, his men running up 'like bloodhounds' under heavy fire.[24] By sheer determination and weight of numbers they drove the Monaghans back through the streets, killing their adjutant, Captain Henry Evatt. The insurgent casualties were heavy, for this was the most serious engagement of the northern rising, but in the long run the United Irish attack could not be sustained. Confusion followed when the bugle calls of the retreating infantry were mistaken for the arrival of reinforcements, and the opportunity was seized for a counter-attack. As so often happened in 1798, the training of seasoned troops prevailed in the end, and the insurgents were soon streaming away from the town in all directions. Some reached the safety of Slieve Croob to the south, but many were cut down by the pursuing cavalry, despite Nugent's order to them to be merciful. Among those who perished in this way was a young girl from north Down called Betsy Gray who has become a legendary figure in the literature of the rising.

After 13 June retribution in the north was as pitiless as elsewhere in Ireland. Both McCracken and Munro were captured and hanged, along with scores of less well-known rebels. A few of the principals, like Simms and Steel Dickson, escaped the gallows because evidence could not be brought against them Others were permitted to emigrate to the United States, or were accepted by the king of Prussia, to the satisfaction of the British government.[25]

It is sometimes argued that, of the three insurrections in 1798, the northern one was the closest in motivation to the original objectives of the United Irishmen. There is an element of truth in this, for the rural population in eastern Ulster was more receptive to the doctrines of Tom Paine and radical propaganda widely disseminated by the *Northern Star,* which had an impressive circulation until its presses were wrecked by the Monaghan Militia in 1797.[26] But this view must be qualified in several respects. With the social shift in the personnel of the movement, the content of radicalism had changed too. Munro's manifestos talk more about tithes than about Rousseau and the social contract. Though the Rights of Man are still invoked, they begin to sound more and more like the rights of workers, which will soon be demanded by trade unions emerging after 1800. Hope writes a good deal about employers as well as landlords, which is something of a new departure.

Again, the northern rebellion had an unexpectedly narrow and sectarian character. Apart from one assembly near Maghera in County Derry, which soon dispersed, the revolt was entirely confined to Antrim and Down, the area east of the Bann, and even there to districts which were almost exclusively Presbyterian. About twenty Presbyterian ministers and probationers were directly involved, of whom two were hanged. There is a strong sense (as to some extent in Wexford) that the men of the cloth are the last leaders on whom the people can rely, though it must be remembered that they are a small minority, roundly condemned by their brethren in the Synod of Ulster. In Antrim and Down tribal religious loyalty was a vital factor, and one could argue that the men who turned out in June 1798 were simply obeying a stubborn Presbyterian loyalty to principles many of their social superiors had now abandoned. Though there was some Defender participation in the rebellion in both counties, the absence of Catholic insurgents in large numbers, in contrast not only to what was happening elsewhere in the country, but to the composition of the United Irish organisation in Ulster, was significant and perhaps ominous for the future. It is hard to escape the conclusion that if the insurrection had occurred a year or two earlier, the consequences might have been very different.

UP NOT OUT:
WHY DID NORTH-WEST ULSTER NOT RISE IN 1798?*

Breandán Mac Suibhne

FROM THE WINTER OF 1795–6, magistrates' reports and informers' statements increasingly mentioned men being 'put up'; the United Irishmen were building a paramilitary organisation and to be 'up' was to be a sworn member. Until recently, however, historians concentrated more on the men who turned 'out' in the military engagements of 1798 than those who were 'up'. Even in histories that claimed a broader focus, Antrim, Down and Wexford bulked large; in other words, *the rebellion* set the agenda for the history of *rebellion*, a subject that concerns a longer period and a greater space. Historians are always drawn to 'moments of high drama' yet, for Ulster, the flash and bang of 'Antrim and Down in '98' only really obscured the bigger picture in the 1890s when the centenary fanned popular interest. Earlier writers had appreciated that the risings did not mark the geographical limits of sedition. Most importantly, Revd Classon Emmet Porter (1814–1885) had traversed the province in the mid-nineteenth-century interviewing old rebels – many of whom had not turned out – and produced an insightful series of biographical sketches.[1] This made sense: although the only 'turn outs' occurred in Antrim, north Down and, even less impressively, south Derry, delegates from Louth and all Ulster counties, except Cavan and Fermanagh, had attended the final meetings of the Provincial Committee of the United Irishmen and committed to rise.

The pre-occupation with 'the rebellion' that developed around the centenary bequeathed a teleology to revisionist history – the only real risings in Ulster were in Antrim and Down and, therefore, there can not have been much commitment to the United Irishmen elsewhere in the province. A. T. Q. Stewart proclaims the perception of widespread sedition in Ulster a mirage: 'in the north, only Belfast and its hinterland in Antrim and Down produced United Irishmen in large numbers'.[2] Nancy Curtin eschews the notion that local social structure, culture and politics might explain spatial variations in United Irish strength and pronounces 'distance from Belfast' the key explanatory factor. This requires the attribution of impressive membership returns for counties far beyond Belfast to 'a fantasy among the republicans'; the interpretation of paramilitary activity in the spring and early summer of 1797 as 'breaches of discipline'; and total disregard for the attendance record of county delegates at provincial meetings in the year prior to the risings; for example, Donegal delegates had a more impressive attendance record than those of Cavan, Monaghan, Fermanagh and Derry.[3]

Recently, historians have begun to look beyond the men who turned out to those who were up and to develop more sophisticated approaches to causation. Notions of rebellion as an import from America or France or a hangover from 'arguing over wine' in Belfast are being abandoned and there is a new concern with elaborating the social bases of 'uniting'; a new paradigm is replacing revisionism's *sonderweg* for Antrim and Down.[4] In this context, the advanced politics of north-west Ulster – the region centred on Derry city that extends from the Sperrins in the east, south to Bearnas Mór and west to Na Rossa – are of particular interest. In this region, a 'potatoed, corned and peopled country' between Letterkenny, Limavady and Strabane formed an advantaged core zone, the inhabitants of which were predominantly Protestant with Presbyterians out-numbering Episcopalians in all localities (indeed, the district was 'more Presbyterian' than the immediate hinterlands of Belfast, Newry or Enniskillen each of which contained several parishes where Episcopalians were dominant). Critically, a profound tension had characterised the 'whole Protestant community' in this area since the early 1700s. Notwithstanding the centrality of the siege of Derry in the 'Glorious Revolution', William King, the bishop of Derry, became a vocal proponent of the legislation that ejected Dissenters from the polity. Dissenter resentment went beyond opposition to rectors and tithes to a more general antipathy to Episcopalians. Dialect verse – a self-conscious amplification of social and cultural difference – was a conspicuous feature of regional print culture from the 1730s. Faction-fighting between the 'Scotch laddies' of Strabane, a Presbyterian town, and the 'English' of Lifford, its Episcopalian suburb, continued until the late 1700s. By the 1750s a levelling sub-culture had developed that included a cult of Oliver Cromwell; Dissenters toasted the Protector and named their sons after him. As the Protestant bloc fractured – and as the emergence of an English-speaking Catholic middle class fractured 'the other' – Planter-Gael dichotomies became anachronistic. From the 1770s, Patriots conceived their ideological project as drawing a 'veil of oblivion' over divisive settler and native narratives of the Irish past and raising 'a prouder story'; in effect, the construction of an inclusive Irish identity. In the 1780s some volunteer companies gave this project practical expression: they ostentatiously recruited Catholics; accepted donations from priests for the purchase of arms; paraded at the Catholic bishop's house to celebrate Patriot victories; supported the extension of the franchise to propertied Catholics and raised money for the erection of chapels, in some cases even attending mass when they opened.

Although radicalism lost steam in the mid-1780s, its revival was earlier in the north-west than elsewhere in Ulster. Derry Patriots commemorated the siege with massive festivals of liberty in 1788 and 1789 in which the Catholic bishop and clergy participated. Advanced politics were evident in Bastille Day celebrations in Derry and Limavady; the publication in Derry in 1791 of Tom Paine's *Rights of Man, Part I* (well before a Belfast edition appeared); enthusiastic participation in the new volunteers of 1792–3; bare-faced support for France in the war with Britain and the militancy of the *London-Derry Journal* before its sale in 1796. Reflecting this 'rebelly' milieu, men from the north-west were prominent in the United Irishmen in Dublin and Belfast. Oliver Cromwell Bond, Dublin's hawkish leader, was a native of Saint Johnston where his father was Dissenting minister for half a century. William Sampson, the Belfast-based republican propagandist, was a member of an old Derry family. Revd James Porter of Greyabbey, another propagandist, was a native of Ballindrait. Dr Alexander Crawford, the United Irish leader in Lisburn was a brother of Revd William Crawford of Strabane, spent much time in the town and married a local woman. Henry Haslett, owner-cum-editor of the *Northern Star*, was from Clooney, Limavady.

Not surprisingly, from the winter of 1795 – and particularly from the following summer — the United Irishmen developed a formidable presence in the north-west. By the end of 1796, Joseph Orr, a wealthy Derry brazier, was on the organisation's national executive and county delegates to the Provincial Committee claimed over 8,000 men in Derry, 3,000 in Donegal and 6,550 in Tyrone; (at this stage, the Tyrone and Derry figures included many men west of Limavady and Omagh and all Donegal's 'Unites' were in the north-east).[5] The arrival of the French fleet at Bantry Bay in December transformed north-west Ulster. The French connection confirmed, croppies commenced nightly raids for arms and began to cut trees to make pike-shafts. Inevitably, there were fatal clashes. In January at least five men died when the military ambushed United Irish 'squads' operating from the republican village of Newbuildings.[6] Earlier that week there had been an actual 'insurrection' in Fánaid. Supported by 20 Manx Fencibles, Revd William Hamilton, the local rector, had arrested several rebel leaders. Two hundred croppies then mobilised and besieged Hamilton and the fencibles for two days in an attempt to release the prisoners; they only withdrew when reinforcements arrived from Letterkenny. The military swept the parish for arms and suspects – captured weapons included a cannon – and, for a few weeks, Hamilton appeared to be stemming the tide of sedition in Fánaid; however, on 2 March the United Irishmen assassinated him at Sharon, outside Newtowncunningham.[7] 'Hamilton's fate' shocked Dublin Castle; General Lake was immediately instructed to disarm Ulster and shortly afterwards martial law was formally declared. The impact of martial law was uneven. In the city, the United Irishmen had made great efforts to 'corrupt' the Tipperary Militia. Fearing summary punishment under martial law, three militiamen now gave information against six middle-ranking rebels, all respectable traders.[8] In contrast, martial law had no clear impact in the countryside. Rebel numbers peaked shortly after its introduction at about 10,000 in Derry, 10,000 in Donegal and 13,000 in Tyrone yet the rebels maintained a high level of paramilitary activity – arms raids; arms manufacture; drilling; punishing informers – until June 1797.[9]

The deep roots of rebellion in the north-west and the high level of rebel activity in 1797 raise an obvious question: why did the region not rise in 1798? This chapter argues that two factors were decisive; first, class-based divisions emerged within the United Irish organisation on the issue of rising without French support and influential figures who had the authority to lead a regional rising held back; second, an intensification of counter-insurgency activity in late May 1798 made even local outbreaks unlikely.

DIVISIONS ON THE ISSUE of foreign aid owed much to events in summer 1797. Initially, the United Irishmen had drummed into recruits that they would only rise when the French landed. In April 1797 the Ulster Executive had informed the Provincial Committee that a landing was imminent and issued instructions for the election of officers and the arrangement of plans for attacking the 'king's forces'. Across the north, the United Irishmen were ready by May.[10] When the French failed to appear, the Ulster Executive resolved to rise without them. In the first week of June, the Ulster and Leinster Executives met in Dublin. Leinster refused to rise and the northern men, including Joseph Orr, went home 'to begin the business themselves'.[11] At this stage, the croppies were champing at the bit. In the second week of June, Sir George Hill, MP for Derry city, spent three days in Inis Eoghain with the Derry Yeomanry and Cambridgeshire Cavalry searching for arms taken from a party of 15 Culdaff yeomen and burning houses; he thought the people 'wild absolutely to turn out' and found it 'too tantalising' to see 'large numbers beyond attack' in the mountains.[12] However, on his return to Derry, Hill learned that paramilitary activity had suddenly ceased across Ulster; rebels were coming in, dumping weapons and taking the oath of allegiance. Hill and other loyalists correctly interpreted this 'mysterious silence' as a ploy to lull them into a false sense of security before a rising yet all came to naught.[13] Some Antrim colonels refused to rise, arguing that 'it was imprudent to act ... without foreign aid'. A provincial meeting at Randalstown failed to bring them back on board. The moment passed. At the end of June unrelated circumstances threatened the arrest of Antrim, Down and Armagh leaders and they fled to England.[14]

In the confusion that followed the abandoned rising, the Tipperary Militia again proved the weak link in Derry. Several militiamen confessed that they were to have mutinied, killed their officers and opened the city gates to the rebels. An investigation led to Corporal Thomas Patterson.[15] Patterson revealed that Christopher Hardy, a wealthy saddler and machine inventor, had put him up. Hill was stunned; he had always considered Hardy a friend. Indeed, Hardy was then in Dublin, where he was arrested on 2 July, collecting £1,200 for government saddle contracts.[16] In Derry, Joseph Orr received early word of the arrest, went to Hardy's house, burned his papers and then escaped with 'a number of others'; by the end of the year, he was in France.[17] Hill now moved against the leaders left in the city and arrested Robert Moore of Molenan and William McClintock. A successful ironmonger and merchant, Moore had been active in regional politics since the late 1770s; he had been a volunteer officer, a founder of the chamber of commerce and a treasurer of the poor house and infirmary. A man of untainted respectability, he had been a Derry delegate and was to have given the 'necessary instructions' for the rising in the north-west.[18]

The failure to rise in 1797 turned key figures against conspiracy without action and against action without a sure chance of success. The crown's case against Moore was weak; indeed, the 'Democrats' alleged that he was held in gaol – despite an offer of £2,000 bail – to prevent his running against Hill in the August election.[19] Released in September, he was now more cautious. Approached to resume his role as county delegate, he refused, saying that he would not act 'until they were in the field'.[20] Similarly, there is some – admittedly slight – evidence that Alexander Montgomery, Donegal's Patriot MP, refused to lead the United Irish army in Ulster; years after the event, his natural son, Richard, a Dublin playboy known as 'The Buck of Raphoe', claimed to have been present 'when Lord Edward [Fitzgerald] disclosed his plans to his father'; Montgomery, whose support for the rebels was well-known, tried to dissuade Fitzgerald, 'telling him he had none on his side that he could trust' and when offered 'command of the men in the north' he declined 'on the score of old age'.[21]

There was no resumption of paramilitary violence after June 1797; arms raids and drilling ceased and informers who had moved into the

towns went home and lived 'unmolested'. The United Irish organisation remained intact in Donegal and Tyrone: county delegates rout-
inely attended provincial meetings from June 1797 until May 1798.
However, although the paucity of information on delegates before
summer 1797 makes comparison difficult, they were almost certainly
from a lower social rank than those of winter 1796–7. George Buchanan, a Donegal delegate in winter 1797, was a 45 year old 'country-
man' who lived 'within about a mile of Raphoe'. Andrew Stilley of
Guystown, a cousin of Revd James Porter and Donegal delegate in
May 1798, owned a 'large mill' but was not near as wealthy as Robert
Moore. John Wilson, a regular Tyrone delegate, was a 'horse jockey
or horse dealer'. Significantly, none of the Donegal or Tyrone delegates had achieved prominence in 'public life'; leadership had passed
to the middle, or even lower middle, strata of society.[22] In Derry the
movement was in total disarray. Beside the arrest of the city leaders,
three high-placed informers in the south of the county – Joseph
Ledlie, Denis Lynch and Charles McFillin – and three full-time agents
employed by Hill were feeding the authorities detailed information.
No Derry delegate appeared at a provincial meeting from June 1797
until March 1798 when Billy McKeever of Maghera presented himself.[23]

McKeever's attendance reflected a re-organisation as the croppies
again prepared to rise. Delegates for Derry, Donegal and Tyrone
agreed to rise; indeed, on 10 May they even chose representatives for
a provisional 'national assembly or parliament'. The south rose on 23
May but the Ulster Executive did not issue any orders to the northern
rebels. The provincial committee re-assembled in Armagh on 29
May. The Derry, Donegal and Louth delegates were confident they
could disarm the military in their counties. The delegates from Down,
Antrim, Armagh and the 'upper half of Tyrone' were less optimistic.
Still, with the exception of the Down delegate, all believed that 'the
people they represented would act'. The Down and Antrim 'colonels'
were to meet the following day to devise 'a general plan of insurrection'. This plan would be sent by express to the 'adjutant generals'
throughout the province; all counties would then rise together.[24]

Significantly, Lord Cavan, the military commander at Derry, remained confident that there would be no regional rising without foreign aid. The north-west, he predicted on 3 June, would remain 'perfectly quiet ... unless the French make their appearance'; if they did, he continued, 'I should have ... more than doubts what the conduct of the inhabitants would be'. However, Cavan did concede that even without the French, there might be 'much trouble' – local outbreaks – in the rugged, predominantly Catholic, peninsulas of Fánaid and Inis Eoghain and also in Donagheady, a mountainous, mainly Presbyterian district on the right bank of the Foyle.[25]

Cavan's assessment is revealing; these districts had been very active in 1797 yet they were outside the rebel heartland – the rich flax-lands in the Liberties of Derry and the Laggan district of north-east Donegal – and their rebel leaders were from a lower social bracket than men like Moore and Montgomery who, having been involved in public life for a generation, could more easily have brought out large numbers. The wealthier men had always been reluctant to rise without the French; in December 1796, Harry Alexander, a city MP, had observed that 'numbers of men of property' had joined the United Irishmen, 'some from an attachment to the republican principles, others from fear of plunder or personal danger', and that having 'embarked in one vessel with a populace who look only to plunder and idleness, they already begin to quarrel for the helm. It is not the interest of the rich to encourage predatory outrage and the lower are too impatient for the revolutionary advantages of constitutional innovations'; 'the business will soon be settled one way or the other,' he predicted, 'without a landing of the French it will die away; with a landing the spirit will be difficult to be resisted'.[26] In late May 1798 – when the arrest of Edward Fitzgerald and the threat of a Franco-American war were the big stories in the newspapers – it was difficult to forecast national or international developments and this difficulty, coupled with the vacillation of the Ulster leadership after the south rose, made it even less likely than at any time in the previous year that hard men in the middle-strata of the Laggan, like Stilley, or wild men in Fánaid, Inis Eoghain and Donagheady would convince these 'men of property' to turn out.[27]

LORD CAVAN DID NOT even have 'much trouble' in Fánaid, Inis Eoghain and Donagheady. The only hints of a turn out were reports of men gathering outside Strabane; on 9 June there were 'a thousand ... seen in a large field in Magherycoltan (close by Taggert's bleach-green)' and three days later, Col Kearney mounted an officers' picket guard on the "different avenues" to the town having received information that "cou'd not be doubted" of large bodys ... seen in the night collected at the foot of Meenashesk ... and to all appearance armed and ready to march down and surprise the town'.[28] Although the reluctance of wealthy leaders to act without the French may have prevented a regional rising, the absence of local outbreaks owed more to an intensification of the counter-insurgency effort in late May.

News of the Wexford rising reached Derry on Saturday 26 May. Although confident that there would be no regional rising, Cavan immediately stepped up counter-insurgency activity. He issued a pro-clamation informing 'those disaffected persons (which I hope are few) within my district of command, that I have received orders to execute the most rigid and exemplary punishment by martial law against any person whatever that may attempt to disturb the publick peace'. He warned men out on recognisances to be '*particularly* tranquil and orderly' or become 'the first objects of justice'. The following day, he offered an amnesty to anybody surrendering arms and on Monday he ordered that a return be made to the mayor of all strangers in the city, mentioning their names and business, whence they came and where they were going.[29]

Cavan marked the crackdown by making courts martial a con-spicuous feature of the counter-insurgency effort. Court-martialling of republican prisoners began on Saturday 2 June. That morning, Cavan presided in the mayor's office at the trial of Dan McCarron of Carrigans and Thomas Clarke, a United Irish leader from Swatragh who had been awaiting trial for over a year; McCarron was charged with administering the United Irish oath to a private in the Tipperary Militia and Clarke with 'disorderly practices'. Both men were con-victed. The court sentenced McCarron to 1,000 lashes and Clarke to 500. They were marched down to the quay where the troops of the garrison and the yeomanry cavalry had drawn up. McCarron was tied and lashed 345 times; Clarke's punishment was postponed. One act punctured the pomp. As McCarron was about to be lashed, the mate of an American ship docked at the quay, was heard to utter 'some words of a treasonable nature', 'outrageous expressions against his Britannic Majesty and the Government of his kingdoms'. He was taken from his ship, marched into the circle, tried at the drum head and sentenced to 500 lashes. However, as he was an American, Cavan forgave the offence on condition he remained on his ship during her stay in port.[30]

Cavan's tactics appeared to be pay dividends. 'A vast quantity of arms, consisting of guns, pistols, bayonets, swords, &c.' was delivered up at the mayor's office on Monday 28 May and the following Saturday a party of the Derry Cavalry brought in 'a large quantity of arms given up at Muff'.[31] Over the next two weeks military and yeomanry parties brought in 'vast quantities of arms': in the week of 5 to 12 June, the Limavady yeomanry alone brought in 'a very considerable number of pikes and some pike handles' and 'six carts laden with guns'.[32]

The surrender of arms may have reflected a recognition that a rising would be pointless. When news had arrived of Wexford, Cavan had placed 'almost the whole of the yeomanry corps' on permanent duty under the command of Captain Maxwell of the Aberdeen Fencibles and ordered 'country corps' into Derry and key towns, including Omagh, Newtownstewart and Strabane.[33] At the same time, he had instructed Hill, as captain of the city yeomanry, to form a supplementary corps to serve in the city and liberties; all recruits had to swear that they had never been United Irishmen or taken their oath of secrecy.[34]

These orders were critical. With the exception of Hill's corps and a few other town-based units, Cavan did not trust the yeomanry; like other leading loyalists, he believed the republicans had 'corrupted' most corps. Despite 'numerous' applications, he had refused to give yeomanry corps powder to practice firing blank cartridges: 'I think it useless to give it such troops', he had explained to General Knox, his counterpart in mid-Ulster, in August 1797.[35] That summer he had dismissed yeomen who refused to take the oath of allegiance and he had disbanded the Cumber Cavalry after learning that 'they were [united] to a man except the officers'.[36] Indeed, as late as February 1798, Cavan had penned a deeply negative assessment of the corps in his district: the yeomanry 'puzzle me much,' he wrote to Knox, 'I have not a corps of them as loyal as you have, and with a few exceptions, I would wish to disarm those I have'.[37] Hence, in calling the country corps into the city and major towns, where British troops were quartered, Cavan's purpose was less to have the yeomen's guns protect the towns than to protect the towns from the yeomen's guns.[38] Reflecting the success of the move (and, paradoxically, the depth of sedition), a large number of yeomen ordered into Derry soon after 'laid down their arms and returned to their homes rather than remain on permanent duty in established quarters'. Cavan was delighted and began replacing deserters with men whose 'steadiness and loyalty' he could depend on.[39]

Consequently, when word came through of the chaotic developments in Antrim and south Derry, the crown was well-placed to meet any local outbreak. Admittedly, there was considerable alarm among loyalists – they fled to the city and towns from the countryside – but alarm soon abated as news of the devastating counter-attack came within hours of the first reports of the rising; news of the rising arrived in Strabane on the night of 8 June and reports of the rout came the following morning.[40] If 1,000 croppies did assemble to attack Strabane on 9 or 12 June, they would have known something of events further east and that troops would move quickly against them from Derry, Letterkenny, Newtownstewart and Omagh; moreover, even 1,000 men would have had difficulty taking Strabane, then garrisoned by the Somerset Fencibles, the Queens County Militia, two troops of the Cambridgeshire Cavalry and some 200 yeomen.[41]

Counter-insurgency activity remained intense. Cavan ordered lists of inhabitants to be posted on all houses in the city; he cautioned people 'on no account to harbour strangers of any description, without giving immediate notice of their arrival to their immediate commanding officer' and he advised that they stay in their homes except when employed in the fields, carrying supplies to the army or going to their usual markets. Cavan also imposed new restrictions on blacksmiths and threatened them with summary execution at their own doors if they made pikes.[42] Pickets mounted on the approaches to towns and patrols through the countryside made important arrests. In the second week of June the *London-Derry Journal* reported that 'some persons in attempting to escape to Scotland have been apprehended' and the following week that 'several persons' charged with 'treasonable offences' had been arrested when 'about to escape for America'.[43] One of the most intriguing arrests was made in Strabane. On the night of 17 June yeomen on guard-duty stopped Patrick Gallagher, a local man who had been living in Dublin. On searching him, they found some letters from his brother John, one of Lord Edward's bodyguards. 'Patrick and the letters,' the arresting officer reported, 'were sent early this morning with a party of dragoons to Derry and will I suppose be flogged till he confesses'.[44]

Courts martial continued. Thomas Clarke, whose sentence had been postponed, was lashed on Saturday 9 June. New charges were then laid against him but he died in gaol three days later. 'White arsenick' was found in a paper in his pocket and 'when poured down the throat of a dog the animal died soon after in strong convulsions'. The following week, two brothers called Gray were arrested in the city on suspicion of involvement in 'treasonable practices'. One of them confessed that they had both borne arms at Maghera and had been deputed by Billy McKeever, the rebel leader, to collect reinforcements from Derry. His brother was tried, convicted and sentenced to death but as his own brother's evidence had convicted him, Cavan mitigated the punishment to 1,500 lashes; on 18 June, Gray received 300 lashes on the quay.[45]

By this stage, the Ulster risings had been crushed. People who had been 'on the spot' were reaching the north-west with accounts of floggings, executions and house-burnings.[46] Newspapers carried similar reports, emphasising the fate of well-known rebel leaders.[47] Locally, the croppies were lying low if not down; on 23 June '150 pikes and 2 car load of arms were surrendered from the town of Castlefin' after a United Irish meeting – Hill, however, learned from the blacksmiths and 'very few of them we have prevailed on to confess' that they retained most of their pikes – and the following week two of the principal inhabitants in each townland in Tamlaghtfinlan entered into recognisances for the good behaviour of their neighbours.[48]

As the threat of local outbreaks receded, loyal civilians became more active. From 1 July parochial meetings began to pass resolutions thanking the military and yeomanry corps for preventing a rising.[49] The Roman Catholic clergy made particularly early and conspicuous demonstrations of their loyalty. On 26 June the Derry clergy issued a 'small pamphlet' entitled *Instructions addressed to the Roman Catholics of the Diocese of Derry, by their pastors*.[50] On Sunday 1 July Dr Charles O'Donnell – appointed bishop of Derry two weeks earlier – read the pamphlet to a 'large congregation' in the Long Tower church. Other priests did likewise 'at their respective places of worship' and distributed copies *gratis* among their 'hearers'. The *Journal* – which carried the *Instructions* on its front page – trusted that 'there will not be a Catholic, who hears or peruses these *Instructions,* who will not carefully attend to the pastoral affection which they breathe, and profit by the precepts of piety and wisdom which they contain'.[51] The *Instructions* were emphatic: rebellion was morally wrong. There were two key premises. First, render unto Caesar; Catholics must be 'obedient and submissive, in the temporal order of things, to all those whom Providence has placed over you in civil authority'. Second, times had changed; 'members of the Catholic Communion' were not oppressed under 'his present Majesty'; they had chapels and a seminary at Maynooth; they had permission to practice at the bar and to hold civil or military offices and they could confidently invest in property:

> We enjoy numberless blessings and privileges to which our forefathers were strangers. They laboured under various penal restrictions, and they continued Loyal. Religion taught them to do so. The restraining penalties have been, nearly, all done away under the benevolent Reign of his present Majesty. We enjoy RELIGIOUS LIBERTY without restriction. We thank Providence and our Rulers for it – we have our Chapels to shelter us from the inclemency of the weather, and we are never to forget, that our Protestant Brethren of every description, contributed to our comfort in that respect, with a most bountiful and liberal hand. Our Young Men, destined for the Ecclesiastical state, are not under the necessity of repairing to foreign countries for their education as formerly. The present Government has at a very considerable expense erected a College for them, and generously contributes its bountiful supplies for their support. The people of our Communion are not excluded from

the Bar; they hold CIVIL and MILITARY offices under the CROWN; and may lay out their money at pleasure in the purchase of property. All these benefits and [many others] were unknown to our ancestors. We enjoy them through his Majesty's humane and bountiful interference with his Parliament. Abstracting then, from every other obligation of Loyalty, gratitude calls for our attachment to his Government.

Finally, the *Instructions* denied that priests had accepted government salaries and declared that those who 'engaged in the horrid act of Rebellion' would be deprived of 'the holy Sacraments, instituted by your DIVINE REDEEMER for your salvation' and 'die without consolation'.[52]

In the weeks that followed publication of the *Instructions*, loyal priests stepped forward. On 5 July Abercorn's agent received a loyal declaration signed by Catholics from Dr Arthur McHugh – 'the Popish priest of that part of your Lordship's estate in the parish of Urney ... as loyal a priest as in the kingdom' – who asked him to forward it to Abercorn to be passed to Pelham or Castlereagh. He sent the resolution, but not the roll of signatures – 'it was too bulky to send' – and advised Abercorn to flatter the priest with a reply; receiving a reply from Castlereagh within three weeks, McHugh published it in the press. Charles McBride, the priest at Baron's Court, gave Abercorn's agent a similar resolution with 1,400 signatures asking that it be sent to Lord Cornwallis.[53]

DESPITE A GENERAL ACCEPTANCE by mid-June that even local outbreaks were now unlikely, there was no relaxation of the counter-insurgency effort. Rather, it took on the character of a terror as the crown's objectives shifted from the prevention of a rising to the destruction of the rebel organisation.[54] The first house-burning occurred after the real danger had passed; on 14 June, the home of John Horner of Carnet, Limavady was torched during a raid when pikes and other weapons were discovered (Horner, the son of an old volunteer leader, escaped and remained at large 'attended by a guard of fellows in the mountains' until summer 1799 when he negotiated 'voluntary exile' to America).[55] Massive displays of military strength were calculated to overawe rebel communities; on 12 July, 'almost the entire' garrisons of Derry, Strabane, Newtownstewart and Omagh marched to Saint Johnston – Oliver Bond's hometown on the Foyle – for a field day that Cavan had announced a fortnight earlier.[56] Finally, military and yeomanry parties began to round up suspects. Although nobody had turned out west of the Sperrins, the gaols of Omagh, Lifford and Derry filled with 'rebels'. 'Prisoners are brought in here every day', Abercorn's agent wrote from Strabane as late as 28 June. In that letter, he mentioned 'a fellow of the name of McFarland ... charged with having used treasonable and seditious language last Sunday at the meeting house in [Donagheady]'.[57] Critically, however, many men were taken up for 'old offences'; for example, in late June, the 'discovery' of a 'conspiracy' to assassinate Capt. Tom Smith, a Rathmullan revenue officer who had taken an active part against the croppies, resulted in about a dozen arrests — the 'conspiracy' had occurred at United Irish meetings in January 1797.[58] At Derry, courts martial continued until the end of July, losing some legal trappings when they moved from the mayor's office to Neilson's Hotel and inferior officers replaced Cavan as president. There were also courts martial at Magilligan, Limavady and Strabane, where courts martial sat for over ten days in September, and again at Derry in November. Some convicts were lashed. Others were transported for life; in September a shipload of prisoners sailed for America.[59]

Terror numbed rebel communities. Men who escaped conviction were 'persuaded' to 'trot off'. Robert Moore reluctantly 'banished himself from his Majesty's dominions' that summer and settled in Baltimore.[60] James Friel, a 'spoiled priest'-cum-schoolmaster who had been the most conspicuous Catholic in the Fánaid 'Unites', left in September, eventually settling in New York, where – ironically, after two spells in *príosún dubh Leifir* – he became clerk to the inspector of state prisons.[61] Samuel Alexander of Newtowncunningham, a sheriff's deputy who had drilled croppies in Castle Cunningham, went to Philadelphia; his people remembered that he 'had the pluck of a game cock' and rode to Derry 'in daytime, at a moderate pace on his own beast, not at night as was the custom with suspects'.[62] Still, not all left. Andrew Stilley, a Donegal delegate in May 1798, remained at home and a rebel. In 1801–2 he regularly visited Napper Tandy in Lifford

Gaol; in 1808 Dublin informers reported that he 'frequently' visited the capital where he stopped at the Castle Hotel in Temple Bar, a den of sedition; in 1815 he attended the duel between O'Connell and D'Esterre at Naas; and in 1845 he talked candidly to Classon Porter.[63] Still, by late 1798, transportation and 'voluntary exile' had removed respected leaders from communities across the north-west. Perhaps Henry Joy McCracken was right and the 'rich' had betrayed the 'poor'; however, they suffered for waiting for the French.

Table 1 — Counties represented at meetings of the Ulster Provincial Committee, 14 July 1797 to 29 May 1798

Date	14.7.97	14.8.97	14.9.97	14.10.97	14.11.97	14.12.97	14.1.98	1.2.98	27.2.98	24.3.98	1.4.98	17.4.98	19.4.98	10.5.98	29.5.98
Venue		A	B	C	C	D	C	E	F	G	H	F	I	C	F
Antrim								N/A							
Armagh								N/A							
Cavan								N/A							
Derry								N/A							
Donegal								N/A							
Down								N/A							
Fermanagh								N/A							
Louth								N/A							
Monaghan								N/A							
Tyrone								N/A							

Key: A — Randalstown; B — Samuel Thompson's, Scotch St, Dungannon; C — Mrs McCall's, Scotch St, Armagh; D — McDermon's, Randalstown; E — McClean's, Shanes's Castle; F — William Campbell's, Thomas St, Armagh; G — Samuel Greaves's, The Moy; adjourned to Blackwater Town; adjourned again to Mrs. McCall's, Armagh; H — Hagan's Tavern, Belfas; I — Hay's Tavern Belfast.

County Delegates and Visitors

14 July 1797; 14 Aug. 1797
County Delegates: N/A but included *Down* Nicholas Maguan, Saintfield
14 Sept. 1797
County Delegates: *Antrim* Robert Hunter, Belfast (secretary); James Stewart, Glenarm; *Armagh* John Jackson, Armagh; *Donegal* John Wilson, Magheracreggan; William Crawl; *Down* Dr Philips, *Bangor;* Nicholas Maguan, Saintfield, (chairman); *Monaghan* John Crawford; *Tyrone* John Cunning, Stewartstown; James McCricket, Dungannon
14 Oct. 1797
County Delegates: *Antrim* Robert Hunter, Belfast (secretary); *Armagh* John Jackson, Armagh (chairman); *Donegal* John Wilson, Maghercragan; *Down* John Kelso, Jr., Drumbridge; Nicholas Maguan, Saintfield; *Tyrone* John Kennedy, Coalisland

Visitor: Mr. [?Henry] Ogleby, Dublin; representative of Leinster Executive 'sent down to hold conference with Jackson of Armagh on some business with which he was entrusted by the Ulster Executive from Belfast previous and preparatory to the next Ex. meeting on Monday'.

14 Nov. 1797

County Delegates: *Antrim* James Stewart, Cushendal; Robert Hunter, Belfast (secretary); *Armagh* James Jackson, Armagh; William McCormick, Blackwatertown (chairman); *Donegal* George Buchanan, Raphoe; *Down* John Kelso, Drumbridge; Nicholas Maguan, Saintfield; *Monaghan* James Maxwell; *Tyrone* John Nicholas, Newtownstewart or Stewartstown; John McCardock, near Dungannon

14 Dec. 1797

County Delegates: *Antrim* James Stewart, Cushendal; Robert Hunter, Belfast (secretary); *Armagh* James Wilson; *Donegal* George Buchanan, Raphoe; *Down* David Thompson; Nicholas Maguan, Saintfield; *Monaghan* John Crawford; *Tyrone* John Wilson; James Bell (chairman)

Visitor: Dr. Magee, Randalstown

14 Jan. 1798

County Delegates: *Antrim* James Stewart, Cushendal; Robert Hunter, Belfast (secretary); *Armagh* William Jackson; James Moore; *Donegal* William Gallagher, 'near Omagh'; *Down* ___ O'Pray (chairman); Nicholas Maguan, Saintfield; *Tyrone* John Nixon, Thomas Bell; Mr Davidson

1 Feb. 1798

County Delegates: N/A but included *Down* Nicholas Maguan, Saintfield

27 Feb. 1798

County Delegates: *Antrim* Robert Hunter, Belfast (secretary); *Armagh* Jonathan Richardson (chairman); ___ Nicholson; *Donegal* John Welsh, Strabane; *Down* Nicholas Maguan, Saintfield; David Thompson; *Tyrone* Francis McMullan, Dungannon; James Borland, near Omagh

Visitors: John Kelso [Down]; Douglas Davison [Tyrone]; ___ Wilson of Killybagh; [Wm. or Mr.] Donnelly

24 Mar. 1798

County Delegates: *Antrim* Robert Hunter, Belfast (secretary); *Armagh* John Nicholas; John Moore, Richill; Jonathon Richardson, Loughgall; *Derry* Billy McKeever (alias Campbell), Maghera; *Down* Nicholas Maguan, Saintfield; *Tyrone* Francis McMullan; Douglas Davison; ___ Clark, near Omagh. Also James Gillen [?Armagh] and ___ Jameson

Visitors: 'Doctor Irwin', a 'fictitious name his real name being Swift son to the onranoble Dain Swift' attended as representative of Leinster Executive

1 Apr. 1798

County Delegates: *Antrim* Robert Hunter, Belfast (secretary); *Armagh* ___ Wilson; *Derry* Billy McKeever (alias Campbell), Maghera (chairman);

Down Nicholas Maguan, Saintfield; Andrew Todd, Jr.; David Thompson; *Tyrone* ___ McCarrel; ___ Clark, The Crew

17 Apr. 1798

County Delegates: *Armagh* John Wilson, Newtownhamilton; Allen Donaldson, Newtownhamilton; *Derry* Billy McKeever (alias Campbell), Maghera; Mr. Smith; *Donegal* John Marshall; *Down* Nicholas Maguan, Saintfield (secretary); *Louth* ___ [?Devany]; *Monaghan* Mr. Porter, Monaghan (chairman); John Crawford, Monaghan; *Tyrone* John Montgomery, The Crew; [?William] Clark, The Crew

  Comment: 'At a provincial meeting held at Armagh the 17th April [1798] Nicholas Maguan was sent by Hunter of Belfast to adjourn the same because Robert Simms had not arrived from Dublin. Accordingly the adjournment was made to Belfast, Thursday the 19th April'.

19 Apr. 1798

County Delegates: *Antrim* Robert Hunter, Belfast (secretary); *Armagh* and *Tyrone* Allen Donaldson, Newtownhamilton; *Derry* and *Donegal* Billy McKeever (alias Campbell), Maghera ('Campell represented Donegal and Derry, the representative of the former having given him that trust'); *Down* David Thompson; Nicholas Maguan, Saintfield (chairman); *Louth* ___ [?Devany]; *Monaghan* John Crawford, Monaghan

10 May 1798

County Delegates: *Antrim* Thomas Bashford, Belfast (secretary); *Armagh* John Wilson, near Killybagh; Alexander Donaldson; *Derry* Billy McKeever (alias Campbell), Maghera (chairman); *Donegal* 'James Stiller', 'beyond Omagh' [Andrew Stilley, Guystown]; *Down* David Thompson; Nicholas Maguan, Saintfield; *Louth* John Conolly (alias Conlan), Dundalk (chairman); *Monaghan* William Cunningham, Ballybay; *Tyrone* John Wilson, 'near Omagh'; John Montgomery, Stewartstown

29 May 1798

County Delegates: *Antrim* Thomas Bashford, Jr (secretary); *Armagh* Alexander Donaldson, near Keady; John Moore, Wasteland, near Richill (chairman); *Derry* Billy McKeever (alias Campbell), Maghera; *Donegal* John Patterson, 'beyond Omagh'; *Down* Nicholas Maguan, Saintfield; *Louth* John Conolly (alias Conlan), Dundalk; *Tyrone* James Piller, Jr, The Moy; John Wilson

Sources: Statements of Nicholas Maguan, Saintfield, who turned informer in summer 1797; PRONI Clelland Papers D714/2/7 [14 Sept.]; D714/2/8A [14 Oct.]; D714/2/9 [14 Nov.]; D714/2/10a [14 Dec.]; D714/2/14 [14 Jan.]; D714/2/15A [27 Feb.]; D714/2/17 [24 Mar.]; D714/2/20a [1 Apr.]; D714/2/21 [10 May]; D714/2/23 [29 May]; HO 100/76/132 [17 Apr.; 19 Apr.]; Secret Committee, pp. 102–19; extracts from Revd Classon Emmet Porter's 1845 interview with Andrew Stilley in Young, Ulster in '98, pp. 18–19.

WEXFORD IN 1798: A REPUBLIC BEFORE ITS TIME

Brian Cleary

OVER RECENT YEARS HISTORICAL research into 1798 has opened up a reassessment of events in Wexford and their relationship to those elsewhere. It is no longer tenable that the huge events occurring there did so without any political framework or objective or that they took place as an isolated and anomalous phenomenon unconnected with United Irish activity in the rest of Ireland.

Late eighteenth-century Wexford was a relatively sophisticated polity which had enjoyed the influence of a radical press in the early 1790s and was quite exceptional as a county, in that as much as a third of its ruling Protestant establishment favoured full political inclusion of Catholics. Indeed it was with their help that Wexford had played a frontline national role in the franchise campaign in 1792 and the Fitzwilliam campaign in 1796.

Contemporary assumptions in Dublin Castle that no United Irish organisation existed in Wexford in 1798 were gravely mistaken. On the contrary, the county was comparatively well prepared to participate in the general United Irish plan to overthrow the sectarian aristocratic regime in Dublin Castle and replace it with a pluralist democracy free of English interference.

The interpretation that Wexford in '98 was nothing more than a maelstrom of uncontrollable insurrectionary or sectarian impulses is misleading and inadequate. This is not to say but that a significant insurrectionary element must be factored into in the course of the rising there, and as for sectarianism, it is difficult to see how the dismantlement of a sectarian state could avoid having a sectarian dimension to it, once that dismantlement was opposed. Nevertheless the fact is that these matters were peripheral to the central drama – namely – the effort to raise the individual from the position of subject to the rank of citizen in Ireland's first republic.

Unlike other counties the campaign in Wexford opened with a

string of victories at Oulart Hill, Enniscorthy and The Three Rocks. These forced the military and civic authorities to evacuate Wexford town on 30 May and thereby afforded the revolution that critical respite in which to consolidate and establish.

Hectic improvisation and hurried meetings followed. A historic assembly of the principal inhabitants of town and county was convened on the night of 31 May which, acting in the name of the people, took civil and military power in County Wexford and they authorised bodies and personnel to exercise these powers on their behalf. Thus began the *Wexford Republic*. Though some no doubt harboured deep misgivings about the ultimate success of the revolution on a national basis they held their peace and Christopher Taylor, who printed the various proclamations circulated under the Republic, caught the popular contemporary atmosphere when he had 'Printer to the Wexford Republic' emblazoned in gold lettering on his printshop door in Main Street.

Revd George Taylor of Ballywalter, a Methodist minister, wrote the first Wexford history of 1798 and came very close to the meaning of these events. Taylor says that:

> No sooner had the rebels entered the town than they immediately began to re-organise the state. *A Grand National Committee* was set up and a *Committee of Five Hundred* and a *Council of Elders* and the premises of Mr Cullimore was commandeered and *was known* as the *'Senate House'*.

Given Taylor' references to the Senate House and also to 'the rebel senate' elsewhere in his text, and because the term Senate succinctly conveys the revolutionary dimension to what was taking place there, the name 'Senate' is used in this article to describe these meetings where the leading citizens were brought together in numbers to legitimise decisions of the Republic in the name of the people.

The first meeting of the Wexford Senate took place on the evening of the 31 May and continued the following day. General Tom Cloney, victor of The Three Rocks on 30 May records (1830) how he 'received the thanks of a very general meeting of the principal inhabitants of Wexford on the following night, on which occasion the celebrated Captain Keugh presided'.

The historian Edward Hay, a key United Irish leader in the county himself and subsequently an architect of Catholic Emancipation under O'Connell wrote in 1803:

> These circumstances produced a general meeting of the principal inhabitants on the first of June, wherein Mr. Harvey was called on to act as commander in chief, and *various other appointments and regulations took place* for the maintenance and supply of the *country* [Read 'were made' for 'took place'.]

When we examine these appointments and regulations we find ourselves at the birth of a popular revolution as the people formally assume military and civil power in the county.

1 **A Council of Elders**, or *committee of general regulation* as Hay calls it, was formed as an executive committee to act on a day to day basis in the name of the Senate. It was the supreme committee under the Senate. It was ultimately responsible for everything including courts and prisons. The commander-in-chief was the president of this council, thus linking the all-important army with civil administration which was minimal anyway in the late eighteenth-century. Its remit was intended to be county-wide and on the few occasions that the sparse records provide, we see it striving to impose its will, all be it with great difficulty, in Enniscorthy and indeed as far north as Gorey.

This committee met in Lett's house in George Street. The Letts were republican and closely related to Bagenal Harvey. This committee was altered on 13 June to become *The Council for Directing the Affairs of the People of the County Wexford*. In the histories it is often referred to, perhaps deliberately, as 'the committee'. The reference in Mrs Brownrigg's diary refers to it properly as the council which she visited on 2 June. It is interesting as a glimpse inside the council chamber:

> I arrived at Mrs. Letts, where Centinals were placed, colours flying and all proper dignity preserved. The Centinals stopped me so I asked for Mr. Harvey. He immediately came out and took me into a parlour where sat Keugh and Fitzgerald with various papers on a green table before them ... Harvey wrote an order for my trunks and I departed. So ended my visit to the Council.

2 **The Wexford army.** Beauchamp Bagenal Harvey was appointed
   commander-in-chief of the Wexford army. Other officers were
   also appointed. By this act they made official the establishment
   of the army itself. It comprised some 20,000 men at maximum,
   including a substantial number of Protestants. It was set up in
   two divisions, each comprising men from one side only of the
   river Slaney which roughly bisects the county. Both armies
   functioned as separate field-armies and in fact never fought
   together. Their main contact with the Republic was through
   the commissariat and through the council. Many Senate members would have been serving in the armies.

3 **The Wexford navy** was established. It comprised four oyster
   boats each with a twenty-five man crew. John Howlin, former
   privateer in the War of American Independence, was appointed admiral. Next day, 2 June, the navy captured a ship carrying
   Lord Kingsborough, colonel of the North Cork Militia at the
   harbour's mouth. He was to play an important part in the Republic's capitulation three weeks later. For his capture, John
   Scallan who seized his ship, was later made admiral. Scallan
   died at sea about 1835 as captain of a West Indies freighter. The
   capture of three barrels of gunpowder on a Guinea cutter was
   an extremely critical contribution from the Wexford navy to
   the Republic's arsenal. One barrel was all that could be spared
   to the northern army for the Battle of Arklow. Cargoes of various foodstuffs were also captured and brought into the town.

4 **A Committee of Public Safety** was established in place of the
   sectarian corporation. A Protestant, Matthew Keugh was appointed chairman of this high-powered committee. A thorough-
   going revolutionary, he was ex-officio commandant of Wexford town. Under the committee each ward raised its own company of soldiers: the John St Corps; the Selskar Corps and the
   Faythe Corps. These elected their own officers and carried out
   regular guard duty in the town day and night. They had a remarkable record in the protection of persons and property

until the Republic began to collapse. Their temporary absence from the town during the Battle of Horetown permitted others to open the prisons and execute some seventy prisoners on Wexford Bridge. The committee carried out two executions during the life of the Republic. Both were Catholic and both informers who had been tried and convicted by courts of the Republic.

A similar type committee operated in Enniscorthy of which very little is known. Its record is very different to that of Wexford. A tribunal was set up to try loyalists and many executions took place on Vinegar Hill. The relationship between the Enniscorthy committee and the council in Wexford is unclear but a very weak control is the most that can be claimed for the council in this case.

5 **A commissariat** was established to supply the army and navy with *matériel* and Wexford town [Pop. 10,000] with food. It had two representatives in every parish in the county who tried to oversee the supply of foodstuffs from the countryside. This committee became very large during the three weeks of the Republic and performed various functions through its network. It was chaired by Cornelius Grogan of Johnstown Castle who was later executed. A few rationing coupons used for the houses in the town have survived. Many of Wexford's leading businessmen served on the commissariat and some suffered death like Grogan on Wexford Bridge after the rising.

These were the principal proceedings of the first meeting of the Senate. There was no formal proclamation of the Republic like the proclamation of the Republic of Connacht in Castlebar two months later by General Humbert. This may reflect the expectation of the formation of a national revolutionary government in Dublin. It may equally reflect a longheaded caution – the formal declaration of the *de facto* republic then existing offered no material advantage; but in the event of defeat such a declaration when read at the courts martial that would inevitably follow could cost many lives on the scaffold.

Revd George Taylor's reference to a Grand National Committee being formed can reasonably be interpreted as a resolution declaring allegiance to future revolutionary government in Dublin. Any attempt to launch the Grand National Committee from Wexford, with Wexford acting *in loco Dublinensis* seems far-fetched, and had this been so, then we should surely expect a much quicker advance on New Ross and Arklow by the Republic's armies.

For those involved in the Senate the reality was that they were architects, however doctrinaire, of a new political entity which derived its legitimacy from the people assembled. It was their own: taking its power from themselves. In the turmoil of the times it is easy to miss this point, especially as in time of war much of an executive nature was carried out on the march by the army. The source of authority is the point at issue. They sanctioned these 'appointments and regulations' by the authority of a popular Senate acting in the name of the people in June 1798: and in this event the age of the *citizen* arrived in Ireland.

On repeated occasions the council and the army had recourse for authority to this Senate of principal inhabitants – whom indeed we should now style 'principal citizens'. *It is this recourse to the people for authority that made it a Republic as distinct from a mere military government.* The preciously few items of correspondence surviving from the Republic show some of the leaders addressing or referring to themselves or others as 'Citizen'. The first meeting of the Senate was probably the high point of the Republic. Alas, very soon the military and political weaknesses became visible and developed inexorably, and in a real sense we see the reason for the title of this essay: *Wexford in 1798: A Republic before its Time.*

The first Senate meeting was over when on 2 June the arrest of Lord Kingsborough already mentioned brought confirmation that things had gone badly elsewhere. Kingsborough's information soon caused a fundamental change in policy in Wexford with New Ross and Arklow now becoming regarded as prime targets through which the revolution must spread westwards into Munster and northwards to revive Dublin.

New Ross on 5 June was a bloody day with brave Unitedmen charging cannon belching grapeshot. Thirty per cent of the southern army fell in the fierce attacks. In Arklow on 9 June the northern army was also repulsed. There the fighting was equally fierce around the barricades in Main Street. Losses were not so heavy as at Ross, but as both sides hung on by their fingernails the shortage of powder forced the Unitedmen to withdraw and the town was held for England.

Repercussions were inevitable after these two major defeats. With the revolution hemmed in and the prospect of a revolutionary government in Dublin evaporating, cracks appeared in the unity of the Republic's leadership. Poor discipline and insubordination, ever a problem, now deteriorated to the point that the southern army was almost dissipated and the northern army becoming steadily estranged from the leadership in the council in Wexford town

Concerned at these developments the council moved to tighten their fragile hold on affairs. The Senate was convened on 13 June. Hay records the meeting with surpassing coyness saying: 'On 13th of June several persons from the different encampments, led by the most benevolent motives, as if by preconcerted agreement, waited on the commander-in-chief, in Wexford to consult on the best mode of keeping the unruly rabble in some order'.

After meeting with Harvey they went to the Senate to do things democratically. The restoration of discipline generally was the main purpose for this meeting but the development of a capability to engage in negotiations in the name of the whole county seems to have been the other unspoken half of its inspiration. The survival of the Republic or its ability to negotiate from a position of cohesiveness, if not to say strength, depended on discipline. The council's attitude to acts of indiscipline was now made clear when they ordered a public inquiry into the burning of Scullabogue Barn. In the event the Republic did not survive long enough to implement it. However the fact that it was made means that pogrom was not policy, and on the contrary shows their abhorrence and remorse. This was then followed by the establishment of *The Council for Directing the Affairs of the People of the County Wexford*.

In its name the new council made it clear that it claimed the allegiance of the whole county. Comprising eight men, four Catholics and four Protestants in a county of 90% Catholics, it was the essence of United Irish philosophy. Its cross-denominational composition was a statement to the whole country that the new order would not be the other side of the coin of the Penal laws. Instead it was a call to Catholic, Protestant and Dissenter to unite as Irishmen. All three were represented. The Catholics were: Edward Hay, Ballinkeele; Robert Carty, Birchgrove; Robert Meyler, Gurteenminogue; and Edward Kearney, Wexford town. The Protestants: Beauchamp Bagenal Harvey, Bargy Castle; William Hatton, Clonard; Matthew Keugh, Wexford town and Nicholas Gray, Whitefort, the one Presbyterian on the new council. Harvey, who had lost the command of the southern army after New Ross and had been replaced as commander-in-chief by Fr Philip Roche, retained the presidency of the new council, with Nicholas Gray as its secretary.

From the outset the new council was beset with difficulties. Concensus within the Republic on the outcome of the war was breaking down and not unreasonable suspicions appear to have developed between elements in the northern army and the council on the issue of *secret* negotiation of an end to hostilities. On the supply side the gunpowder factory set up in Wexford town was not successful, its powder lacked force and was no match for that of the enemy. Pike production and repairs were satisfactory but muskets damaged by inexperienced usage were not always repairable. Huge efforts were made to improve supply to the armies.

On 14 June the new council met a delegation from the prisoners in Wexford at the prisoners request. Thirteen enemy officers held at Wexford expressed the view that if crown forces continued to shoot rebel prisoners then nothing could save themselves in time. Moves were made for a deal on prisoners with Dublin Castle which might open contacts for wider negotiations. The effort failed when the Dublin bound emissaries were stopped at Enniscorthy by men who were determined to fight and felt betrayed that an ulterior motive pertaining to capitulation was secretly involved.

This type of suspicion partially undermined the authority of the Republic once victory became doubtful, especially in the northern theatre. Obedience to superior officers in the army and obedience to authority generally was paramount if the Republic was to survive or treat with the enemy from strength. To reinforce their authority by fastening obedience of the army the new council issued United Irish paths to be taken by every officer and private not yet sworn, and a general United Irish Test to be taken by the public at large *[Fig. 1, p. 110, published courtesy of the National Museum]*. The new oaths issued by the council had good effect. As crown forces gathered on Wexford's borders for the showdown, Gray, secretary of the council, wrote on 16 June to Philip Roche, the new commander-in-chief desperate for reinforcements for his southern army which had almost melted away since the battle of Ross:

> Dear Citizen, ... We have, however, now issued orders, desiring all un-married men to repair to camp immediately: *we did so before*, but they were not fully obeyed: at the present time particular obedience *will be enforced*, and we trust you will shortly find at your camp a number of fresh young fellows, as well appointed and provided as our best efforts can accomplish ...

Gray's words were no empty claim. Obedience was enforced with such effect that four days later this army was back in shape sufficiently to fight the Battle of Horetown which lasted four and a quarter hours when the shortage of gun-powder again forced the Wexfordmen to withdraw. The southern army was back in business as Gray had predicted. The Republic's writ still ran.

On 19 June as events moved inexorably towards the great encounters of Horetown and Vinegar Hill, crown forces advanced from Waterford, New Ross, Bunclody, Carnew, Tullow, Tinahely and Arklow. General Needham's advance from Arklow towards Oulart left a trail of devastation for a mile on either side of him. No prisoners were taken. The people fled before him on the clogged roads and ended up in the area between Oulart, Enniscorthy and Wexford town. The situation was wildly unstable and open to manipulation.

Very late that same day, 19 June, an order came from the Three Rocks camp for all armed men in Wexford town to appear there by day-break. Committee of Public Safety companies were then stripped from the town to further strengthen the southern army against General Moore for the Battle of Horetown to the south-west. This left Wexford town open to the many nameless people who had de-

By Order of the *Council* for directing the Affairs of the *People* of the County WEXFORD.

OATHS to be taken by all the UNITED ARMY, in the most public and solemn Manner.

TEST OATH.

IN the awful Presence of God, I, A. B. do voluntarily declare, that I will persevere in endeavouring to form a Brotherhood of Affection among *Irishmen* of *every* religious Persuasion; and that I will persevere in my Endeavours to obtain an equal, full, and adequate Representation of *all* the People of Ireland.—I do further declare, that neither Hopes, Fears, Rewards, or Punishments, not even Death, shall ever induce me, directly or indirectly, to inform on or give Evidence against any Member or Members of this or similar Societies, for any Act or Expression of theirs, done or made collectively or individually, in or out of this Society, in Pursuance of the Spirit of this Obligation. So help me God.

OATH OF A PRIVATE.

I, A. B. do solemnly and sincerely swear, and take God, and his only Son our Lord Jesus Christ, to witness, that I will at all Times be obedient to the Commands of my Officers—That I am ready to lay down my Life for the Good of my Country—that I have an Aversion to Plunder, and to the spilling of innocent Blood—that I will fight couragiously in the Field, and have Mercy where it can be given—that I will avoid Drunkenness as tending to Disorder and Ruin—that I will endeavour to make as many Friends and as few Enemies as possible—that above all, I detest a Coward, and that I will look upon him as an Enemy who will stand back in the Time of Battle.—So help me God.

OATH OF AN OFFICER.

IN the awful Presence of God, who knows the Hearts and Thoughts of all Men, and calling my Country to witness, I, A. B. Officer in, &c. do solemnly swear, that I do not consider my Life my own when my Country demands it—That I consider the present Moment calls for a Proof of the Sincerity of that Sentiment; and I am ready and desirous to stand the Test; and do aver, that I am determined to die, or lead to Victory; and that all my Actions shall be directed to the Prosperity of the common Cause, uninfluenced by any inferior Motive: And I further declare my utter Aversion to all Alarmists, Union Breakers, and Cowards, and my Respect and Obedience to the Commands of superior Officers.—So help me God.

Done at the Council Chamber,
Wexford, June 14, 1798.

By Order of the Council,

B. B. HARVEY, President.
NICHOLAS GRAY, Secretary.

Figure 1

manded swifter retribution for the lawless oppression of the days and weeks prior to the rising. The house-burning, whippings, pitch-capping and the shooting of some hundreds in their own doors before their families tends to be forgotten because the victims have no names. But their dark harrowing experience provided the insurrectionary impulse which may well have forced the outbreak of the rising, and it remained the main reason for an incessant demand for retribution from the Republic and resulted in recurrent challenges to the authority of the council during the lifetime of the Republic. Pressure was maintained on Harvey and Keugh to have the guilty punished. Harvey, a barrister, stood firmly for due process against such demands.

Many executions had taken place in Enniscorthy where the local committee in charge of the town took a very different attitude to that in Wexford; perhaps because the north of the county had suffered much worse in the pre-rising period. As early as 7 June General Edward Roche of the northern army, issued a strong exhortation to his own men for discipline and urged them to remember the cause for which they were sworn and united. It is the finest document from the Wexford Republic *[Fig. 2, p. 112]*. This was followed with the despatch by the council of a special guard of 130 gunsmen from Wexford to Enniscorthy which ended the executions on Vinegar Hill.

In Wexford town executions of loyalists were avoided until the situation was exacerbated by the behaviour of Needham's forces. Then the worst happened. Harvey's policy of due process was finally overborne. Some seventy loyalist prisoners were brought before a hastily constituted tribunal and were put to death on the bridge, innocent among the guilty. The manner of their deaths was gratuitously cruel and constituted a human and political tragedy.

It was an evening of intense drama. The town was traumatised by the executions on the bridge. The like had not been seen in the town since Cromwell. A great battle was in progress at Horetown and another preparing for the morrow on Vinegar Hill: two of the biggest battles in Irish history. English gunboats hung offshore. The light of democracy was flickering to extinction when about ten at night the first men brought back news of the indecisive field of Horetown. In

111

TO THE PEOPLE OF IRELAND.

Countrymen and Fellow Soldiers!

YOUR patriotic exertions in the cause of your country have hitherto exceeded your most sanguine expectations, and in a short time must ultimately be crowned with success—Liberty has raised her drooping head; thousands daily flock to her standard; the voice of her children every where prevails—let us then, in the moment of triumph, return thanks to the Almighty Ruler of the universe, that a total stop has been put to those sanguinary measures, which of late were but too often resorted to by the creatures of government to keep the people in slavery.

Nothing now, my countrymen, appears necessary to secure the conquests you have so bravely won, but an implicit obedience to the commands of your chiefs; for, through a want of proper subordination and discipline, all may be endangered.

At this eventful period, all Europe must admire, and posterity will read with astonishment, the heroic acts achieved by people, strangers to military tactics, and having few professional commanders. But what power can resist men fighting for liberty!

In the moment of triumph, my countrymen, let not your victories be tarnished with any wanton act of cruelty; many of those unfortunate men now in prison were not your enemies from principle, most of them, compelled by necessity, were obliged to oppose you; neither let a difference in religious sentiments cause a difference amongst the people. Recur to the debates in the Irish House of Lords of the nineteenth of February last, you will there see a patriotic and enlightened *protestant bishop* (Down, and many of the lay lords) with manly eloquence, pleading for catholic emancipation and parliamentary reform, in opposition to the haughty arguments of the lord chancellor, and the powerful opposition of his fellow courtiers.

To promote an union of brotherhood and affection amongst our countrymen of all religious persuasions, has been our principal object; we have sworn in the most solemn manner, have associated for this laudable purpose, and no power on earth shall shake our resolution.

To my *protestant* soldiers I feel much indebted, for their gallant behaviour in the field, where they exhibited signal proofs of bravery in the cause.

Wexford, June 7, 1798.   EDWARD ROCHE.

Figure 2

112

the Cape of Good Hope Inn an anxious Kingsborough sent for Edward Hay to discuss terms of capitulation to be sent to General Lake the commander of the English forces. Hay, a member of the council, insisted that the matter be put to the people and agreed to assemble as many members of the Senate as he could. Those he gathered however would naturally not dare agree anything until the outcome of Vinegar Hill was known. They stalled for time. Hay tells us that they agreed to meet again the following morning 'at Captain Keugh's house, where the subject would be taken into consideration by a general assembly, which could not be formed at that time of night'.

At 3am on the fateful 21 June, Kingsborough had Hay roused again. Hay again insisting on the need to have the concurrence of the people if the capitulation on terms was to carry. This meeting was protracted and before it ended Hay could hear the opening salvoes of Lake's cannon at Vinegar Hill. That made it 7am. A meeting of the Senate then took place in Keugh's house. The windows rattled as English gunboats bombarded Rosslare Fort. The Senate ruled that three deputations should be sent, one to each approaching army, and that Kingsborough should remain in the town and assume military authority while the former Mayor Jacob should resume office. Because their numbers were depleted the Senate decided to put these proposals to the armed corps of the town assembled on Common Quay for the purpose. To save the town the people approved the terms by acclamation.

A deputation then communicated this to Kingsborough who on accepting the military authority of the town asked Captain Keugh for his sword. Keugh, regretting that it could not be surrendered to the approaching armies, presented the sword of the Republic 'with the greatest formality'. The former Mayor Jacob, who had joined the Republic as a medical doctor, agreed to re-assume his former office of mayor. Thus with the sword and mayoralty returned to those who held them prior to the revolution the Wexford Republic had come to an end.

The northern army which had seen the worst of the oppression prior to the revolution now arrived having extricated itself from Vinegar hill. They rejected the terms. Lake, still at Enniscorthy also rejected them. Wexford town was occupied by General Moore before Lake left Enniscorthy. The northern army of the Republic moved out of Wexford as Moore approached the town. They then split in two with Fr John Murphy going north-east as far as County Laois and Anthony Perry's force going north as far as Ardee. Between them they fought as many battles after Vinegar Hill as were fought before – ten. Their heroic deeds in that sad dénouement are only now beginning to be researched and written as is the case with the Wexford Republic itself. The work is only beginning, encouraged by the bi-centenary.

The Wexford Republic remains a tantalising image not yet quite clear in its full detail. It must rank as one of the great legacies of that exciting generation and era which produced the United Irishmen. If it was unsophisticated, it was the first. If ineffective betimes, it was beset. If there was vengeance, there was outrage. If it was in fact premature, it had a modern vision: and if that vision continue, it will come to pass.

GENERAL HUMBERT'S CAMPAIGN IN THE WEST

Harman Murtagh

EVENTS IN THE WEST of Ireland in 1798 centred around the landing of just over 1,000 French troops in Mayo towards the end of August. For a fortnight they conducted a lively campaign with the support of local rebels, until they were surrounded and captured by superior government forces in County Longford as they attempted to march towards Dublin.[1]

The background lay in the efforts of the United Irishmen, chiefly through Theobald Wolfe Tone, their 'ambassador incognito' in Paris, to persuade the French government to invade Ireland and assist the republicans to overthrow British rule.[2] Tone's negotiations resulted in Hoche's unsuccessful Bantry Bay venture of 1796 and an abortive expedition from the Batavian Republic (Holland) in 1797. By 1798 Ireland ranked lower in French priorities, and news of the rebellion came as a surprise. Much of the French army was absent in Egypt with Napoleon, the navy was weak and the public finances in disarray.

Nevertheless, the French responded as best they could. Plans for an expedition of 8,000 men were initiated.[3] Meanwhile, in a desperate attempt to keep the Irish rebellion alive, smaller forces from Rochefort, Dunkirk and Brest were ordered to sail more or less simultaneously to the west of Ireland, where they were to link up in Donegal. The commander at Rochefort was General Jean Joseph Amable Humbert, a thirty-year-old uneducated former skin dealer from the Vosges, whose energy, bravado and physical courage had quickly raised him to general in the heady early days of the revolutionary army.[4]

Humbert hankered after an independent command, and to the dismay of the other generals he put to sea on 6 August without waiting for the Brest fleet which was to carry General Hardy, the overall commander, with the bulk of the French forces. By sailing when he did, Humbert forfeited the advantage of surprise, and Hardy was intercepted and defeated by the English navy off Lough Swilly in October. Another squadron reached the coast of Mayo too late to be of any value, and preparations were abandoned for a larger expedition from Brest under the Irish-born General Kilmaine.[5]

Humbert landed at Kilcummin near Killala in County Mayo on 22 August. 'The army of Ireland', as he grandiloquently titled his force, was comprised of 888 infantry, principally the second battalion of the 70th demi-brigade, together with 42 inexperienced artillery-men, 57 cavalry mostly from the 3rd Chasseurs, and a staff of 35 officers.[6] An observer noted that except for the grenadiers, in appearance 'they had nothing to catch the eye. The stature for the most part was low, their complexions pale and sallow' and their blue uniforms much the worse for wear.[7] Although young, most were seasoned veterans, confident of the superiority of French arms and inured to hardship. Amongst a handful of Irishmen to accompany the expedition were Bartholomew Teeling, the radical son of a Lisburn linen draper, Tone's brother, Matthew, and the Mayo-born Captain Henry O'Keon, an ex-priest whose fluency in Irish, English and French made him invaluable.

The infantry was armed with flintlock muskets, best discharged in volleys of about two per minute, and with a range of less than 200 metres. They also had bayonets and swords, and the cavalry was equipped with sabres, pistols and carbines. The artillery comprised three 4-pounder field guns. Local horses were commandeered for cavalry and transport, but insufficient numbers were available, and the artillery and ammunition wagons were sometimes dragged by hand. Although there was a shortage of bread, the seizure of livestock ensured that victuals were plentiful, and the French rated the Irish beef and mutton delicious.

The rebellion in Ireland was well over before Humbert left France. Connacht had remained quiet throughout the disturbances of the early summer. The United Irishmen were poorly organised in the province, and their allies, the Defenders, remained weak after tough counter-insurgency measures in 1795.[8] However, there was widespread sympathy for the rebel cause, and in Mayo the French were welcomed with enthusiasm. Cries of *Erin go bragh* and *vive la republique irlandaise* greeted them on the march, and people knelt by the roadside to pray for their success.[9]

Having occupied Killala, Humbert called on the Irish to join him. A small number of Catholics of gentry and middle-class background volunteered their services and were made officers. They included James Joseph MacDonnell, a lawyer and an old associate of Tone, who was the leader of the United Irishmen in Mayo.[10] Command of the Irish was given initially to Matthew Bellew, an ex-Russian army officer, who had been invalided home in a deranged state having been blown up by a Turkish mine.[11] His instability, compounded by an addiction to drink, rendered him unfit to play a role of any consequence. His appointment was a severe embarrassment to his brother Dominick, the Catholic Bishop of Killala, who afterwards found it difficult to shake off allegations of collusion with the rebels, even though, like the rest of the Irish Catholic bishops, he had little sympathy with republicanism.[12] The thirty or so priests of his diocese were divided. Some sought to dissuade their parishioners from involvement, but half a dozen or more, together with a similar number from the neighbouring dioceses, were implicated in Humbert's campaign, mainly by indications of approval and the encouragement of recruiting.[13] No Protestants joined Humbert.

In all 6–700 volunteers enlisted with the French at Killala and another 3,500 at Castlebar, including some captured soldiers of the Longford militia. The recruits were divided into companies of forty to fifty men. The bulk were from the poorest peasantry, and there were amusing scenes as they rushed to dress in their new blue uniforms, while an officer banged helmets onto their heads with his fist. The French found the process of turning such rustics into disciplined soldiers a frustrating experience.[14] Linguistic difficulties and a shortage of officers impeded training, while the recruits were prone to desert as soon as they had collected their uniforms and some loot. A colony of Ulster weavers, under the command of Teeling, formed the most reliable unit. They were refugees from Orange persecution who had settled in Ballina and were much 'addicted to speculate in politics'. The 3,000 muskets which Humbert distributed were almost enough to arm his Irish allies, and the use of pikes was probably mainly confined to fringe groups. A green colour was unfurled, depicting the harp with the motto *Erin go bragh*.

The French landing was viewed as a serious crisis by the Irish government, especially as early reports exaggerated Humbert's strength. An experienced soldier, Lord Cornwallis, had just been appointed viceroy and commander-in-chief. He had close to 100,000 men under his command, and a further 10,000 came from Britain in September.[15] However, only just over 10% were regulars. The rest of his troops comprised the Irish militia, a largely Catholic force officered by Protestants; English and Scottish fencibles – soldiers who volunteered for service only in the British Isles; and the Irish yeomanry, a local defence force of part-time largely Protestant volunteers. An effective part of Cornwallis' strength lay in his artillery.[16] The battalion six-pounders and curricle guns of the Royal Irish Artillery had a round-shot range of 6-800 metres, and also fired case and grape – discharges of quantities of musket balls devastating to massed opponents at close quarters. Scarlet was the predominant uniform colour of the government soldiers, except for the artillery and some of the cavalry who wore blue.

At the time of the French landing the government had less than 4,000 troops in Connacht, of whom militia and yeomanry formed a large proportion. General Hutchinson, the commander, divided his forces and took up station with only 1,700 men at Castlebar, where he was joined by General Lake, the conqueror of Wexford.[17] Humbert's orders were to exercise caution, but having captured Ballina, he boldly took the offensive. With 800 French and the same number of Irish, he marched overnight, via the mountain road through Barnagehy, arriving at Castlebar on the morning of 27 August. Lake and Hutchinson were taken by surprise, with barely time to draw up their forces in traditional linear formations on the hilly ground north-west of the town.[18] Humbert attacked immediately with the Irish in the centre, flanked by the French on either side. The government artillery, positioned in front of the infantry, was well served: Humbert's Irish broke and fled before a hail of fire, and the French halted under cover of a ditch. They were rallied by General Sarrazin, Humbert's second in command, who led them along a sunken path to threaten the flank of the government line. The militia showed their in-experience and nervousness by panicky musket fire while the French were still out of range. When Sarrazin's men charged forward with fixed bayonets to the cry of *vive la republique*, the government cavalry galloped away, and the Kilkenny and Longford militias fell back in disorder, abandoning the artillery. The French pressed home the attack and drove the government forces from the town in the igno-minious flight that has come to be known as the 'Races of Castlebar'. Humbert lost about sixty Frenchmen killed and 120 wounded, in-flicting similar casualties on the enemy, and capturing five colours, with most of his opponents' artillery and baggage. Jubilantly he re-ported to France that with 2,000 reinforcements and 15,000 more muskets, he would free Ireland within a month.

Virtually the whole of Mayo now came under Humbert's con-trol. Trees of liberty were erected in the towns, and drink flowed freely in the rowdy atmosphere surrounding the celebration bonfires. With the normal forces of law and order overthrown, looting inten-sified, and there was widespread destruction of property. A number of big houses suffered major damage, although Westport House was preserved through the timely intervention of James MacDonnell. Only Wexford and Wicklow surpassed Mayo in the compensation after-wards paid to 'suffering loyalists'. Some Protestant churches were vandalised and Protestants feared for their lives, but the destruction and intimidation was probably more social than sectarian. Although Catholics wore scapulars as a badge of identity, there was not a strong tradition of religious animosity in Mayo; no Protestants died except on the battlefield, and Catholics with property also suffered.

The French were struck by the wretched living conditions of the peasantry, and by the contrast between rich and poor. There was a suggestion that a redistribution of land 'would communicate through the kingdom like an electric spark', but Humbert had proclaimed an 'inviolable respect' for property, and in keeping with the conservative instincts of the United Irish leadership he made no move to en-courage a radical overthrow of the existing social order.[19] Some of his officers were detached for duty to the main towns, and they took an active role in restoring order. Mayo was divided into regional departments, each with a responsible local Catholic as magistrate to organise security patrols. Humbert set up a twelve-man provisional government for Connacht at Castlebar, tasked with organising the military power of the province and with providing subsistence for the French and Irish troops.[20] The president was John Moore, who had been educated in France and was the son of a wealthy local landowner.[21]

Humbert spent a week at Castlebar. In military terms, a rapid renewal of the offensive would have been the proper course of action, but he delayed for news of his victory to trigger widespread rebellion. However, it soon became clear that Irish republicans had little appetite for fresh hostilities, certainly not until more significant forces arrived from France. Outside Mayo, there was no response in Connacht. In Roscommon, where a strong rebel organisation was reputed to exist, the United Irish leader, an ex-French army officer named Plunkett, lost his nerve and surrendered to the government. Sligo was still cowed after its disarmament in 1797, and in Galway the United Irishmen, who were not numerous, drilled with farm implements and waited on events.

Cornwallis was shaken by news of the Castlebar defeat, which he feared would be followed by further French landings and fresh rebellion. It was essential to deny Humbert a second victory, and the viceroy warned the government commanders to avoid battle until sufficient forces were concentrated to make success a certainty. He requested reinforcements from London and placed the yeomanry throughout Ireland on permanent duty. Then, proceeding 'with extraordinary, perhaps with excess of caution', he made elaborate dispositions for his campaign.[22] Soldiers on detachment throughout Leinster were ordered to congregate at fixed stations. General Nugent moved to Enniskillen to block any thrust into Ulster. General Hewett assembled forces from the south and east at Portumna.[23] Cornwallis himself, with a force of 7,000, took personal charge of the offensive against Humbert. He had no faith in Irish troops, whom he regarded as undisciplined and untrustworthy, and he delayed his advance until Scottish and English units could join him. He reached Tuam on 2 September and consulted with Lake. It was decided that Cornwallis would move against Castlebar from the south, while the 2,500 remaining government troops in Connacht would unite under Lake at Frenchpark and advance from the east. A strong cavalry reconnaissance would precede Cornwallis, under the command of Colonel 'Black Bob' Craufurd, a daredevil expert in mobile warfare. This force comprised Hompesch's Dragoon Riflemen, a German regiment in British pay, and the 1st Irish Fencible Dragoons – Lord Roden's Foxhunters – who astonished the French by jumping stone walls 'like goats'.[24]

Meanwhile Humbert was being forced to scale down the optimistic plans he had made after the victory at Castlebar. Initially he had hoped to drive the government forces beyond the Shannon, and join with insurgents to advance on Dublin for a decisive result. Next, he considered digging in at Castlebar, making it the rallying point for Irish rebels until reinforcements came from France. But, as Cornwallis closed in, it was clear that defending Castlebar was not a realistic military proposition. Hardy had not appeared. Humbert's French were too few, and there was no time to train the wild Irish or construct adequate fortifications. Ruling out a retreat to the western mountains, Humbert decided to break out of Mayo by a fast march through County Sligo. The idea came from Sarrazin, who claimed afterwards that from the start the objective was Dublin, which the French believed was lightly defended. Doubtless, this daring manoeuvre would have held appeal for Humbert. However, it seems likely that at the outset he did not exclude the possibility of heading north. In the event he adopted Sarrazin's full concept out of desperation, as circumstances developed on the march.

The French evacuated Castlebar on 3–4 September, accompanied by only 600 of the Irish under MacDonnell. Humbert slipped around General Lake who had advanced to Ballaghadereen and brushed off an attack by the local yeomanry at Tubbercurry, where he was joined by some of the Irish from Ballina. In thirty hours he covered the forty miles to Collooney. His men had just started to rest, when they were attacked by the Limerick militia which formed part of the garrison of Sligo. A sharp, hour-long engagement ensued. Amidst noisy exchanges of cannon and musket fire, the outnumbered militia were repulsed and then overwhelmed in a characteristic flanking movement by Sarrazin. Great personal courage was displayed by

Teeling in disabling one of the militia cannon.

Cornwallis was uncertain of French intentions, although he considered 'every point of direction for their march ... equally desperate'. He ordered Lake to pursue and harass Humbert. Craufurd's cavalry, which had entered Castlebar, was sent to reinforce him, followed by the light infantry. Events now took another turn with republican uprisings in support of the French in Longford and north Westmeath.[25] These were poorly organised affairs which were quickly suppressed by locally available government forces. However, Humbert turned south at Dromahair in an attempt to unite with the insurgents, while Cornwallis moved east across the Shannon with his own force, and was sufficiently alarmed to order the Guards Brigade into Westmeath. The security of Dublin became a concern, and although the city was defended by six regiments and 5,000 yeomanry, barges were assembled on the Grand Canal for the transport of reinforcements, should this prove necessary.

Meanwhile Humbert pushed his exhausted column forward. All the captured artillery was dumped, and the soldiers took it in turn to ride the available horses. There was criticism amongst officers and men that a host of blunders had been made, their government had abandoned them, and their lives were being needlessly sacrificed. It took the combined efforts of Humbert and Sarrazin to shore up the flagging morale. There were several minor engagements with Craufurd's cavalry which continually harassed the extended Franco-Irish column. The country people were too terrified of retribution to give any military support, but they supplied food, and the women 'showed us the care which they have for children, brothers and friends'. A promised rendezvous with the remnants of the defeated Longford insurgents failed to materialise.

Humbert's campaign ended at Ballinamuck in County Longford on 8 September. With Cornwallis blocking the French advance at Ballinalee, Lake attacked the rearguard of Humbert's column which capitulated at the first assault. Humbert drew up the rest of his force on a hillside and put up a token fight. There were casualties on both sides, but when further resistance was futile he surrendered unconditionally. The surviving 800 French were made prisoners-of-war

122

and brought to Dublin, where they were feted as heroes before going on to England. The officers were soon exchanged, but it took much longer for the rank and file to be repatriated. In France there was little appreciation of their efforts. Humbert received no further promotion and eventually emigrated to America, where he died penniless in 1823. No mercy was shown to the Irish who had accompanied him to Ballinamuck. Several hundred were slaughtered on the battlefield or as they fled, and a large number of prisoners were hanged, including Teeling and Matthew Tone.

The bloodshed continued with the suppression of the remaining insurgents in Mayo. Ballina was recaptured, and General Trench then led a force of 3,000 against Killala which was defended by 800 rebels, under the remaining French officers. On 23 September the town fell to simultaneous attacks at both ends, and scenes of appalling carnage ensued as fencible cavalry sabred 400 rebels to death in the streets. In Erris and Tirawley, throughout the following week, houses were burned, villages wrecked and peasants killed, some of them naively still wearing their French uniforms. Prominent insurgent leaders were hanged, including General Bellew and two of the priests who had supported Humbert. Others went on the run, and a few, like James Mac-Donnell who had escaped from Ballinamuck, got away to exile in France. President John Moore was captured at Castlebar and died in prison. An amnesty was only finally declared in 1799, and even then its application was selective.

The defeat of the French was followed by recriminations. Humbert was reported to have said that the Irish had deceived him abominably, robbing him of everything they could get hold of and behaving in a cowardly manner.[26] Other officers claimed the French had been misled about the extent of the support they could expect in Ireland. The truth was that Humbert's expedition was not a rational operation of war, but a foolhardy adventure, too late and far too little to assist the Irish republicans or threaten the government regime. The French troops were the best soldiers on either side in 1798, and Humbert's lively campaign has always bedazzled commentators. However, there is some justice in the criticism that he was given too much rein by Cornwallis' excessive caution. The whole episode proved that retaining control of Ireland was a far greater strategic necessity to Britain, especially in wartime, than 'liberating' it was to the French. In any case the disorganised and demoralised French navy was in no condition to transport a sizeable army to Ireland, or sustain it there, even if such a force had been available in 1798. For all their diplomatic success in Paris, the United Irishmen's policy of reliance on France was a strategic mistake. The impossibility of co-ordinating military planning between France and Ireland proved fatal to the insurrection and indeed to Humbert. The involvement of the French further hardened the attitude of the government and its conservative allies in Ireland. Humbert's expedition is widely commemorated. But for the people of Mayo in 1798, their month of 'liberty' was a futile tragedy – bloody, destructive and divisive.

THE PRIME INFORMANT:

THE LIFE AND TIMES OF 'THE SHAM SQUIRE' FRANCIS HIGGINS
(1746–1802)

Thomas Bartlett

BY THE MID-1790S THE gravity of the threat posed by the United Irishmen had been starkly revealed to both the British government and Dublin Castle. There was clear evidence that the United Irishmen were in secret communication with the French government, the Directory, and that they were actively soliciting an invasion force from that quarter. In Britain itself, there were disturbing reports that Irish republicans were infiltrating English and Scottish radical political groups and seeking to make common cause with them. In Ireland, the United Irishmen were busy swearing in new members, suborning from their duty members of the armed forces, and attempting to form an alliance with the rural insurgents known as Defenders.

The challenge which the United Irishmen mounted to the connection between Britain and Ireland, and indeed to the imperial state of Britain in its war with revolutionary France, elicited by way of response a series of measures that were calculated to draw the teeth of the United Irish threat. Harsh new laws – among them, an Arms Act, a Gunpowder Act and an Insurrection Act – were brought in which prescribed severe punishments for a range of offences which had hitherto been treated as mere misdemeanours. In addition, new forces were created: in 1793 an Irish Militia was set up, in 1796 an Irish Yeomanry was embodied, and throughout 1797, reinforcements of Scottish and English Fencibles flooded into Ireland. These military forces were everywhere encouraged to act vigorously, and Dublin Castle turned a blind eye to the excesses they visited on the civilian population. Moreover, a new (or newish) concept – that of Protestant ascendancy – was quickly espoused by Dublin Castle, and the rough measures of the foot soldiers of that ideology – the members of the newly-formed Orange Order – were connived at or even encouraged. The non-sectarian programme of the United Irishmen would be combated by the avowed sectarianism of Dublin Castle; and everywhere the notion of *disunited* Irishmen would be pitted against that of *united* Irishmen. Lastly, in its campaign against the United Irishmen, Dublin Castle made extensive use of spies and agents, informers and informants in order to penetrate to the very heart of that organisation and discover its secrets in order to disrupt and defeat its plans.[1]

Later commentators have been uniformly impressed with the effectiveness of the castle's spy network. The historian, Richard Madden who wrote extensively on the United Irishmen in the mid-nineteenth-century claimed that 'every important proceeding of the United Irish was known to the government';[2] and another nineteenth-century writer, William John Fitzpatrick, drew the moral for later aspirant revolutionaries: 'The organisers of illegal societies will see that in spite of the apparent secrecy and ingenuity of their system, informers sit with them at the same council board and dinner table, ready at any moment to sell their blood, and that the wider the ramifications of conspiracy, the greater becomes the certainty of detection.'[3] Fitzpatrick spoke with great authority on the matter of informers and informants, for he had spent many years researching this topic, publishing *The Sham Squire and the Informers of 1798* (Dublin, 1869), and *Secret Service under Pitt* (Dublin, 1892). In these, and in other works, he set out to name those who had betrayed their comrades, to cite the sums paid to them, and to reveal the secret history of the 1790s. In particular, Fitzpatrick focused his energies on laying bare the extraordinary career of one of the leading Dublin Castle informants, Francis Higgins, known colloquially as the Sham Squire or Shamado. Higgins, the editor of the *Freeman's Journal,* 'ran' a number of agents and informers in the Dublin area and it was through one of them, Francis Magan, a Catholic barrister, that he procured the vital information divulging where the United Irish chief, Lord Edward Fitzgerald, was in hiding. Coming as it did on the heels of a series of arrests of key personnel, Lord Edward's capture on 19 May 1798 was a devastating blow to the Dublin and Kildare United Irishmen, and on its own, may have rendered their insurrection abortive. A consideration of Higgins' life and letters is therefore timely.

IN A SHORT PROFILE OF FRANCIS Higgins published in 1799, at a time

126

when Higgins was proprietor of the *Freeman's Journal,* the journalist Henry MacDougall snidely commented that his subject's career 'is a singular instance of what may be done in life by strict attention to private ends without regard to the means which so often retard the advancement of men of principle'.[4] Much of MacDougall's information concerning Higgins derived from a sensational series of articles about him published in 1789 by a rival editor, John Magee, proprietor of the *Dublin Evening Post.* While Higgins denied some of the stories Magee dragged up about his past, and others were passed off as youthful folly, the essential accuracy of MacDougall's judgement can scarcely be questioned.

Higgins' family had hailed originally from Downpatrick, County Down, and his father, Patrick, having conformed to the Established Church, found employment as a clerk in a law office in Dublin in the 1740s.[5] On the death of his father – it was constantly alleged that he was murdered to conceal information that had come into his possession concerning an important lawsuit – the young Higgins found himself literally out in the street. Beginning as an errand boy, shoeblack and waiter in a porter house, he worked his way up to an employment in the office of Daniel Bourne, attorney-at-law. There he allegedly discovered a talent for forgery and determined that this would be his pathway to success. He set out to procure himself a rich Catholic heiress and, having been accepted into the Catholic Church, he furnished himself with the necessary documentation to prove that he was a Catholic of property and a worthy catch in the marriage lists. A contact with a Jesuit, Fr Shortall, led to an introduction to William Archer, a wealthy Catholic merchant, on the lookout for a suitable suitor for his daughter, Mary. Further elaborate deceptions followed: Higgins produced forged documents which showed he had property in County Down worth £250 a year, that he had a lucrative employment in the revenue service, and that he was himself heir to a fortune.[6] He even took care to be seen exiting from a house on fashionable St Stephen's Green which he claimed he was set to inherit, though in fact he only knew one of the servants there, and he made his entrance and exit when the real owners were away. Completely taken in, Archer overruled his daughter and ordered her to marry

Higgins. After the marriage the truth speedily emerged that Higgins, so far from being a well-off and worthy son-in-law, was in fact an unscrupulous fraudster. Mary Archer fled and reportedly died soon after. William Archer took an action against Higgins, accusing him of attempting to 'cheat, cozen and defraud' him, and of seeking to 'aggrieve, impoverish and ruin' his daughter, Mary. In January 1767, Higgins was found guilty of fraud and lodged in Newgate Gaol: at his trial, the judge denounced him as nothing but a 'sham squire'; and this nickname was to dog him for the rest of his life.

When Magee in 1789 dragged up this unsavoury story from Higgins' past, Higgins was forced to concede that most of it was accurate, passing it off as a youthful error. Magee, however, followed up his account of Shamado's fraudulent marriage with even more scurrilous accusations which Higgins denied but refused to rebut in detail. Magee claimed that Higgins during his time in gaol, in a plot line that could have been taken from John Gay's *The Beggar's Opera* (1728), had become enamoured of the gaoler's daughter, and that this 'Mac-Heath' and 'Lucy Lockit' were duly married. Furthermore, following another spell in prison for an excise fraud, Magee alleged that Higgins went to work as a sort of enforcer for Charles Reilly of Smock Alley who ran a public house and gambling den, infamous as a haunt of 'sharps, scamps and flashmen'. Reilly was soon forced out, and Magee contended that Higgins took over both the business and Reilly's wife, whom he claimed died soon after of a disease contracted from Higgins: the premises were subsequently let out as a brothel.[7] There may be some truth in this last accusation, for Higgins was an associate of some very questionable individuals and a friend of Dublin's most notorious madam, Mrs Margaret Leeson.[8]

Less controversially, an investment made by Higgins in the clothing trade paid off about this time, and he became master of the guild of hosiers, and active in Dublin corporation politics.[9] The law now beckoned and, building on his knowledge picked up in Bourne's office (and taking advantage of his friendship with the dissolute John Scott, Lord Clonmell, chief justice of King's Bench), after a short period of study, in 1781 Higgins became a solicitor. However, his career was by no means done, for with a nose for profit, politics and influence that did him credit, he spotted that control of a newspaper would assuredly hasten his rise in society, bring him to the attention of Dublin Castle, and – very important – intimidate his enemies. He obtained an editorial position on the *Freeman's Journal* in the late 1770s and some time later advanced a sum of money to its proprietor. When the owner defaulted on payment, Higgins had him committed to the debtors' prison. In return for authorising his release, Higgins forced him to sell the newspaper, allegedly at a fraction of its value. Concluding his profile of Higgins, MacDougall commented: 'From his law practice, his gaming room contributions and newspaper, the Sham now enjoys an income that supports a fine house in a fashionable quarter [St Stephen's Green] of a great city whence he looks down with contempt on the poverty of many persons whose shoes he has formerly cleaned'.[10] Long before that date, Higgins had also become a key informant of Dublin Castle, running as many as seven agents in his own private intelligence network, and regularly supplying the castle with the fruits of his, and their, labour: it is to his activities in this regard that we now turn.

EXACTLY WHEN FRANCIS HIGGINS began to work in the castle's interest has not been positively established. He appears to have begun to write for the *Freeman's Journal* in the late 1770s, a time when that newspaper was very much an opposition mouthpiece. His later claim that he was single-handedly responsible for bringing the paper over to the government side should be treated with some scepticism. However, in 1783 Higgins' conduct at the newspaper was noted approvingly by the then lord lieutenant, Lord Northington and there is no doubt that by 1784, the *Freeman* was firmly in the castle camp.[11] The large volume of government proclamations published in its pages from then on was visible proof of this: and so too was its declining readership which in its turn made a generous government subsidy ever more vital. In 1785, during the controversy over the so-called 'Orde's commercial propositions', the *Freeman's Journal* took a decidedly pro-government stance, so much so that Higgins himself (or so he claimed) was threatened with 'tarring and feathering' for supporting the 'English interest'. The newspaper also backed the castle during the regency crisis brought on by George III's insanity in 1788; and throughout the 1790s it took a pro-administration line, being determinedly hostile to the United Irishmen, the French, and Henry Grattan; and being paid an annual subsidy, through the publication of government proclamations, to the value of at least £1,000.[12]

In addition, Higgins by his own account had materially assisted government in various other ways over the years. He had given forewarning of an attempt by the Dublin United Irishmen to mob the new lord lieutenant, Earl Camden, on his arrival at Kingstown in early 1795, and thus he had enabled evasive action to be taken.[13] He had been active in Dublin city politics in the government interest during the 1780s and 1790s, carefully scrutinising candidates and the coalitions behind them.[14] Again, as a lawyer, he had been – so he claimed – instrumental in having a troublesome and costly lawsuit against the Stamp Commissioners quashed. Higgins had acted for the plaintiffs in this matter but when it had looked as if his clients would in fact prevail in the £100,000 lawsuit, he had unscrupulously advised them to hold off, thus enabling the government to bring in retrospective legislation which had the effect of killing off the claim against the Commissioners.[15] Lastly, and less legally, he had recruited fifty louts – at the request of Richard 'Dasher' Daly of the Theatre Royal – to attend other theatres in Dublin with orders to pounce on those who refused to take their hat off for the singing of the newly-popular loyalist anthem, 'God save the King'.[16]

IN THE FIRST OF HIS extant letters, Higgins had remarked to his contact in Dublin Castle, 'I could be useful':[17] and from 1795 until his death early in 1802, he wrote some 160 letters, probably many more, giving detailed information to the castle on the activities of both the Catholic Committee and the United Irishmen.[18] His position as proprietor of the *Freeman's Journal* was of great assistance in this regard, for he was in an ideal position to pick up snippets of intelligence in the course of his work. He was also useful in presenting the castle's point of view, if so desired. In late December 1796, he wrote to Edward Cooke, under-secretary at Dublin Castle, seeking advice on the proper line to take in the *Freeman's Journal* on the threatened French landing at Bantry Bay; and when there was a rumour of peace with the French in September 1797, he asked Cooke to 'have the goodness to say in what manner the *Freeman* should report it'.[19] In addition, as a noted, even notorious, *bon viveur* as well as the owner of a leading newspaper, he aroused no suspicions when he frequently hosted large dinner parties at which, as the claret and brandy flowed freely, tongues became loosened. 'I had a party yesterday,' he told Cooke in December 1797, 'who when they got wine did not disguise their opinion but openly spoke out that before six weeks there would be a flame in the country.'[20] A few months later, clearly having enjoyed a heavy night's drinking, his letter to Cooke petered out with the comforting news that 'there will be no insurrection or rising of the lower ordeal [sic!] of the people on Patrick's day. I am ashamed to write more, I am so sleepy. Adieu, God Bless you, my Dear – F. H.'[21]

Higgins was also in demand as a dinner guest, for neither his open support of government nor his unedifying past brought him social opprobrium, and he was by all accounts a most amusing companion. He often found himself at the same table as those who were the castle's opponents. On one occasion in August 1796, he had dinner at the house of a Mr Crilly, a wealthy Catholic merchant, and among the company were three Catholic priests. Later, he wrote to Cooke describing the mood of the Catholics at the prospect of a French invasion.[22] In September 1797, he dined at the home of Peter Burrowes, a legal adviser to the United Irishmen, and present there also were Lord Wycombe, son of Lord Shelburne, and Travers Hartley, MP for Dublin city.[23] On another occasion, he supped at the house of the barrister and politician, Charles Kendal Bushe.[24] After every such event, he let Cooke know what had transpired. Cooke would have found particularly valuable Higgins' denunciation of the subversive language of Leonard MacNally, the United Irish barrister. MacNally – or 'JW', as he signed his letters – was one of the castle's leading informers, and Higgins' strictures on him would have confirmed to Cooke that MacNally's double-role was not suspected.[25]

However, Higgins was not content merely to brief Cooke on the latest political gossip and social chit-chat to be picked up in the coffee houses and at the dinner table. He also managed a network of informers throughout Dublin, and further afield, who supplied him with crucial information about the United Irishmen and the Catholic Committee in the capital, and this information was promptly relayed to Dublin Castle. 'From the numbers that I hold intercourse with and who frequently call,' he told Cooke in April 1797, 'I receive intelligence of every transaction going forward in the city and of the meetings holding for the most wicked purposes.'[26] Two of Higgins' men – Glenville and Kennedy – had already infiltrated the so-called 'National Guard' in early 1793, and continued to operate as confidential agents, reporting to Higgins alone, throughout the 1790s. In mid-1798, another agent, Myler, 'a shrewd, keen fellow', infiltrated one of the Funeral Societies – a cover for the United Irishmen – which had sprung up in Dublin. Other agents, mostly United Irishmen themselves, provided Higgins with those 'printed papers, emblems, cockades etc.' which he duly passed on to Cooke and which found their way into the Secret Committee reports, or into Cooke's private museum of United Irish material.[27] Moreover, Higgins was able to exert pressure on some of his tenants who rented property from him in the Liberties. One United Irish sergeant refused to tell Higgins what he knew, but Higgins was quietly confident of turning him: 'He owes me now for rent £25, therefore [I] have some kind of binding over him', he noted.[28] All in all, at any one time in the 1790s, Higgins had between four and seven agents, possibly as many as ten, on his payroll who reported to him on a weekly basis.[29]

From Higgins' letters, it is evident that Cooke made frequent use of his services, and those of his agents and informers. In May 1797, Cooke set him on the trail of the United Irishman and woollen draper, Edward B. Gilternan: Higgins reported that he 'made strict enquiry after him from those whom I can depend on who are his neighbours'.[30] There were similar requests from Cooke seeking information on the noted subversive, Fr James Coigley, one 'Murphy' (Higgins rightly complained that this was too common a name for him to act on), and the United Irish organiser from County Monaghan, Edward Carolan.[31] Very often, Higgins' information was passed on in person to Cooke for he was a frequent visitor to the castle. However, it is clear from Higgins' letters that waiting on the overworked Cooke could be a frustrating business: In March 1798, he remarked that 'I had the honour this week of limping to your office four different days this week and also this evening but without the pleasure of seeing you'. A few days later, he threatened Cooke that 'the next time I call at the castle, I will bring my bed and stay until I have the pleasure of seeing you'.[32]

Higgins had especially good informants in Catholic circles in Dublin. He told Cooke that he held 'strict intimacy and intercourse' with two of the select committee of the Catholics, and he was in the confidence of Fr Caffry, OFM, of Church Street, who, though a 'violent republican', spoke openly to Higgins because 'I have known him since a boy and have done several things to serve his family'.[33] Fr Peter Moran, a Franciscan of Adam and Eve's chapel, was another informant who supplied Higgins with 'most interesting intelligence' in 1798.[34] With such contacts, Higgins was able to supply Cooke with a detailed report of a Catholic meeting in October 1796, including the precise sum awarded John Keogh to undertake the legal defence of those taken up as Defenders.[35] In April 1797, following a breakfast held by the Catholic Committee, Higgins informed Cooke that 'one of the persons who was at the breakfast called and told me every particular'.[36] Cooke was especially impressed with such information, and in late 1801, in a letter to his successor as under-secretary, Alexander Marsden, he supported Higgins' claim for a pension, stating that he 'has certainly been of use ... [and] ... will know pretty accurately what the Catholics are about'.[37]

Undoubtedly Higgins' major service to Dublin Castle was his procurement of Francis Magan. He was a young, and allegedly briefless, barrister who in early 1797 held a modest position in the Dublin United Irishmen. Higgins had been on terms of intimate friendship with Magan's father for many years, and Thomas Magan apparently died in 1797 owing him money.[38] His son, Francis, had been a casual informant of Higgins for a short while but Higgins (and Cooke) soon realised his importance, for Francis was evidently well positioned for promotion within the ranks of the Dublin United Irishmen. In March 1797, Higgins wrote to Cooke about 'a young barrister from whom I have received information'. He suggested that the lord chancellor,

Lord Clare who knew his father, or the Earl of Carhampton, then commander-in-chief of the Irish army, 'to whom his [Magan's] father and [him]self owed obligation respecting a lease granted by his lordship' should speak to Francis.[39] Some six months of tortuous negotiations (including at least two meetings with Cooke) followed: 'You cannot believe what pains I am obliged to use,' complained Higgins, 'to get him at all to listen to the proposal or come into terms.'[40] In November 1797, Francis Magan agreed to become an informer. His terms, wrote Higgins, are 'inviolable secrecy ... that his name would never be used to a third person', and, inevitably, reward; his only motive was claimed to be a desire to save lives.[41]

In early January 1798, Magan had a lengthy – and secret – meeting with Cooke. No record appears to have been kept of this interview but it was clearly for the purpose of enabling Magan to reveal all he knew about the United Irishmen's organisation in the city, and their plans for insurrection. Typically, Higgins, with his voracious appetite for information, was by no means satisfied with Cooke's efforts at debriefing: 'Permit me ... to mention that you have not half sufficiently examined Magan', wrote Higgins, and he offered to supply further questions for Cooke to put to him.[42] Cooke had heard enough, however, to realise that Magan was a major catch for the castle, and with Higgins as his controller, Magan was brought onto the payroll, Cooke awarding him an immediate £200 out of the Secret Service funds. Higgins now urged Magan to put himself forward for promotion from the Baronial Committee to the Provincial Directory of the United Irishmen; but Magan may have been reluctant to move so high and in the end he appears to have served only on the Dublin City committee of the United Irishmen. This position was, however, sufficiently elevated for him to be privy to the whereabouts of the United Irish military commander, Lord Edward Fitzgerald, on the run since he had escaped the swoop on Oliver Bond's house on 12 March 1798. Higgins urged Magan to keep his eyes and his ears open for any hint of the place of concealment of 'the generalissimo of the murderous crew of United Irishmen', as Higgins called him.[43] Cooke promised £1,000 for Magan ('without the mention of his name or enrolment of it in any book on having the business done') if he would discover Fitzgerald's hiding place.⁴⁴ For a time there was no word, for the fugitive's security was quite effective: 'Lord Edward skulks from house to house,' fumed Higgins, '[he] has watches and spies, armed, who give an account of danger being near'.⁴⁵ On 18 May 1798, however, Magan had a stroke of good fortune, for he was asked to conceal Lord Edward that night in his own house on Ussher's Island. This vital information was transmitted by Higgins to Cooke who was urged to guard all approaches to the house:

> ... Place Watches after dark this night near the end of Watling St on two houses up in that street from Ussher's Island and towards the Queen's Bridge, and a third in Island St, the rere of the Stables near Watling St and which leads up towards Thomas St and Dirty Lane; and at one of these three places they will find Lord Edward, disguised – he wears a wig, or may be otherwise metamorphosed, attended by one or two, but followed by several armed banditti with new daggers. He intends to give battle if not suddenly seized.⁴⁶

That night, Major Henry Sirr and his patrol narrowly failed to take Lord Edward; after an exchange of pistol shots, he made off; but because of the heavy military presence he could not flee the district. Next evening, on receipt of precise information from Magan, Sirr and his colleagues went directly to Thomas Street and there seized Lord Edward after a desperate struggle in the house of Nicholas Murphy, feather merchant.⁴⁷ His capture dealt a devastating blow to the United Irish plans for insurrection, and was well worth the £1,000 reward which Magan now claimed.

There was, however, some delay in paying over the money, and Higgins wrote several acrimonious letters to Cooke pleading for payment of the reward. 'I am tormented out of my life by M[agan] and hope you will have the goodness to let me have the money for him, as I do most solemnly assure you I was obliged to advance before and since the business £400 merely to keep him steady and active'.⁴⁸ Eventually, the money was paid to Higgins on 20 June 1798, and he appears to have forwarded it to Magan, who may have used it to pay off his father's debts.⁴⁹

THE CAPTURE OF LORD EDWARD Fitzgerald marked the high point in

Higgin's career as spy-master. From this point on, his letters, by and large, are taken up with incessant demands for the fulfilment of promises concerning remuneration and with ever lengthier rehearsals of his services to the castle over the years.[50] In 1801, he eventually secured a pension of £300 for his work, but he did not live long to enjoy it. His health, never very good, had begun to deteriorate badly in the late 1790s: he suffered constant and severe pain from 'flying gout' and rheumatism; by early 1801, he had 'bloodshot eyes, horribly swelled and painful', and he was spitting blood.[51] He died on 19 January 1802. Higgins' passing was suitably Gothic: his nineteenth-century biographer, W. J. Fitzpatrick recalled that as a boy in Dublin, he often heard the expression, 'it is as awful a storm as the night the Sham Squire died'.

Neither Higgins nor Magan were unmasked during their lifetime, nor indeed till long after their death. Magan continued as a castle informer, though without much energy, occasionally writing about Catholic politics in the early nineteenth-century, for he was quite active in that area.[52] He was awarded a pension of £200 a year, and on occasion received lump sums of £100 and £500 from the Secret Service funds, presumably for specific pieces of information. He never married and lived as a semi-recluse in his house on Ussher's Island until his death in 1843. By his will, he left his large fortune to his sister.

On Higgins' death, his most recent will was found to be missing from the bank where he had deposited it, and an earlier will, dating from 1791, was deemed valid. He bequeathed money to various charities, among them the Charter Schools, the debtors' prison, and the Lying-in hospital. He also left £30 for a tombstone, 'solid and durable with brick and stone or all stone work', to be erected over his grave in Kilbarrack churchyard, near Howth.[53] When Higgins' past services to the castle came to light, the tombstone was smashed and bits of it were hurled into the sea. What was left was daubed with the words, 'Here lies the monster Higgins, Lord Edward Fitzgerald's informer'.

SCOUNDRELS ALL – PRIESTS AND PRELATES IN '98

Dáire Keogh

NO IMAGE OF 1798 has proven more enduring than that of Fr Murphy at the head of the 'mighty wave'. While such depictions reflect popular perceptions of the rebellion as a priest led, principally Wexford, phenomenon they mask the real significance of an insurrection which was political in its inspiration and execution. That such misconceptions survive, however, is a measure of the success of the post-rebellion propaganda which sought to strip the events of that year of their political significance by presenting them in ways which served the intentions of various partisan commentators.

Sir Richard Musgrave, for example, the great loyalist historian of the rebellion, attempted to place '98 within a ghastly trinity of horrors which included the events of 1641 and 1690. Within this reading the presence of priests amongst the rebel leadership facilitated his attempt to present the insurrection as a popish plot. The rebellion, Musgrave believed, had sprung from the 'envenomed hatred' of the Protestant state and the British connection which the clergy had inspired in their people; once in battle the priests exhorted their troops, 'often horse-whipping, and even threatening the runaways with swords and pistols'.[1]

A similar economy of truth is reflected in several of the accounts written by implicated radicals in their attempt to distance themselves from political conspiracy. Accounts like those of Thomas Cloney and Edward Hay consciously depoliticise the Wexford rebellion – both play down United Irish activity in County Wexford and both writers present themselves as reluctant rebels in a spontaneous rising.[2] In this endeavour, the prominent role of priests in the Wexford campaign provides Edward Hay with a useful scapegoat, which hides the political inspiration of the rebellion. Hay's willingness to exploit their presence led Bishop Caulfield of Ferns to the belief that the purpose of Hay's *History* was to 'build a loyal reputation on the ruins of the friars and clergy'.[3] The bishops, of course, were equally anxious to distance themselves from the rebellion. Caulfield, appalled by the 'shocking number' of priests 'who had most wickedly volunteered in the damned rebellion', set about saving the reputation of the Church.[4] These considerations led Archbishop Troy and his confreres to dismiss the rebel clerics as unemployed, suspended, giddy, drunken characters; they were, Caulfield declared, 'the very faeces of the Church'.[5]

The debate on the role of the clergy was re-opened in 1863 with the publication in Paris of Miles Byrne's *Memoirs*. Byrne consciously singled out the rebel priests for attention condemning earlier accounts of the rebellion and the misrepresentations of Catholic historians who had tarnished the reputation of those priests who fought so bravely at the head of the people, in their effort to expel the common enemy'.[6]

The timing of the publication of Byrne's *Memoirs* was a source of embarrassment to the Church, then pre-occupied with the challenge of the Fenians. In the wake of the failed rising of 1867, the Wexford Franciscan, Patrick Kavanagh attempted to reconcile the activity of the rebel priests with the Church's condemnation of oath-bound societies. The result was a history of 1798 which portrayed the priests as involuntary rebels, reluctantly leading their flocks against tyranny and oppression.[7] This image has survived in popular lore, and Kavanagh was almost single-handedly responsible for the measure of acclaim accorded in the popular memory to 'Brave Father Murphy', the curate of Boolavogue. Patrick McCall's stirring anthem, written in the 1890s, copper-fastened this image of Fr Murphy which has complicated the general appraisal of clerical involvement in the rebellion.

SUCH SIMPLISTIC ANALYSIS HIDES the true nature of clerical participation in the radical politics of the 1790s. Even the most fleeting examination of the sources indicates the complexity of their involvement – seventy, or almost 4% of Ireland's 1,800 priests were called upon to account for their behaviour in 1798. Some of these played a prominent part in the rebellion, many had slight connections with the rebels and others were implicated on the basis of the vaguest passing reference.

Yet, as Louis Cullen has argued, 'one of the many striking things about 1798 is the prominence of clergymen from all three major religious groupings'.[8] That priests were conspicuous amongst the rebels, however, is not surprising given prominence of clerics in late eighteenth-century society.

The history of Presbyterian participation in the politics of the 1790s is well documented; histories of the decade are replete with reference to Presbyterian divines, William Steel Dickson, Thomas Birch and Samuel Barber.[9] Curtin estimates that almost one-third of the Presbyterian clergy were identified with the United Irish Society at some point in its history; of those twenty-four ministers, licentiates and probationers were implicated in the rebellion.[10] Their prominence facilitated Richard Madden, the great historian of the United Irishmen, in his attempt to re-assert the political significance of 1798. While recent writing suggests that 7% of the Presbyterian clergy participated in the rebellion, Madden stressed the apparent proportionate equality of Presbyterian and Catholic clerical involvement in his attempt to dispel sectarian interpretations of 1798.[11]

The role of the Anglican clergy in the rebellion is more problematic. Steps have been made by Patrick Comerford towards an assessment of the clergy of Ferns, but a broader analysis of the Church has still to be written.[12] This task, as Cullen observes, has been thwarted by the concept of *Protestant Ascendancy*, an overused label which suggests Irish Anglicans were monolithic in their support of the establishment.[13] On the contrary, Anglican ranks included the full spectrum of political opinion and it was from their number that several of the most conspicuous United Irish leaders were drawn. Amongst the clergy, too, political differences are immediately apparent; while the bench included the hard-line Charles Agar, liberal opinion was represented in Bishop Stock of Kilalla. The lower clergy, too, were divided in their politics; while many explicitly opposed the policies of the government Revd William Jackson became an agent of revolutionary France.[14]

No Anglican cleric appears to have joined the rebel army in 1798; although Revd Henry Fulton was transported to New South Wales in 1799 for seditious activity. Clerical participation was more conspicuous amongst the magistracy where, again, contrasts may be drawn between the dreaded Charles Cope, whose reputation for pitch-capping was renowned, and the liberal Francis Turner. Again, in the aftermath of the rebellion, there were striking contrasts in the accounts written by Bishop Stock, who adopted a whiggish line, and that of Revd George Taylor of Ballywalter who observed that 'none of the rebels were so blood-thirsty as those who were most regular attendants at the popish ordinances'.[15] These superficial observations illustrate the variety of opinion within Anglican ranks, but the absence of a thorough study of the Church of Ireland in the age of revolution represents a significant lacuna in our understanding of period.

THE ROLE OF THE CATHOLIC clergy in the rebellion has received fuller attention, yet many aspects of their participation require further examination.[16] That the hierarchy presented a united front in 1798 is not surprising. Since the outbreak of the Revolution the bishops had waged a war of words against what one of their number called 'the French Disease' and its associated radicalism.[17] Yet, behind the ritual of condemnation, there are clear indications that there were differences of opinion amongst the bishops and contrasts between their public and private positions.

The loyalism of Archbishop Troy of Dublin is renowned; dismissed by the former United Irishman Watty Cox for his 'pious alliance' with the government, even the rabidly anti-Catholic Patrick Duigenan acknowledged his 'steady' loyalism.[18] A close reading of Troy's writings, however, present a more nuanced indication of the archbishop's politics. The force of his celebrated *Pastoral Instructions on the duties of Christian Citizens* (Dublin, 1793), particularly his reference to Catholics as 'an enslaved people', created alarm amongst loyalists who perceived it as 'a political tract ... hostile to the establish constitution in Church and State'.[19] In his private correspondence, too, there are glimpses of frustration, most notably in his analysis of the Armagh troubles which he attributed to the 'supine neglect of the magistrates and prejudice of the gentry'.[20] In public, however, Troy remained constant in his support of the regime and failed to condemn injustice and the increasingly tyrannical policies of the castle.

Of the hierarchy, Bishop Thomas Hussey of Waterford and Lismore was unique in his public criticism of the administration. His protest came in response to a court martial at Carrick-on-Suir which sentenced Private Hyland of the Irish Light Dragoons to 200 lashes for refusing to attend Protestant services. Having made unsuccessful representations to Edmund Burke, Earl Fitzwilliam and Lord Camden, Hussey published a pastoral address in April 1797 which not alone addressed abuses in the army, but delivered a stinging assault on the establishment, the penal laws, the 'junta' and the Church of Ireland which he disparagingly described as 'a small sect'.[21]

Loyalist reaction to the bishop's incendiary was immediate in its condemnation. This response, which Hussey characterised as 'vomiting ... malice', was understandable, but the reaction of the Catholic hierarchy presents a novel insight into their thinking.[22] Bishop Carroll of Baltimore read it with 'pleasure and approbation', while Troy's principal objection was that it contained 'too much vinegar' which was 'not sufficiently tempered with oil'. 'Terms less strong and more conciliatory', he believed would have been 'equally effectual without giving offence'.[23] If there was disagreement amongst the bishops, then, it was on the question of prudence rather than on the content of Hussey's pastoral.

Such distinctions raise questions about the accepted interpretation of the political philosophy of the Catholic hierarchy which is often presented in rigid ideological terms. One suspects that a rigorous examination of Episcopal correspondence will challenge these assumptions and reflect the pragmatic priorities of the hierarchy. While the bishops were forthright in their opposition to the excesses of the French Revolution, oath bound societies and rebellion, evidence suggests Episcopal sympathy for the political aspirations of the original Society of United Irishmen. Hadn't Francis Moylan's brothers fought alongside George Washington? Hadn't Dr Troy proclaimed the bishops as 'second to no description of Catholics [in the demand] for emancipation'.[24]

Obviously an examination of the politics of the lower clergy presents additional problems, not least of which is their number. By far the greatest obstacle to an assessment of their role, however, is the absence of reliable source material. We have already discussed the partisan priorities of the contemporary commentators like Musgrave who cast the priests as 'the chief abettors of this nefarious conspiracy' and Miles Byrne who condemned the 'earnest endeavours' of the clergy which had kept the Irish in thraldom and saved 'the infamous English government in Ireland'.[25]

With the notable exception of James Coigly, none of the seventy clerics implicated in the rebellion left any memoir and explanation has been drawn from indirect sources. The most comprehensive study of the Wexford clergy has focused on the extensive Caulfield-Troy correspondence in the Dublin Diocesan Archives, but this evidence must be set against the background of the post rebellion polemic and Bishop Caulfield's attempt at damage limitations. These considerations have lead Whelan to revise his original interpretation published 1987.[26]

Yet even James Coigly's substantial *Life,* which chronicles the details of the priest's life from his youth in County Armagh to his death on a scaffold on Pennington Heath in 1798, requires careful reading.[27] Coigly was clearly a United Irishman, his activity amongst the Defenders is well documented as were his frequent missions to the radical societies in England and France. The priest was finally arrested, together with Arthur O'Connor, in Margate on 28 February 1798 as he prepared to cross the channel. Amongst his possessions was found a seditious address from the 'Secret Committee of England' to the French Directory; it was this document which sealed his fate. Given his close connections with the opposition in England, Arthur O'Connor was a more significant prisoner, so his acquittal was a source of acute embarrassment to Pitt's government. Coigly, an arch propagandist, appreciated this irony and exploited the interval between his conviction and execution in order to expose the tyranny of government. So, far from an appeal for clemency, Coigly's *Life* is a political tract intended to highlight his imminent judicial murder, the behaviour of governors of Ireland, whom he called 'nefarious villains, public plunderers ... proconsuls fit for Nero or Caligula, or bashaws fit for Ottoman Sultans', and the outrages of the Orange Order which he compared to the 'tyranny of Robespierre'.[28]

The Coigly case became a *cause celebre*. Tone, who was no friend of priests and this one in particular, recorded his death in his journal:

Quigley has been executed, and died like a hero. If ever I reach Ireland, and that we establish our liberty, I will be the first to propose a monument to his memory; his conduct at the hour of death, clears everything. 'Nothing in his life became him, like his leaving of it'.[29]

In the aftermath of the rebellion, however, there was little enthusiasm for erecting monuments to fallen heroes.

Coigly apart, of those implicated in the rebellion the best documented priest is certainly John Martin, an Augustinian friar from Drogheda.[30] His radical career bears similarities to that of Coigly. Martin was active amongst the Defenders in County Louth. He took the United Irish oath in 1797 in order to 'put all units on a level', to 'dissolve all establishments' and to 'obtain ... rights' for 'an injured people'. From that time, Martin busied himself in the promotion of the 'brotherhood of affection', preaching throughout Armagh, Louth, Meath and Dublin and organising radical structures in Drogheda. During the rebellion, Martin received an important commission from the United Irish Committee, based in Thomas Street Dublin. Following the reverses suffered by the rebel armies at Tara and the Curragh the United Irish military plans were thrown into disarray; the exception to this was Wexford, where insurgent numbers were higher than elsewhere, but even they had failed to break into the neighbouring counties.

Within this context, Martin was commissioned to ride south, to meet with Joseph Holt and to co-ordinate a concerted assault on Dublin. The friar, however, was captured by the yeomanry at the Meeting of the Waters in County Wicklow and it is his subsequent confession which provides us with the details of his short-lived radical career. Obviously such sources, extracted at the mouth of a cannon, demand careful reading. Martin's confession, for example includes a lengthy denunciation of the United Irish system:

He now hates the United Irishmen because they have not stood together and that he considers them as a cowardly rabble, he conceived that they would all have fought and died in the cause. That he did not intend to take arms himself, but he intended to have instigated the people with a fine death in the cause. That he had read Machiavel [sic] and that Machiavel taught that they should spare no time whatever to effect the object they had depended on.[31]

Nevertheless, carefully read, Martin's confession, like Coigly's *Life*, provide us with an insight into the possibilities and nature of clerical involvement within the United Irish ranks. Neither fit the stereotypical image of 'rebel priest'; neither were popish fanatics, 'giddy drunkards' or 'reluctant rebels' driven to insurrection by the persecution of the regime. Both were consciously political, committed to the United Irish cause and active in the promotion of the brotherhood. Given these considerations, it is not surprising that both Coigly and Martin have been virtually forgotten, lost behind the image of Fr Murphy's 'mighty wave'.

A SIMILAR LACK OF reliable sources has made it difficult to assess the motivation of the loyal priests – just as the myth of the 'rebel priest' needs re-examination, so too does the image of unswerving clerical loyalty. Just as clerical disaffection had taken many forms, the loyalty of the lower clergy was also reflected in different ways.

There were, for example, priests who opposed the radical politics of the age upon ideological grounds. On the eve of the rebellion, Fr William Gahan, of John's Lane, Dublin, published a pamphlet entitled *Youth Instructed* which contained a blunt rejection of Tom Paine and 'his idle speculations, wild ideas and conjectures'.[32] This Counter-Enlightenment tract, represents a rare example of published comment from the lower clergy on the radical literature of the period. Yet, despite its conservative content and tone, Gahan's pamphlet is difficult to categorise. Certainly, it contained valuable material for the loyal preacher, but its purpose was most likely pedagogical. The author had no apparent loyalist or political agenda, nor was his text directed to a popular audience.

Other priests adopted high profile loyalist positions – few more conspicuous than Fr Patrick Ryan, parish priest of Coolock, County Dublin. This future bishop of Ferns, achieved great distinction amongst conservatives as a result of his active co-operation with the Fingal Yeomanry Corps and the Beresfords in their campaign disarming the district.[33] Many priests voluntarily co-operated in the campaign to secure loyal declarations in the spring of 1798, but there is evidence that priests were victims of loyalist intimidation. William Farrell, the Carlow United Irishman, recalled in his memoirs threats made by Captain Swayne, of the City of Cork Militia, to the aged Fr Higgins at Prosperous County Kildare to insure loyal declarations; 'if you don't have it done,' he warned the aged priest, 'I'll pour boiling lead down your throat'.[34] Others responded to more subtle persuasion and the names of as many as ten priests appear on the lists of recipients of secret service money during the rebellion.[35] Several of the clerical informers paid a price for their co-operation Thomas Barry of Midleton claimed that his living was destroyed, while the body of Michael Phillips, a Franciscan, was taken from the Lagan in January 1796.[36]

By far the largest group amongst the clergy, however, were those who merely laid low and avoided taking any part, either for or against, the rebellion. Their inactivity has supported the image of a loyal clergy in '98. But equally, their silence has been interpreted as providing tacit support for the rebel cause. The last word, then, has not been said about the role of the Catholic clergy in 1798. It is a complex story, which deserves renewed attention and a careful reading of the sources available.

PARTNERS IN STRUGGLE: THE WOMEN OF 1798

Mary Cullen

SO FAR RELATIVELY LITTLE has been published dealing specifically with women and 1798. Helena Concannon's *Women of 'ninety-eight* was published in 1919, and in this bicentenary year we welcome *The women of 1798* edited by Dáire Keogh and Nicholas Furlong in which ten authors examine a range of different aspects of the subject. Obviously further research will reveal much more yet already, drawing on these and other published work, it can be argued with some confidence that women as well as men were active in all aspects of 1798.

When addressing this topic one is faced by two main problems. The first is that, as always, the better off and better educated have left more records of what they did and thought than have the poorer and less well educated. The second is that such sources as exist have usually been compiled within a mindset that sees males as the active agents of change in human history and females almost solely in support and follower roles. The second problem is compounded by the fact that many historians still work within a somewhat similar mindset.

The foundation of the United Irishmen grew directly from the broad eighteenth-century debate around Enlightenment emphasis on the rational nature of all human beings and republican emphasis on virtuous government in which both the interests and the voice of the people as a whole could be expressed. It seems clear that women were more active participants in this political debate than has usually been recognised.

A recent study of British politics during the period found that aristocratic women were increasingly influential. While they might actually *say* that women were not suited to politics, in reality many were actively involved in on-going political discussion with other women and with men, offering political opinions and advice through letter writing, salons, *tête-à têtes*, discussions, and so on. Many had a solid educational base and 'many were widely read, particularly in the works of the French Enlightenment ... in history and to some extent in English and Scottish moral philosophy and political economy'.[1] Indeed it appears that these women were often more widely read, especially in Enlightenment literature, than the men.

In the light of this we can note Stella Tillyard's assessment of Emily duchess of Leinster. The duchess was clearly a powerful influence on her favourite surviving son, Lord Edward Fitzgerald, one of the most radical and egalitarian of the United Irish leaders. English by birth and upbringing she quickly developed an active interest in Irish politics. She appears to have read more widely in politics than her husband who 'turned [political pamphlets] over to Emily',[2] and in their correspondence she offered political advice while excusing her interference. She moved from a family-based interest centred on the liberal politics of her husband, her brother-in-law, Henry Fox, and her nephew, Charles James Fox, to more radical constitutional issues including the relationship of king, parliament and people and whether parliament existed for king or people. Tillyard sees her as becoming increasingly more radical, 'not only idealistically interested in liberty, but also prepared to countenance civil rights – access to offices, courts, information and religious emancipation – for a far wider section of the people than enjoyed them at the time.'[3] She seems to have supported Edward's political stance up to mid 1794, and even his wish to see the French example followed in Ireland. When she realised that the United Irishmen and radicalism were now heading for rebellion her enthusiasm waned, though not her political sympathies. She made a significant statement of these sympathies after Edward's death. On the cover sheet binding a bundle of his last letters she copied a passage from a political pamphlet written by Joseph Priestley in 1768, and underlined some of his phrases. In *An essay on the first principles of government; and on the nature of political, civil and religious liberty* Priestley argued that rebellion was justified if a government was oppressive and hence unconstitutional:

> if the bold attempt be precipitate and unsuccessful the government will be sure to term it rebellion, but the censure cannot make *the thing itself less glorious*. The memory of such brave tho' unfortunate friends of

liberty and of the rights of Mankind as that of Harmodious and Aristo-
geiton among the Athenians and Russell and Sidney in our own country,
will be held in everlasting honour by their grateful fellow citizens, and
History will speak another language than laws.[4]

When we turn to what little is known so far about the political
thinking of middle-class women in United Irish circles we find them
making no pretence that women were not interested in or suited to
politics. Martha McTier was an informed and vigorous contributor
to debate and discussion. Her letters to her brother William Drennan
of the United Irishmen are regularly used by historians as a source for
what happened and what people thought. For example, when dis-
cussing the extraordinarily enthusiastic reception in Ireland of Tom
Paine's writings *Common Sense* and *The Rights of Man* David Dickson
quotes Martha McTier's comment on *The Rights of Man* as catching
the essence of the enthusiasm: 'I never liked kings and Paine has said
of them what I always suspected, truth seems to dart from him in
such plain and pregnant terms, that he, or *she* who runs may read'.[5]

We probably know more about Mary Ann McCracken than any
of the other women in United Irish circles thanks to Mary McNeill's
biography.[6] A member of a middle-class Belfast Presbyterian merchant family, she was well-educated, attending with her brothers a
progressive co-educational school. The McCracken home was a
centre of United Irish political discussion and planning. She was
particularly close to her brother Henry, and Nancy Curtin notes that
she seemed 'quite comfortable lecturing her elder brother on the
subject of politics' and appears to have been far better read than he in
the classic republican and radical texts.[7] In a recent article John Gray
argues that her commitment to United Irish aims was deeper and
tougher than it appears in McNeill's biography.[8] Gray queries the
basis for believing she cherished an unrequited love for Thomas
Russell, and sees her continued and active support of Russell and
Robert Emmet after the execution of her brother Henry as politically
rather than romantically driven.

The political activity of Margaret Bond brought her to the attention of Dublin Castle.[9] The Leinster directory of the United Irishmen, of which her husband Oliver was a member, often met in the

Bonds' house. So formidable was her reputation that in 1898 when a grandniece of Oliver Bond wished to distance her great-uncle from the United Irishmen she did so by asserting that Margaret Bond had been a 'rampant rebel' who held United Irish meetings on her husband's property against his wishes.[10] She is also famed for smuggling writing materials, newspapers and communications from friends into the United Irish leaders in Kilmainham Jail hidden beneath the crust of a freshly baked pie.

Another recent article broadens the participation of women in the radical political debate to include women like Mary Leadbeater of Ballitore and her circle of Quaker women friends. Kevin O'Neill notes that while Quakers were of more recent English descent than most Irish Protestants and maintained their English links more than most, yet '[f]rom a Catholic perspective the Friends of Ballitore were neither landlords, magistrates, soldiers or tithe collectors – the normal rural functions of the Anglo-Irish. Instead they were farmers, teachers, millers and most of all, neighbours'.[11] While Quakers were completely opposed to the use of violence by either the government or its opponents they strongly supported the ideas of liberty, equality and fraternity and agreed with the United Irish in placing the blame for the miseries of Ireland firmly on the shoulders of its government. Quakers, both men and women, were actively involved in the political debate in the years preceding 1798. Leadbeater herself read widely in French and English political philosophers from Edmund Burke to Mary Wollstonecraft, and William Godwin's *Political Justice* was the most quoted work in her diaries in the 1790s. Both she and her husband were on terms of intimate friendship with their neighbour Malachi Delaney during the early 1790s and while he was actively recruiting for the United Irishmen in 1796 and 1797. Delaney led the United Irish in the fighting in the Ballitore area in the following year. 'During those years, in word and action, she was an advocate of radical equality in Irish society.'[12]

THE SAME FACTORS THAT fostered United Irish republicanism also stimulated feminist assertion. Enlightenment and republican thinking encouraged challenges to the long-standing model of women's role which defined women in terms of relationship and service to men, as wives, mothers, daughters or sisters. The impetus underlying feminism has always been to challenge such reductionism and assert the autonomy of women as self-directed human persons. Both the American and French revolutions encouraged demands for practical as well as intellectual change. In late eighteenth-century Ireland women, in common with women in western societies in general, had few civil or political rights. A central issue was the position of married women. Under the English common law when a woman married she lost her separate legal identity which merged with that of her husband. Both her person and her property came under his full legal control. Within a system based on the principle that only those who were economically and socially in a position to exercise independent judgement could be trusted with political rights the legal position of married women ruled them out. In practice all women were excluded from holding public office, sitting in parliament or voting in parliamentary elections.

Among the best known feminist writings was Mary Wollstonecraft's *A Vindication of the Rights of Woman* (1792) which argued that women as well as men shared rational human nature and so should be educated to become responsible and autonomous adults who made responsible and virtuous decisions about their lives and actions. In revolutionary France quite a few radical women went further to assert the right to full political participation but were rejected and suppressed by the male leadership. In Ireland, where growing calls for reform and more radical change provided an opening, it appears likely that many United Irish women would have urged feminist claims. Wollstonecraft's book was widely read and discussed by both women and men. Certainly Mary Ann McCracken is on record as having put the challenge to the United Irishmen. A wonderful letter of 16 March 1797 to her brother Henry in Kilmainham Jail links a number of aspects of her thinking. First she tells him of local political developments, including the growth of support for the United Irishmen. Then she mentions the Societies of United Irishwomen:

> I have a great curiosity to visit some female societies in this Town (though I should like them better were they promiscuous, as there can

be no other reason for having them separate but keeping the women in the dark and certainly it is equally ungenerous and incandid to make tools of them without confiding in them). I wish to know if they have any rational ideas of liberty and equality for themselves or whether they are contented with their present abject and dependent situation, degraded by custom and education beneath the rank in society in which they were originally placed; for if we suppose woman was created for a companion for man she must of course be his equal in understanding, as without equality of mind there can be no friendship and without friendship there can be no happiness in society. If indeed we were to reason from analogy we would rather be inclined to suppose that women were destined for superior understandings, their bodies being more delicately framed and less fit for labour than that of man does it not naturally follow that they were more peculiarly intended for study and retirement, as to any necessary connection between strength of mind and strength of body, a little examination will soon overturn that idea, I have only to place the McCombs, Val Joice and our worthy Sovereign opposite Mr O'Connor, Mr Tone and our dear departed Friend Dr Bell (three little men possessing genius) to show the futility of such an argument ... I hope the present Era will produce some women of sufficient talents to inspire the rest with a genuine love of Liberty and just sense of her value without which their efforts will be impotent and unavailing ... I think the reign of prejudice is nearly at an end, and that the truth and justice of our cause alone is sufficient to support it, as there can be no argument produced in favour of the slavery of woman that has not been used in favour of general slavery and which have been successfully combated by many able writers. I therefore hope it is reserved for the Irish nation to strike out something new and to shew an example of candour generosity and justice superior to any that have gone before them – as it is about two o'clock in the morning I have only time to bid you goodnight – Believe me. Yours affectionately Mary.[13]

It will be interesting to see how this picture develops as information on a larger number of women emerges. For instance, Mary Leadbeater and some of her Quaker women friends were actively involved in printing and circulating anti-slavery literature,[14] and participation in the anti-slavery movement is recognised as a breeding ground for feminist awareness. As for the United Irishmen themselves, Nancy Curtin sees their republican ideology as excluding women as full citizens while seeing them as having a supporting role in the republican campaign. However it appears that individual men may have pondered and perhaps supported women's claims. For example, in 1793 Thomas Russell, travelling in County Antrim to organise the United Irish movement, gave the question some thought. A diary entry for 11 July reads:

> Should women be learn[e]d? Is their a difference of mind? Why not as of body? Has it ever occur[r]ed to anatomists to observe is their any difference in the brains of men and women children [*sic*]? Women in public offices as clever as men. Queens, poetesses, etc., etc. In merchants' houses keep the accoun[t]s as well as men. Why not mathematicians?[15]

THE SUPPORT GIVEN TO UNITED Irishmen by their wives, mothers and sisters is the central theme of Helena Concannon's book. In view of the model of women's role noted above, many historians of women are understandably uneasy with looking at women only in the context of their relationship with men. Yet male-female relationships and sex-based divisions of labour need to be re-examined and analysed rather than ignored. One flaw in the model is that it tends to see 'men's work' and 'women's work' as mutually exclusive, with men's work regarded as the more important. Another is to see women's work and support of family members as 'natural' and instinctive rather than an active, self-directed and positive contribution without which a political or social movement could not have functioned.

In this context Nancy Curtin notes the sheer physical and mental strength involved in Matilda Tone's sacrifice of a normal domestic life, her acceptance of her husband's long absences, her shouldering of the full responsibility for their children and the worries about money, her unfailing support of her husband's undertakings which she carried to the extent of concealing the fact that she was pregnant when he left America for France on behalf of the United Irishmen.[16] Recognition of the importance of this type of contribution to any movement and its incorporation into historical analysis will be one key component in writing a more inclusive history. At the same time this recognition should not obscure Matilda Tone's personal contribution to political discussion and United Irish thinking and planning.

Mary Ann McCracken too gave a sister's support to her brother right to the scaffold. When Henry Joy McCracken was in hiding after the Battle of Antrim she found him and organised help in food and clothing. She arranged for his escape to America by ship but he was arrested on his way to the appointed rendezvous. She visited him in Belfast Jail and was present at his trial for treason. She was with him in his cell on the day of his death and walked with him, her arm in his, to his place of execution before the Market House on 17 July. She only left then because he could not bear that she should witness his death. She later brought up his illegitimate daughter Maria who became her close companion.

NANCY CURTIN MENTIONS THREE main ways in which women participated in the United Irish movement; as members of oath-bound Societies of United Irishwomen; as active recruiters; and as passive recruiters in the role of symbols of endangered Irish womanhood. She describes the United Irishwomen as

> a kind of female auxiliary which attended to fund raising and providing amenities for imprisoned United Irishmen and their families. These women might also undertake the dangerous business of gathering information and carrying secret messages within the vast network of local United Irish societies. Women as well as children were certainly required to take the United Irish oath of secrecy, forbidding the swearer to reveal the secrets of the organisation and the identity of its members. Such an oath was also a prerequisite for membership of the organisation.[17]

Rose McGladdery, Mary Ann McCracken's sister-in-law, is said to have been a sworn United Irishwoman before her marriage to William McCracken. She carried intelligence then and later brought information in and out of Kilmainham when William and Henry were imprisoned with other United Irish leaders.[18]

Further research may throw more light on these societies, their number and the number of members, their location and more on their activities. As noted above, Mary Ann McCracken was suspicious of separate male and female societies on the grounds that the men were not keeping the women fully informed or involved. However separate 'auxiliary' female organisations often contribute more substantially than is recognised to a cause and participation in them can increase political awareness and lead some of the women involved to question contemporary gender roles.

There were different grades of oaths and it appears possible that some women may have been sworn into the central United Irishmen.[19] Miss Moore of Thomas Street in Dublin told Dr Madden that she took the United Irish oath and that, to her own knowledge, several women were sworn members. She herself administered the oath to William James MacNeven. Her father James Moore was a United Irishman and a friend of Lord Edward Fitzgerald. Fitzgerald stayed at the Moores' house more than once while in hiding and she carried messages for him. He was there around 16 May 1798 when a carpenter at Dublin Castle heard that James Moore's house was to be searched. He carried the warning and James Moore went into hiding leaving responsibility for the safety of the commander-in-chief to his wife and daughter. Miss Moore arranged to bring him to a house on Usher's Island belonging to Francis Magan, who, unknown to the United Irish, had become an informer. Both women set out with Fitzgerald and an escort of two male companions for an evening stroll. They were met by Major Sirr and his men, informed by Magan. Lord Edward and Miss Moore escaped and she took him instead to the house of Murphy the feather merchant. When the next day Magan came to ask why his visitor had not arrived, she told him what had happened, and that evening Fitzgerald was taken.[20]

Recruiting for the United Irishmen was a specific female activity. One way in which this could be done was by persuading militiamen to change their allegiance. Curtin quotes a militia officer in Derry complaining of a 'practice of having an intrigue with a girl and swearing the man to secrecy when the matter [the aims and goals of the United Irishmen] should be divulged in confidence.'[21] Another way was by exerting moral pressure. Charles Teeling, of the Antrim Catholic family who were forgers of links between the United Irish and the Defenders, wrote that 'the enthusiasm of the females exceeded the ardour of the men; in many of the higher circles, and in all the rustic festivities, that youth met with a cold and forbidding reception from the partner of his choice, who, whether from apathy or timidity, had not yet subscribed to the test of union.'[22]

Overall information on the activities of women in the broad United Irish and Defender movements is scattered and scarce. That women were active is clear but the information comes in glimpses or snapshots through passing references. One report will tell of women supporters of the United Irish going through towns and villages singing seditious song. Another will speak of women wearing green ribbons, handkerchiefs and shoe laces to show their political allegiance. So far we have no records in their own words of what these women did and what they thought. This is all the more frustrating as research is showing that the Defenders were far more politically aware and politically motivated than had been realised.

WHEN WE COME TO THE rebellion itself there is a striking contrast between United Irish ideology of women's role and popular memory as recorded in story and ballad. The first portrayed women as symbols of Ireland, or as heroic mothers urging on their sons for the cause, or as beautiful maidens turned into wandering maniacs by the brutality of the soldiery.[23] It never represented them as actual combatants. Popular memory, on the other hand, has remembered individual women who took part in physical combat as heroines, and often as Joans of Arc leading the men into battle. This contrast raises some interesting questions for historians.

Best known of all is Betsy Grey who fought at the Battle of Ballynahinch in County Down. 'The popular memory has preserved a vision of her, a bright-faced, beautiful girl, dressed in green silk, mounted on her gallant mare, and brandishing her burnished sword above her head, while side by side with Munro she led one victorious charge after another.'[24] According to Concannon her lover Willie Boal and brother George Grey were sworn United Irishmen, and it is believed that Betsy was also. The story as told to Madden by Mary Ann McCracken is that Betsy Grey went to the camp on the Saturday before the battle with some supplies for her brother and sweetheart and insisted on staying to live or die with them. They procured her a pony and she went into action on it bearing a green flag. After the defeat they were overtaken in flight by a party of Hillsborough yeomanry who killed all three.[25]

Molly Weston of Westmeath who fought and died at the Battle of Tara was famed for recruiting United Irishmen. Folk memory recalls a handsome and accomplished horsewoman, dressed in a green riding costume with gold braid and a green cocked hat with a white plume. Armed with sword and pistols she rode to battle with her four brothers. She too is remembered as a leader, rallying the pikemen and leading repeated charges. Her four brothers were reported killed but Molly Weston was never seen again.[26]

Mary Doyle, who appears to have seen lengthy military service in Wexford, is remembered for a specific military achievement. When the rebel army attacked New Ross it was defeated and reduced to a tattered remnant. Immense amounts of ammunition and powder had been used and hundreds of guns and pikes lost. Only one of the artillery pieces was saved and that by the 'heroic efforts' of Mary Doyle.[27]

Many other women fell in active combat. The names of some are remembered, such as that of Ruth Hackett who was killed at Prosperous in County Kildare,[28] but many others are not. For instance, at the battle of Vinegar Hill the women 'were not content to leave the fighting to the men. They mingled with them, encouraging them and fought with fury themselves. Several were found slain among the fighting men, where they had fallen in crowds, felled by the delayed bursting of the bomb shells.'[29]

Obviously the participation of women in war goes far beyond the actual wielding of pike or gun in battle. The rebel camps contained large numbers of women. For example, that under Fr John Murphy at Oulart Hill in County Wexford held four and five thousand people, one thousand fighting men, and the rest women, children and the elderly.[30] The work done by the women in these camps has yet to be recorded in a systematic way but some indications of their activities survive. Anna Kinsella records that cutting the cross belts from the bodies of fallen dragoons was 'a common task for camp followers, many of them apparently women', and that women also appear to have made gun-powder in the camps.[31] Some, like Suzy Toole, the 'moving magazine' of County Wicklow, 'secured ball cartridge and ammunition from disaffected soldiers ... [and] provided intelligence on the movements of the King's troops'.[32]

Such activities as acquiring and supplying combatants with food, arms, ammunition and other supplies, carrying messages and gathering information, providing hiding places and safe houses, the dangerous harbouring and hiding of rebels on the run, collecting and burying dead bodies from the field of battle are all seen as part of soldiers' work when done by men in all-male armies. Many individual cases of all these activities being carried out by women are remembered in various parts of the country. The work going on during this bicentenary year in compiling and collating local knowledge and folk memory may provide the basis for more systematic analysis.

Occasional glimpses of rebel women may be found in sources such as the written accounts by seven loyalist or neutral Protestant women in County Wexford of their experiences during the rebellion.[33] Even though some were written or rewritten many decades later, and despite divides of class, religion and political sympathy, these accounts do aim to describe what witnesses actually observed. They show rebel women as independent actors, and in some instances as acting differently to and in opposition to their men. Dinah Goff described one instance where her father was threatened by a company of rebels. As they hesitated as to who would strike the first blow 'some women came in great agitation through the crowd, clinging to their husbands and dragging them away'. On another occasion, where a United Irish officer prevented some rebel soldiers from looting the Goffs' house, she saw 'many wicked-looking women ... [who] made frightful faces and shook their hands at us as we stood at the windows'.[34] There is some suggestion that rebel women may have been at least as ready as their men to throw off the bonds of traditional deference. Jane Barber described how a rebel woman, Molly Martin, mother of one of the Barbers' servants, dressed in new clothes whose source she declined in less than deferential language to explain, nevertheless brought Jane to where her father lay dead, killed by the rebels, and then, with the help of a rebel man, brought her safely home when another rebel man began to beat her. Jane Addams recounted an incident where four women having breakfast in a Wexford alehouse refused to get her a glass of water when she fainted and she had to

157

wait until two men arrived.

On another aspect of the experience of rebel women the brief and ambivalent comment of Elizabeth Richards on the rape of local women by the English and Hessian troops who crushed the rebellion evokes the horror more vividly than many lengthy descriptions: '... all the morning we listened to the shrieks, the complainings of female rebels. They almost turned my joy into sorrow'.[35]

One woman's own voice does reach us even if at second hand. In 1842 Dr Madden found Anne Devlin living in poverty in Dublin. In 1803 at the age of 25 or 26 she acted as housekeeper in the house near Rathfarnham rented by Robert Emmet as a base for planning the proposed rising of that year. She was arrested there after the rising, threatened and tortured with bayonets and half-hanging to make her tell what she knew. She revealed nothing in response to torture, bribes and imprisonment. She was particularly badly treated and her health undermined in Kilmainham Jail where she remained until 1806. In Madden's record of her words the force of personality and the depth of anger which enabled her to survive break through. She regularly abused her chief tormentor, Dr Trevor, the Superintendent of Kilmainham, to his face. 'She knew he was everything that was vile and bad, and it eased her mind to tell him what she thought'.[36] She attributed her survival to an Englishwoman, the wife of a gaoler, who, in Trevor's absence, 'would bring her to her own apartments for an hour or two at a time, and give her wine and nourishing things'. Once Trevor discovered this and 'his rage was dreadful. He cursed her, and she returned his maledictions curse for curse'.[37] In 1843 when Anne Devlin and Dr Madden found the house rented by Emmet she showed not terror but 'as lively a remembrance of the wrongs and outrages that had been inflicted on her as if they had been endured but the day before.'[38]

ALREADY IT IS CLEAR that looking at the participation of women in 1798 will add to our knowledge of the whole United Irish and Defender movements and of what actually happened in 1798. The United Irish and Defender alliance spanned all classes and creeds in a political movement inspired by the idea of republican government. By simply asking the question 'what did women do?' we find that even the limited and scattered information so far available points to their active participation with men across the board. This participation stretches from the intellectual power-house through organisation and planning to partnership in rebellion. The search for answers to the question also broadens the focus from concentration on a relatively small number of male leaders to include the scale of the contribution at every level by the men and women of all classes who are not seen as 'leaders'. Above all it challenges us to find out more about who these women were, what they did and why they did it.

1798 AND THE BALLADMAKERS

Tom Munnelly

THE PURPOSE OF THIS essay is not to recount the history of the events of 1798 in any manner which would be accepted by academic historians dealing with state papers, military accounts and political records. Instead I propose to deal with the 'idea' of 1798 as perceived by the people on the ground, some verses are by known poets and some are by the people whose usual role in the history books is that of nameless statistics of fatalities, mere brush stokes in the grander canvas of received history. The story recounted by the historian and the ballad singer are not *always* contradictory, but the latter feels no need to be restrained by dispassionate objectivity.[1]

In his work on *Songs of Irish Rebellion*, the Swiss scholar, Georges-Denis Zimmermann states that 'The events of 1798 were to remain for more than a century one of the principle sources of inspiration for balladmakers'.[2] So, where is 1798 in the context of the folk memory? Is it ancient history? In 1934, the Longford folklore collector, Pádraig Mac Gréine, wrote on the traditions of 1798 in *Béaloideas: The Journal of the Folklore of Ireland Society*.[3] He gave an account of the battle of Ballinamuck which he took down from Patrick 'Grey Pat' Gill of Ballinamuck who got the details from his grandmother who witnessed the event. Grey Pat was then in his late nineties, just as Pádraig Mac Gréine is now. So here in 1998 we have a man who recorded an account of one of the pivotal battles of 1798 from a man who got it from an eye-witness. Even allowing for the longevity of the people concerned, it brings home the fact that 200 hundred years is not such an enormous span of time.

The late eighteenth-century was the age of the pamphleteer and tracts like Thomas Paine's *The Rights of Man* sold in their thousands. Songs on every conceivable event made their way from the urban presses of Britain and Ireland. As is the norm in the broadsheet trade, along with newly composed and journalistic ballads, old songs were reprinted for sale and re-formatted to suit current happenings. Thus a song called 'Derwentwater's Farewell'[4] concerning the execution of the Northumbrian, James, Earl of Derwentwater, who was beheaded on Tower Hill for his part in the Jacobite rising of 1715 becomes 'Bagenel Harvey's Farewell' about the condemned commander-in-chief of the Wexford insurgents.[5] The ballad 'The Croppy Boy', or 'Early, early all in the spring', uses a format already old in European tradition in 1798. Captured by Lord Cornwall and his yeomen, he is led to the gallows where he is betrayed by his lover and denounced by his family.[6]

A handful of such songs of the period entered the oral tradition and stayed in the minds of traditional singers right up to the present day. Such a song is 'Dunlavin Green' which tells how Captain Saunders, suspecting his yeomanry of being secret members of the United Irishmen had them marched to the village green and summarily executed. Though written in English, the malediction heaped on Saunders' head by the anguished balladmaker harks back to a far older tradition:

> Bad luck to you, Saunders, bad luck may you never shun!
> May the widow's curse melt you like snow in the sun,
> The cries of the orphans whose murmurs you cannot screen,
> For the murder of their dear fathers, on Dunlavin Green.[7]

Another song which bears the marks of oral transmission is the ballad on Roddy McCorley, accused of being a Defender and hung on the bridge of Toome in County Antrim. Remarkably, although this ballad has survived in oral tradition for almost two hundred years it did not appear in print until the 1960s.[8] Particularly poignant is the verse wherein the betrayed McCorley laments leaving his Presbyterian brethren:

> Farewell unto sweet Drumail, if in it I had stayed,
> Among the Presbyterians there, I ne'er had been betrayed;
> The gallows tree I ne'er had seen had I remained there,
> For Duffin he betrayed me, and MacErlain he set the snare.[9]

Of the ballads which enumerate the clashes which took place throughout that fateful year, many are difficult to date because lack of evidence of a printing history is no proof that they were not contemporary with the events described or written soon after. A typical example of the journalistic ballad would be 'The Battle of Granard': After the English sack Granard, pikemen march from Kenagh, engage and slay English troopers at Edgeworthstown. The boys from Abbeyderg, Killashee and elsewhere march through Ardagh to the Heights of Granard. After a fierce battle the English are slain.[10]

A song collected in Kildare in 1958 tells of insurgents who decide to fight, in spite of an express message from Dublin ordering them not to do so. They march on Dunboyne. The narrator curses Dublin and Rathoath for not joining them in the fight. He lays an extra curse on Carhampton who burned the holy altars and Dunboyne also.[11] Other songs describe 'The Battle of Ballinamuck',[12] 'The Battle of Ross'[13] and other battles and campaigns.

Of all the ballads which may have been contemporary with the happenings of '98, perhaps the most stirring is the one outlining the career of Fr John Murphy of Boolavogue:

> Come all you warriors and renowned nobles,
> Give ear unto my warlike theme,
> And I will sing you how Father Murphy
> Lately aroused from his sleepy dream.
> Sure Julius Caesar and Alexander
> Nor brave King Arthur ever equalled him.
> For armies formidable he did conquer
> Though with two gunmen he did begin.[14]

The meteoric career of General Henry Munro, leader of the County Down insurgents, came to a tragic end after the Battle of Ballinahinch on 13 June. He made his escape but was betrayed and hung in front of his own house three days later:

> Munro being weary and wanting to sleep,
> He gave a woman ten guineas his secrets to keep;
> When she got the money the devil tempted her so,
> That she sent for the army who surrounded Munro.
>
> The army did come and surrounded them all,
> He thought to escape but could not at all;
> They marched him to Lisburn without more delay,
> And put his head on a spear that very same day.[15]

The beautiful old ballad, 'The Streets of Derry' is frequently associated with 1798. In it the young man about to be executed seeks comfort in turn from his father, mother and sister. The clergyman delays his execution by hearing his confession until finally his true love arrives with a royal pardon:

> As he went walking up the streets of Derry,
> I'm sure he marched up right manfully;
> He was more like a commanding officer
> Than a man to die on the gallows tree.
>
> The very first step he went up the ladder,
> His blooming colours began to fail,
> With heavy sighs and dismal cries,
> 'Is there no releasement from Derry Gaol?'[16]

Alfred Percival Graves' collected 'Little Jimmy Murphy' from a Welsh town crier who got it from an Irish street singer in Liverpool in 1840. The singer recalled that 'the ballad had such a success in the Irish quarter of Liverpool that the coppers positively rained from the windows' when he sang it. In this song the figure of Ireland, Caithlín Ní hUallacháin, becomes the more colloquial Kate Wheelan:

> We marched through the town, we marched through the city;
> Our hands tied behind us, and the ladies cried pity.
>
> Poor little Jimmy Murphy was hanged, not for sheep stealing,
> But courting a pretty girl; her name was Kate Wheelan.[17]

The nineteenth-century being poetically a Romantic age, in Ireland patriotism combined with romanticism and the popular muse poured out an unending corpus of songs and recitations using 1798 as a backdrop. A favourite subject was that of the gallant Croppy pitted against the villainous yeoman. Patrick Pearse himself was particularly fond of the poem of 'Páid O'Donoghue' wherein a yeoman captain orders O'Donoghue, a patriotic blacksmith, to shoe his horse or he will kill him, but O'Donoghue slays the yeoman with his hammer and makes a dramatic escape.[18] 'Seán Crossagh' is chased across the Sperrins by Squire Staples and his men. Crossagh leaps the Roe River, a feat which defeats Staples and, for good measure, Seán shoots an informer while escaping.[19] 'Rory Rua Mac Caul' is less lucky. Although wounded, he escapes from the Battle of New Ross and is sheltered by a kindly woman. Unfortunately for Rory, her husband turns out to be a yeoman, who shoots him dead when he returns.[20] Atypical of the genre, but popular nevertheless, is the long recitation concerning 'Tom Gilheany'. On the run after the Battle of Ballinamuck, he is betrayed by Shufflin Shawn who has given him shelter. The arresting yeoman, Ferguson, instead of killing him, gives him sanctuary in his own home. Years later Ferguson is threatened by hostile crowds at Drumkeenan fair when the noble Gilheany springs from the crowd and rescues him.[21]

If melodrama plays a substantial part in these songs, it is hardly surprising, as so many of them were made in Victorian times. The aim of the songwriter is frequently pathos, but more often than not only bathos is achieved. The 'Irish Patriot Mother' is a creation not even equalled by Country and Western songwriters of today. Combine her with 1798 and the result is, to say the least, lugubrious.

When two young rebels are sentenced to death. A woman, who is mother of one and foster-mother of the other, pleads with the judge for their lives. He says he will free only one of them and asks her to choose. She chooses her foster-son. This so impresses the judge that he frees them both.[22] She in her turn is trumped by the mother of another rebel about to be hung in Kilkenny. She is sent for to persuade her son to confess to the yeomen. As her husband has also been slain by the English, she tells her son to die like his father. She then slips her head through the noose and hangs with her son.[23]

'The Patriot Mother' in another song wishes her captured son's blood would turn to poison should he inform on his fellow pikemen who were with him on the Curragh.[24]

Séamus O'Brien has been sentenced to hang for his part in the rising. His mother pleads for him in court, but to no avail. But, while blessing him on the gallows the priest attending him secretly unties his hands. O'Brien leaps from the gallows and makes good his escape.[25]

The 1840s saw the birth the Young Ireland movement, romantic nationalists who were aware of the power of song in conveying their message to all levels of public opinion. The maxim of the seventeenth-century Scots parliamentarian, Andrew Fletcher of Saltoun, 'If a man were permitted to make all the ballads, he need not care who makes the laws of a nation' inspired the Young Irelanders. Indeed, the quotation is often mistakenly attributed to Davis himself. At this distance it is difficult to comprehend the enormous popularity of Davis, Dillon and Duffy's newspaper, *The Nation*. It had an estimated readership of a quarter of a million, and this among a population not greatly literate. Nevertheless, the establishment were also aware of the subversive power of the balladmaker, and *The Times* of London described the songs of Davis and his colleagues as being 'far more dangerous than O'Connell's speeches'.[26] In fact, when O'Connell and eight other leaders in the Repeal movement were facing state prosecution in 1844, a charge against Gavin Duffy as editor of *The Nation* was that he had circulated the song, 'The Memory of the Dead' among the people 'to poison their minds and to unsettle their allegiance'.[27]

> Who fears to speak of Ninety-Eight?
> Who blushes at the name?
> When cowards mock the patriots fate,
> Who hangs his head for shame?
> He's all a knave, or half a slave,
> Who slights his country thus;
> But a true man, like you, man,
> Will fill your glass with us.[28]

Arguably the most popular of all the songs from *The Nation* poets, 'The Memory of the Dead' was something of a political hot potato for its author, Newryman John Kells Ingram. At any rate it remained anonymous until he included it in his *Sonnets and other poems*, published in 1900, 57 years after its original appearance. By this time he had become a respected academic and had transferred his allegiance to the Unionist Party and opposed Home Rule!

Most of the songs of *The Nation* poets have vanished without a trace, though some remain in oral tradition even yet. Notable among these are 'Tone's Grave' by Thomas Davis and 'The Croppy Boy' by W. B. McBurney. Davis' song on Wolfe Tone is better known nowadays as 'Bodenstown Churchyard':

> In Bodenstown churchyard there is a green grave,
> And freely around let winter winds rave:
> Far better they suit him – the ruin and the gloom –
> Till Ireland, a nation, can build him a tomb.[29]

Of W. B. McBurney who wrote his songs under the *nom de plume* 'Carroll Malone', little is known other than that he came from Down and emigrated to the United States where he died about 1892.[30] With the prevailing fondness for melodrama one can see why the story of the innocent Croppy deceived by the treacherous redcoat disguised as a priest in the confessional had immediate popular success:

> Good men and true in this house who dwell,
> To a stranger bouchal I pray you tell
> Is the priest at home or may he be seen?
> I would have a word with Father Green.[31]

This song has many interesting aspects. The tune utilised is *Cailín ó Cois tSúire Mé,* referred to by Shakespeare in *Henry V*.[32] The version in the Elizabethan manuscript, *William Ballet's Lute Book,* held in Trinity College, Dublin, is the earliest known annotation of an Irish song air.[33]

Many such dramatic pieces survived in the urban parlour as well as the country fireside. In the case of 'The Croppy Boy' James Joyce paints a wonderful picture of a performance of this song in the 'Sirens' episode of *Ulysses*. Ben Dollard, accompanied on piano, entertains the bar of the Ormond Hotel by rendering 'The Croppy Boy' in his 'base barreltone'. The story of betrayal in 1798 causes Bloom to muse on his more recent betrayal by Molly with Blazes Boylan.[34]

But to return to the mid nineteenth-century; events such as the skirmish in Tipperary in 1848 with Meagher and Mitchel and the Fenian uprising of 1867 refocused minds drained of energy by the famine years. In a country where nationalism was ever increasing the heroes of 1798 grew continually in stature.

John Keegan Casey wrote for *The Nation* under the name of 'Leo'. He was a prolific songwriter, but he is best remembered for 'The Rising of the Moon':

'Oh! then tell me, Seán O Farrel,
Tell me why you hurry so?'
'Hush, mo buachaill, hush and listen,'
And his cheeks were all aglow.
'I bear orders from the Captain,
Get you ready quick and soon
For the pikes must be together
By the rising of the moon.'[35]

When Casey died in 1870, aged only 23, so popular was he through his songs and poems that his funeral was enormous. Other poets and songmakers of the period reflected this nationalism and were keenly aware of the approaching centenary of the rising of 1798. Robert Dwyer Joyce penned 'The Boys of Wexford' and 'The Wind that Shakes the Barley' 1798 being the theme in both cases. Ethna Carbery wrote her song on Roddy McCorley:

Ho! see the fleetfoot host of men
Who speed with faces wan,
From farmstead and from fisher's cot
Upon the Banks of Bann.
They come with vengeance in their eyes
Too late, too late are they.
For Roddy McCorley goes to die
On the Bridge of Toome today.[36]

If 1798 can be said to have a belated laureate, that person has to be P. J. McCall. A Dubliner himself, he had strong Wexford connections and his father, John McCall had collected songs on the Carlow/Wexford border in his youth.[37] P. J. McCall wrote many songs about '98, including two of the most popular songs to arise from the entire centenary. They remain in the minds of most people today as the quintessential songs of '98. They are 'Kelly of Killann' and the Daddy of them all, 'Boolavogue':[38]

At Boulavogue, as the sun was setting
O'er the bright May meadows of Shelmalier,
A rebel hand set the heather blazing
And brought the neighbours from far and near.
Then Father Murphy from old Kilcormack

Spurred up the rocks with a warning cry.
'Arm! Arm!' he cried, 'For I've come to lead you,
For Ireland's freedom we fight or die.'

The Wexford songmaker Michael 'Red Mick' O' Brien was also inspired by the advent of the centenary. His most popular song, 'Ballyshannon Lane' is still strong in oral tradition today:

> In '96 when the moon did fix its beams o'er Scullabogue
> And the planet Mars with its twinkling stars denoted where each rogue
> Of Saxon birth had bit the earth and Cromwell's crew were slain
> When the Yeomen fled and left their dead in Ballyshannon Lane.

This is an interesting piece of revisionism in that Scullabogue is not noted as a place wherein rebels suffered great losses in 1798, rather it was the site of the greatest act of savagery in a very bloody campaign. Following news that the Battle of New Ross was not going well for the rebels, loyalists and their families who were rounded up some miles away in Scullabogue, became the victims of reprisal. More than a hundred souls perished in this incident. Thirty-five were shot on the lawn in groups of four. The fate of the remainder was even more appalling. Men, women and children were herded into a thatched stone barn which was put to the torch. As the heat and smoke increased the terrified victims tried to escape by forcing the door open. Those who managed to get their hands through the door had them hacked off by the pikemen. It is said that a two year old child who managed to crawl under the barn door was impaled on a pike with the comment: 'Nits breed lice!' (A phrase earlier attributed to Cromwell.) Though the majority of those massacred at Scullabogue were Protestant, the victims included some Catholics who had fallen foul of the rebels, loyal family servants and even an elderly uilleann piper who had been heard to play 'God Save the King'. When the flames died away and the barn doors were swung back the families inside were so packed together that their charred remains were still standing:[39]

> In Keating's lawn at the morning dawn when the barn was all in flames
> I grieve to tell my three uncles fell, that's Martin, John and James,
> And as my aunt Kate stood by the gate, herself and her child were slain,
> My teeth still cringe to have revenge for Ballyshannon Lane.[40]

Seldom is the rewriting of history as evident as it is in this ballad. It is however, symptomatic of the concealment of an uncomfortable truth which could not be faced. The historian Tom Dunne, describing how the massacre was referred to locally recalled:

> There seems to be a strong local tradition of denial or displacement of the memory of what occurred at Scullabogue. My deceased uncle, Mick Galway of nearby Misterin, told my cousin, Monsignor Dunne, on passing the site, 'there was a barn here where Cromwell burned the Catholics'.[41]

Another theory put about was that the atrocity was actually instigated by castle agents in order to discredit the rebels![42] As recently as 1997 such was perpetuated in no less a source than the *Journal of the Wexford Historical Society* wherein we are told that 'Ballyshannon Lane' 'recalls poignantly the outrages committed by the loathed yeomanry in that remote tree-sheltered byway, north of Carrickbyrne hill'.[43]

The 1798 centenary was important as a focal point for demonstrations of nationalism. Committees were formed throughout Ireland, old patriotic songs were sung and many new ones were written. A century later still it is interesting to examine the songs about the centenary itself. At a formal level you had poets like William Rooney (most famous for writing 'The Men of the West') composing his 'Centenary Ode':

> Ross, Wexford, Gorey, Oulart, Tubberneering,
> And many a Wicklow glen
> That knew the dauntless souls and hearts unfearing
> Of Dwyer and all his men –
> These, through a hundred years of gloom and doubting
> Speak trumpet-toned today,
> Above the cry of creed and faction's shouting
> To tread the olden way.[44]

Such woodenly heroic poems and ballads had a great vogue right through the nineteenth-century and for much of this one. So, it is refreshing when the voice of the people comes through in less pretentious verse. A Crossmaglen song tells how funds were raised to aid the 1898 celebrations:

You gentlemen and sportsmen
And politicians too,
I crave your kind attention
To lines; there's but a few.
I mean to tell you plainly
How in sport we have advanced
To celebrate this '98
We had a challenge dance.[45]

Ballyrush, County Sligo, had more grandiose plans:

The Nationalists from every part assembled on that day
With horseback, foot and wagonettes, in gallant grand array,
And men so staunch from every branch with banner and with band,
To commemorate old '98 for Faith and Fatherland.[46]

The ballad singer documented the events of '98 at the time and through the looking glass of later years. If the reports were partisan, that is the nature of song-making. Long after the events of that fatal summer passed into history they acted as a focus for a nationalism which strengthened throughout the nineteenth-century. The ideals and individuals who strutted the stage in the rising became idealised and acted as inspirational icons for succeeding generations. Many would say their influence has not diminished yet.

NOTES

THE STATE OF IRELAND BEFORE 1798

1   Ruth Delany, *The Grand Canal of Ireland* (Dublin, 1995), pp. 52–3.
2   Jack A. Goldstone, *Revolution and rebellion in the early modern world* (Berkeley, 1991).
3   Stella Tillyard, *Citizen lord: Edward Fitzgerald 1763–98* (London, 1997).
4   This is intrinsic to the Goldstone argument: Goldstone, *Revolution,* pp. 123–5.
5   Dickson, 'Paine and Ireland', in David Dickson, Dáire Keogh & Kevin Whelan, eds, *The United Irishmen: Republicanism, radicalism and rebellion* (Dublin, 1993), pp. 135–44.
6   The term 'national government' is used by Tone in his *Argument on behalf of the Catholics of Ireland* (1791), reprinted in W. T. W. Tone, *Life of Theobald Wolfe Tone...,* ed. Thomas Bartlett (Dublin, 1998), p. 279.
7   See esp. Bartlett, 'The burden of the present: Theobald Wolfe Tone, republican and separatist', in Dickson, *et al., United Irishmen,* pp. 1–15.
8   *Tone life,* p.195.
9   Patrick Byrne, Dublin to Mathew Carey, 28 February 1795 (Lea and Febiger papers, Historical Society of Pennsylvania, Philadelphia). See Vincent Kinane, '"Literary food" for the American market: Patrick Byrne's exports to Mathew Carey', in *Proc. of the American Antiquarian Society,* civ, pt ii (1994), pp. 315–32.
10 Dickson, 'Taxation and disaffection in late eighteenth-century Ireland', in Samuel Clarke & James S. Donnelly, jr, eds, *Irish peasants: Violence and political unrest 1780–1914* (Madison, Wis., 1983), pp. 37–63.
11 Samuel Neilson, Belfast to Tone, 21 November 1792, in *Tone life,* p. 184.
12 Dickson, 'Taxation', p. 57.

FRANCE AND THE 1798 REBELLION

1   T. C. W. Blanning, *The Origins of the French Revolutionary Wars* (London & New York, 1986), chapters 3 & 4.
2   Steven T. Ross, *Quest for Victory: French Military Strategy 1792–1799* (South Brunswick & London, 1973), chapter 4.
3   Jacques Godechot, *La grande nation: l'expansion révolutionnaire de la Franc dans le monde* 2nd. Ed. (Paris, 1983), chapter V.
4   Jean-René Suratteau & Alain Bischoff, *Jean-François Reubell. L'Alsacien de la Révolution française* (Colmar, 1995).
5   Bernard Narbonne, *La diplomatie du Directoire et Bonaparte d'après les papiers inédits de Reubell.* (Paris, 1951), introduction & chapter 2.
6   Ross, *Quest for Victory* chapter 5 *passim.*
7   Ross, *Quest for Victory,* pp. 126–131.
8   *Mémoires du prince de Talleyrand, publiés avec une préface et des notes par le Duc de Broglie* vol. 1 (Paris, 1901), pp. 259–61.
9   Elliott, *Partners in Revolution,* pp. 155–6.
10 For the most detailed analysis of French plans and activity, see Edmond Desbrière, *1793–1805: projets et tentatives de débarquement aux (les britanniques,* 4 vols. (Paris, 1900–2) vol. ii, chapts ii–vii.
11 Archives Nationales, Marine, BB4 122 pièces 302–3: letter of Lowry, Hamilton, Teeling & Orr to the Directors, 28 prairial Year VI.

12   Archives Nationales, Marine, BB4 122, pièces 251–5.

13   Archives Nationales, Marine, BB4 122, pièce 272.

14   Marianne Elliott, *Partners in Revolution,* chapter 7, *passim.*

15   Henry Poulet, *Un soldat lorrain méconnu. Le général Humbert (1767–1823)* (Nancy, 1928).

16   Jean-Paul Bertaud, 'Forgotten Soldiers: the expedition of General Humbert to Ireland in 1798' in H. Gough & D. Dickson (eds.), *Ireland and the French Revolution* (Dublin, 1990), pp. 220–8.

17   Poulet, *Un soldat lorrain,* pp. 20–2.

18   Archives Nationales, Marine, BB4 122, pièce 272.

19   T. C. W. Blanning, *The French Revolution & Germany. Occupation and resistance in the German Rhineland 1792–1802* (Oxford, 1983), pp. 317–336; J. Godechot, 'Les variations de la politique français à l'égard des pays occupés 1792–1815' in *Occupants et Occupés 1792–1815* (Brussels, 1968).

20   T. C. W. Blanning, 'The role of religion in European Counter-Revolution' in Derek Beales & Geoffrey Best (eds.) *History, Society and the Churches. Essays in Honour of Owen Chadwick* (Cambridge, 1985) pp. 195–214.

21   T. C. W. Blanning, *The French Revolutionary Wars 1787–1802* (London, 1996), pp. 238–48.

DUBLIN'S ROLE IN THE 1798 REBELLION

1   Camden to Portland, 11 May 1798 (Public Record Office [London], HO/100/76/170–177).

2   Camden to Portland, 26 May 1798 (PRO[L], HO/100/76/291–292).

3   Samuel Sproule to John Lees, 21 May 1798 (National Archives, Rebellion Papers, 620/51/21).

4   Sproule to Lees, undated, 'Wednesday morning, camp' (Reb. Papers, 620/51/30).

5   Sproule to Lees, 15 & 16 May 1798 (Reb. Papers, 620/51/39 & 31).

6   Sproule to Lees, 23 May 1798 (Reb. Papers, 620/51/18).

7   Sproule to Lees, 23 May 1798 (Reb. Papers, 620/51/25).

8   Sir Richard Musgrave, *Memoirs of the Different Rebellions in Ireland* ... (Dublin 1801), p. 214; Francis Higgins to Edward Cooke, 25 May 1798 (Reb. Papers, 620/18/14).

9   Alexander Worthington to Cooke, 24 August 1802 (Reb. Papers, 620/10/125/4).

10   The Met. Office have informed me that sunset on 23 May is at 8.30pm, Greenwich Mean Time, and darkness, depending on weather conditions, up to an hour later. According to contemporary accounts the weather was fine in Dublin in May 1798 which would place dusk at about 9.30pm GMT. But until 1916 'Dublin Mean Time' (which from 1880 applied to the whole island) was 25 minutes behind GMT which would place dusk in Dublin on 23 May 1798 at 9.05pm, local time. If the Yeomanry assembled at about 9pm in anticipation of a rising at 10pm it bears out Musgrave's claim that 'the rebel drums were to have beaten to arms an hour after ours'.

11   Jonah Barrington, *The rise and fall of the Irish nation* (Dublin 1833), pp. 214–215.

12   Musgrave, *Rebellions,* p. 213.

13   *Ibid.,* pp. 211–213.

14   National Library of Ireland MS 637, p.210.

15   Musgrave, *Rebellions,* pp. 210–215; *Freeman's Journal,* 26 May 1798.

16   NLI MS 637, p. 435.

17 Musgrave, *Rebellions*, p. 217.

18 *Ibid.*, p. 212–213.

19 Camden to Portland, 28 May 1798 (PRO[L], HO/100/76/307–308).

20 Information of John McManus, Mullingar, Co. Westmeath, 10 August 1798 (Reb. Papers, 620/39/166); 'J. W.' (Leonard McNally) to Cooke, undated (Reb. Papers, 620/10/121/153).

21 Cooke to Wyckham, 2 June 1798 (PRO[L], HO/100/77/21–22).

22 *F. Jnl*, 26 May 1798.

23 *Ibid.*, 24 May 1798.

24 'J. W.' to Cooke, undated (Reb. Papers, 620/10/121/155); Camden to Portland, 24 May 1798 (PRO[L], HO/100/76/260–266); *Dublin Evening Post*, 31 May 1798.

25 Higgins to Cooke, 2 June 1798 (Reb. Papers, 620/18/14).

26 Thomas Boyle to Cooke, 24 May 1798 (Reb. Papers, 620/18/3).

27 Examination & confession of John Martin, 11 & 16 June 1798 (Reb. Papers, 620/38/126 & 160); Musgrave, *Rebellions*, p. 316; D. Keogh, 'Fr. John Martin: an Augustinian friar and the Irish rebellion of 1798', in *Analecta Augustiniania*, Vol. LI (1988), pp. 227–246.

28 Sproule to Lees, 25, 26 May 1798 & no date (Reb. Papers, 620/51/20, 26 & 29).

29 Camden to Portland, 4, 10, 11 & 13 June 1798 (PRO[L], HO/100/77/25–28, 114–118, 132–134 & 149–152).

30 NLI MS No. 637, p.435.

31 Higgins to Cooke, 2 & 5 June 1798 (Reb. Papers, 620/18/14).

32 Musgrave, *Rebellions*, pp. 537–8.

33 'J. W.' to Cooke, 12 June 1798 (Reb. Papers 620/10/121/112).

34 Examination of John Martin, 11 June 1798 (Reb. Papers, 620/38/126).

35 'J. W.' to Cooke, 29 June 1798 (Reb. Papers, 620/10/121/118).

36 Musgrave, *Rebellions*, p. 531.

37 Higgins to Cooke, 10 June 1798 (Reb. Papers, 620/18/14).

38 Musgrave, *Rebellions*, p. 476.

39 Thomas Pakenham, *The Year of Liberty: the Great Irish Rebellion of 1798* (London 1969), p. 283.

40 Musgrave, *Rebellions*, p. 294.

41 Higgins to Cooke, 4, 5, 13, 24 & 30 June, 12 & 15 July 1798 (Reb. Papers, 620/18/14); Worthington to Cooke, June 27 1798 (Reb. Papers, 620/56/204); 'N' to Cooke, 6 July 1798 (Reb. Papers, 620/39/28); *F. Jnl*, 31 May & 2 July 1798.

42 *Reports of the Committees of Secrecy of the House of Commons and the House of Lords of Ireland,* appendices dccccxlvi–dcccclix.

43 Document found on John Sheares, no date (Reb. Papers, 620/51/267).

44 Sproule to Lees, 14 May 1798 (Reb. Papers, 620/51/40).

45 *Wilson's Dublin Directory, 1797.*

46 Higgins to Cooke, 5 June 1798 (Reb. Papers, 620/18/14).

47 Higgins to Cooke, 13 June 1798 (Reb. Papers, 620/18/14).

48 Commissary Brennan's book, Ross army and Corbett's Hill, no date (Reb. Papers, 620/51/225).

49 Suspects, 1798–1803, no date (Reb. Papers, 620/12/217); Musgrave, *Rebellions*, p. 230; Sirr Papers, no date (TCD MSS 869/8/160).

50 Higgins to Cooke, 30 June 1798 (Reb. Papers, 620/18/14).

51 Madden Papers (TCD MSS 873/216–245).

52 Higgins to Cooke, 15 July 1798 (Reb. Papers, 620/18/14).
53 *F. Jnl,* 13 October 1798.
54 Higgins to Cooke, 12 July 1798 (Reb. Papers, 620/18/14).
55 Higgins to Cooke, 30 June 1798 (Reb. Papers, 620/18/14).
56 Higgins to Cooke, 15 July 1798 (Reb. Papers, 620/18/14); Boyle to Cooke, 16 June
    & July 1798 (Reb. Papers, 620/18/3).
57 *Memoirs of Myles Byrne* (Paris 1863), vol. 1, pp. 241–8.
58 Marianne Elliott, *Partners in Revolution: the United Irishmen and France* (Yale 1982),
    pp. 304–5.
59 Cooke to Wyckham, 25 June & 17 July 1798 (PRO[L], HO/100/77/ 194–195 &
    248–251).
60 *F. Jnl,* 7 July 1798.
61 Boyle to Cooke, July 1798 (Reb. Papers, 620/18/3).
62 Higgins to Cooke, 22 August 1798 (Reb. Papers, 620/18/14); 'J. W.' to Cooke, no
    date (Reb. Papers, 620/10/121/155).
63 Cooke to Portland, 28 July 1798 (PRO[L], HO/100/77/311–312).

1798 IN ANTRIM AND DOWN

1   *The Autobiography of Theobald Wolfe Tone* (ed. R. Barry O'Brian), ii, p. 336
2   Journal of the Duke of Rutland's tour of the North of Ireland, *Hist. MSS.Com.,*
    14th Report, III, pp. 419–423.
3   A.T.Q. Stewart, *A Deeper Silence,* pp. 154, 162.
4   R.B. McDowell, *Ireland in the Age of Imperialism and Revolution 1760–1800,* pp.
    471–472.
5   D. W. Miller, *Peep O'Day Boys and Defenders* (selected documents).
6   C. Dickson, *Revolt in the North,* p. 119.
7   Marianne Elliott, *Partners in Revolution,* pp 124–162.
8   Dickson, *op.cit.,* p. 117
9   W. E. H. Lecky, *A History of Ireland in the Eighteenth Century,* iv, pp. 414–415.
10 *Ibid.,* p. 413.
11 W. S. Dickson, *A Narrative of the Confinement and Exile of William Steel Dickson,
    D.D.,* p. 43–50.
12 Cleland MSS, D 714/2/23 (PRONI).
13 For the sequence of the Antrim meetings see A. T. Q. Stewart, *The Summer
    Soldiers,* pp. 64–66.
14 Mary McNeill, *Mary Ann McCracken,* p. 172.
15 Massereene/Foster MSS, D 562/3038.
16 Memorandum of Edward James Agnew of Kilwaughter, quoted in Dickson,
    Revolt in the North, p. 224.
17 *Old Ballymena,* pp. 23–45.
18 Report of Col James Durham to General Nugent, Antrim 7 June 1798 (Dickson,
    Revolt in the North, pp. 244–245).
19 James Keen's Narrative (Wesley Historical Society).
20 *Old Ballymena,* p. 37.
21 McCance MSS, D 272/32 (PRONI).
22 There is a memorial tablet to the officers and men of the York Fencibles in
    Comber parish church. The other two officers had unusual surnames, Unite
    and Sparks.
23 A. McClelland, 'Thomas Ledlie Birch, United Irishman' in *Procs. Belfast Natural*

History and Philosophical Society, second series, vol. 7 (1965), p. 31.

24 *McComb's Guide to Belfast.* Narrative of the battle by an unnamed participant, p. 128.

25 McDowell, *op. cit.,* p. 677.

26 The extent of the *Northern Star's* circulation in Ulster is indicated in the distribution books preserved in the Rebellion Papers 620/15/8/1–12 (National Archives).

Up not out: why did north-west Ulster not rise in 1798?

★ For a more detailed analysis, see Breandán Mac Suibhne, 'The United Men and the Maiden City: rebellion and loyalty in northwest Ulster, 1796–8' in G. O'Brien, ed., *Derry: History and Society* (Dublin, 1998).

1 For 'biographical sketches' reprinted from *The Northern Whig*, see Rev. Classon E. Porter, *Irish Presbyterian Biographical Sketches* (Belfast, 1883); *idem, Ulster Biographical Sketches* (Belfast, 1884); *idem, Frederick Augustus Hervey, Fourth Earl of Bristol and Bishop of Derry* (Belfast, 1884); *idem, The Seven Bruces: Presbyterian Ministers in Ireland in Six Successive Generations* (Belfast, 1885). Also see *idem, Congregational Memoirs. Old Presbyterian Congregation of Larne and Kilwaughter* (Larne, 1929; reprinted from *The Christian Unitarian*), pp. 64–76. R. M. Young, *Ulster in '98: Episodes and Anecdotes* (Belfast, 1893) and W. T. Latimer, *Ulster Biographies relating chiefly to the Rebellion of 1798* (Belfast, 1897) draw heavily on Porter's notes and publications.

2 A. T. Q. Stewart, *The Narrow Ground: Aspects of Ulster History, 1609–1969* (Belfast, 1977), pp. 108–9.

3 Nancy Curtin, 'The United Irish organisation in Ulster, 1795–8' in David Dickson, Dáire Keogh and Kevin Whelan, eds., *The United Irishmen: Republicanism, Radicalism and Rebellion* (Dublin, 1993), p. 214; Nancy J. Curtin, *The United Irishmen: Popular Politics in Ulster and Dublin, 1791–8* (Oxford, 1994), pp. 68–70.

4 For example, see chapters by Elliott and Whelan in Dickson, Keogh, Whelan, *United Irishmen*; Kevin Whelan, *The Tree of Liberty: Radicalism, Catholicism and the Construction of Irish Identity, 1760–1830* (Cork, 1996); chapters by Dickson and Whelan in J. A. Murphy, ed., *The French are in the Bay: The Expedition to Bantry Bay in 1796* (Cork, 1997); John Gray, *The Sans Culottes of Belfast* (Belfast, 1998).

5 *Secret Committee*, p. 62.

6 NAI, RP 620/28/166 [Derry], 29 January 1797, Hill to Beresford; Copy of Information of Richardson Boardman, Derry, 29 January 1797; 620/28/241 Information of Richardson Boardman, 5 February 1797.

7 NAI, RP 620/28/195 Fanet Glebe, 2 February 1797, Rev. W. Hamilton to G. Knox; 620/28/259 Fanet Glebe, 12 February 1797, Rev. W. Hamilton to Cooke; 620/28/217 Derry, 5 February 1797, Hill to Beresford; 620/28/230 Derry, Wednesday [n.d.], Hill to Beresford

8 NAI, RP 620/29/99 Information of David Dobbyn, Sergeant, 21 March 1797; 620/29/111 Information of Patrick Hickey, Private, 23 March 1797.

9 NAI, RP 620/29/185 Distribution of military in Ulster and Louth, 5 April 1797.

10 NAI, RP 620/32/144 Copy of further information of Charles McFillin, 28 September 1797.

11 Marianne Elliott, *Partners in Revolution: The United Irishmen and France* (London, 1982), pp. 130–33.

12 NAI, RP 620/31/77 Derry, Monday [recd 12 June 1797], Hill to Beresford.

13   NAI, RP 620/31/181 [Derry], [c. 12 June 1797], Hill to Cooke; 620/31/ 182 Derry,
      [June 1797], Hill to Cooke; 620/31/216 Derry, 10 July 1797, Hill to Cooke;
      620/31/298 Derry, 3 July 1797, H. Alexander to Pelham.

14   Elliott, *Partners in Revolution*, p. 133.

15   NAI, RP 620/31/167 Derry, 28 June 1797, J. Bagwell to ___; 620/31/182 Derry, 29
      June 1797, Hill to Cooke.

16   NAI, RP 620/31/172 Derry, 30 June 1797, Hill to Cooke.

17   NAI, RP 620/31/216 Derry, 10 July 1797, Hill to Cooke.

18   NAI, RP 620/32/196 Derry [October 1797], Hill to Cooke.

19   NAI, RP 620/31/262 Derry, 17 July 1797, Hill to Cooke; for Moore's trial, see
      DEP, 28 September 1797.

20   PRONI, Clelland papers D714/2/8A N. Maguan's report on provincial meeting
      of 14 October 1797.

21   G. S. Montgomery, *A Family History of the Montgomerys of Ballyleck* (Belfast, 1887),
      pp. 23–4.

22   On Buchanan, see PRONI, Clelland papers D714/2/9 and D714/2/10a. On Stilley
      and Wilson, see D714/2/21.

23   *Secret Committee*, pp. 85–7; NAI, RP 620/32/47 Coleraine, 14 August 1797, Hill to
      Cooke; 620/32/61 Derry, 19 August 1797, Hill to Cooke; 620/32/144 Copy of
      further information of Charles McFillin, 28 September 1797; PRONI, Clel-
      land papers D714/2/17 N. Maguan's report on provincial meeting of 24 March
      1798.

24   PRONI, Clelland papers D714/2/20a; D714/2/22; D714/2/23; *Secret Committee*, pp.
      118–9.

25   NLI, Lake corr. Ms. 56/173 Derry, 3 June 1798, Cavan to Knox; Ms. 56/195
      Derry, 16 June 1798, Cavan to Knox.

26   NAI, RP 620/26/150 Derry, 24 December. 1796, H. Alexander to _____.

27   *LJ*, 22 May; 29 May 1798.

28   PRONI, Abercorn papers T2541/IA2/7/13 Strabane, 13 June 1798, Hamilton to
      Abercorn.

29   *LJ*, 29 May 1798.

30   *LJ*, 5 June; 19 June 1798.

31   *LJ*, 29 May 1798.

32   *LJ*, 12 June 1798.

33   NLI, Lake corr. Ms. 56/173 Derry, 3 June 1798, Cavan to Knox; PRONI, Aber-
      corn papers T2541/IA2/7/20 Strabane, 9 June 1798, Hamilton to Abercorn; *LJ*,
      12 June 1798.

34   *LJ*, 5 June 1798; NLI, Lake corr. Ms. 56/173 Derry, 3 June 1798, Cavan to Knox.

35   NLI, Lake corr. Ms. 56/93 Milton, Derry, 20 August. 1797, Cavan to Knox

36   NAI, RP 620/31/216 Derry, 10 July 1797, Hill to Cooke; 620/32/105 Letterkenny,
      8 September 1797, J. Rea to [Pelham].

37   NLI, Lake corr. Ms. 56/138 Derry, 14 February 1798, Cavan to Knox.

38   NLI, Lake corr. Ms. 56/173 Derry, 3 June 1798, Cavan to Knox.

39   NLI, Lake corr. Ms. 56/195 Derry, 16 June 1798, Cavan to Knox..

40   PRONI, Abercorn papers T2541/IA2/7/20 Strabane, 9 June 1798, Hamilton to
      Abercorn

41   PRONI, Abercorn papers T2541/IA2/7/13 Strabane, 13 June 1798, Hamilton to
      Abercorn.

42   Cavan's orders of 11 June in *LJ*, 3 July 1798.

43 *LJ*, 12 June; 19 June 1798.

44 PRONI, Abercorn papers T2541/IA2/7/23 Strabane, 18 June 1798, Hamilton to Abercorn.

45 *LJ*, 19 June 1798; PRONI, Abercorn papers T2541/IA2/7/23 Strabane, 18 June 1798, Hamilton to Abercorn.

46 PRONI, Abercorn papers T2541/IA2/7/23 Strabane, 18 June 1798, Hamilton to Abercorn.

47 *LJ*, 19 June.

48 PRONI, Abercorn papers T2541/IA2/7/24 Strabane, 23 June 1798, Hamilton to Abercorn; SOC I 1017/18 Derry, 10 July 1798, Hill to Alex. Knox; *LJ*, 26 June 1798.

49 Resolutions passed at a meeting of the inhabitants of Glendermot on 1 July in *LJ*, 3 July 1798.

50 *LJ*, 10 July 1798.

51 *LJ*, 3 July 1798.

52 *LJ*, 10 July 1798.

53 PRONI, Abercorn papers T2541/IA2/7/26 Strabane, 5 July 1798, Hamilton to Abercorn; T2541/IA2/7/27 Strabane, 25 July 1798, Hamilton to Abercorn; Edward Daly and Kieran Devlin, *The Clergy of the Diocese of Derry: An Index* (Dublin, 1997), pp. 86; 107.

54 For a detailed analysis of events from July 1798, see Breandán Mac Suibhne, 'The United Men and the Maiden City: rebellion and loyalty in northwest Ulster, 1796–8' in G. O'Brien, ed., *Derry: History and Society* (Dublin, 1998).

55 *LJ*, 19 June 1798. On Horner, see NAI., RP 620/32/48 Coleraine, 25 August 1798, Hill to Cooke; 620/41/30 Derry, 12 November 1798, Hill to Cooke; 620/47/104 Derry, 28 July 1799, Hill to Cooke. Also see Mullin, *Limavady and the Roe Valley*, p. 49.

56 PRONI, Abercorn papers T2541/IA2/7/24 Strabane, 23 June 1798, Hamilton to Abercorn; T2541/IA2/7/26 Strabane, 5 July 1798, Hamilton to Abercorn.

57 PRONI, Abercorn papers T2541/IA2/7/25 Strabane, 28 June 1798, Hamilton to Abercorn.

58 PRONI, Abercorn papers T2541/IA2/7/25 Strabane, 28 June 1798, Hamilton to Abercorn; *LJ*, 3 July; 10 July 1798.

59 *LJ*, 11 September 1798.

60 NAI, RP 620/32/48 Coleraine, 25 August 1798, Hill to Cooke.

61 NAI, RP 620/57/104 New York, 20 November 1799, James Friel to Rev. James Friel, Rossnakill.

62 Family papers in possession (1978) of Mrs J. K. Baird, Dernacally, Carrigans; quoted in S. M. Campbell, 'Laggan Personalities of 1798' in *Donegal Annual* (1978), p. 365.

63 Rubert J. Coughlan, *Napper Tandy* (Dublin, 1976), pp. 206–7; NAI, RP 620/12/217 'Alphabetical list of suspects, 1798–1803' (despite the title, it includes suspects active at specified dates *after* 1803); extracts from Porter's interview with Stilley in Young, *Ulster in '98*, pp. 18–19; 58–60. Also see Porter, *Irish Presbyterian Biographical Sketches*, pp. 16–19.

GENERAL HUMBERT'S CAMPAIGN IN THE WEST

1 General accounts include Charles H. Teeling, *Sequel to the history of the Irish Rebellion of 1798: a personal narrative* (Glasgow, 1876), pp. 300–22; C. Litton

Falkiner, 'The French Invasion of Ireland in 1798' in *Studies in Irish history and biography, mainly of the eighteenth century* (London, 1902), pp. 250–350; Richard Hayes, *The last invasion of Ireland: when Connacht rose* (Dublin, 1937); Général Gastey, 'L'étonnante aventure de l'armée d'Irlande' in *Revue Historique de l'Armée* (Paris), 8th year, no. 4 (December 1952), pp. 19–36; Thomas Pakenham, *The year of liberty: the great Irish rebellion of 1798* (London, 1969), p. 294 *et seq.*

2   See Marianne Elliott, *Partners in revolution: the United Irishmen and France* (New Haven & London, 1982), especially parts 2 and 3.

3   E. Desbrière, *Projets et tentatives de débarquement aux îles britanniques* (Paris, 4 vols, 1900–2), ii, p. 69 *et seq.*

4   Jacques Baeyens, *Sabre au clair: Amable Humbert, général de la république* (Paris, 1981), *passim.*

5   F. W. van Brock, 'Dilemma at Killala' in *The Irish Sword*, viii, no. 33 (winter 1968), pp. 261–73; Desbrière, *Projets et tentatives*, ii, pp. 164–71.

6   Jean-Paul Bertaud, 'Forgotten soldiers: the expedition of General Humbert to Ireland in 1798' in Hugh Gough and David Dickson (eds), *Ireland and the French revolution* (Dublin, 1990), pp. 220–8.

7   Grattan Freyer (ed.), *Bishop Stock's narrative of the year of the French: 1798* (Ballina, 1982), p. 23.

8   Nuala Costello (ed.), 'Little's diary of the French landing in 1798' in *Analecta Hibernica 11* (1941), p. 64; W. E. H. Lecky, *A history of Ireland in the eighteenth century* (London, 1913), iii, pp. 419–20; Patrick K. Egan, 'Progress and suppression of the United Irishmen in the western counties in 1798–9' in *Journal of the Galway Archaeological and Historical Society*, xxv, nos 3–4 (1953–4), pp. 104–34.

9   Richard Hayes (ed.), 'An officer's account of the French campaign in Ireland in 1798' [General Sarrazin's account] in *Irish Sword*, ii, no. 6 (summer 1955), p. 111.

10   Hayes, *Last invasion*, pp. 275–8; Sheila Mulloy, 'James Joseph MacDonnell, "the best-known of the United Irish chiefs of the west"' in *Cathair na Mairt, Journal of the Westport Historical Society*, no. 5 (1985), pp. 67–79.

11   Sir Richard Musgrave, *Memoirs of the different rebellions in Ireland* (2nd edn, Dublin, 1801), pp. 587–90.

12   Brendan Hoban, 'Dominick Bellew, 1745–1812, parish priest of Dundalk and bishop of Killala' in *Seanchas Ard Mhacha* (1972), pp. 333–71; Patrick Hogan, 'Some observations on contemporary allegations as to Bishop Dominick Bellew's (1745–1813) sympathies during the 1798 rebellion in Connacht' in *ibid.* (1982), pp. 417–25.

13   E. MacHale, 'Some Mayo priests of 1798' in *Blianiris*, ii, no. 5 (1991–2), pp. 7–20; Dáire Keogh, *The French disease: the Catholic Church and Irish radicalism, 1790–1800* (Dublin, 1993), pp. 182–6.

14   L. O. Fontaine, *Notice historique de la descente des francais en Irlande ...* (Paris, 1801), p. 46; Nuala Costello (ed.), 'Journal de l'expédition d'Irlande suivi de notes sur le Général Humbert qui l'a command' [Captain Jean Louis Jobit's account] in *Anal. Hib. 11*, pp. 24, 52.

15   Kenneth P. Ferguson, The army in Ireland from the restoration to the act of union (unpublished Ph.D. thesis, TCD, 1980), pp. 179–83.

16   G. A. Hayes-McCoy, *Irish battles: a military history of Ireland* (London, 1969), pp. 282–3.

17 Statement of General Hutchinson, 21 September 1798 (Charles Ross, ed., *Correspondence of Charles, first marquis of Cornwallis,* London, 1859, ii, pp. 409–10); Sir Henry McAnally, *The Irish militia 1793–1816: a social and military study* (Dublin & London, 1949), pp. 133–8.

18 See contemporary plans of the dispositions in T. H. McGuffie, 'A sketch-map of Castlebar, 27th August 1798' in *Journal of the Society for Army Historical Research,* xxvi, no. 107 (autumn 1948), pp. 88–90; and W. A. Maguire (ed.), *Up in arms!: The 1798 rebellion in Ireland: a bicentenary exhibition* (Belfast, 1998), p. 258.

19 F. S. Bourke, 'The French invasion of 1798: a forgotten eyewitness' [Edward Mangin] in *Irish Sword,* ii, no. 8 (summer 1956), p. 293; John Cooney, 'Humbert's expedition – a lost cause?' in John Cooney and Tony McGarry (eds), *Post-Maastricht Europe: papers of the 1992 Humbert Summer School* (Dublin, 1993), pp. 112–3.

20 F. van Brock (ed.), 'A memoir of 1798' [account of Sergt Maj. J. B. Thomas] in *Irish Sword,* ix, no. 36 (summer 1970), pp. 199–200.

21 Patrick M. Hogan, 'The undoing of Citizen John Moore – president of the provisional government of the republic of Connacht, 1798' in *Jn. Galway Arch. and Hist. Soc.,* xxxix (1981–2), pp. 59–72; Sheila Mulloy, 'John Moore of Moorehall (1767–99): the general who wasn't' in *Irish Sword,* xviii, no. 73 (summer 1992), pp. 264–70.

22 *Impartial relation of the military operations which took place in Ireland in consequence of the landing of a body of French troops, under General Humbert, in August, 1798* (Dublin, 1799), pp. 8–28; Carola Oman, *Sir John Moore* (London, 1953), p. 189.

23 Thomas Bartlett, 'Counter-insurgency and rebellion' in Thomas Bartlett and Keith Jeffrey (eds), *A military history of Ireland* (Cambridge, 1996), p. 286.

24 G. A. H[ayes]-McC[oy], 'Fencible corps in Ireland, 1782–1803', in *Irish Sword,* ii, no. 6 (summer 1955), pp. 140–3; M. E. S. Laws, 'Hompesch's Dragoon Riflemen' in *ibid.,* no. 8 (summer, 1956), p. 297.

25 Liam Cox, 'Westmeath in the 1798 period' in *ibid.,* ix, no. 34 (summer 1969), pp. 1–15.

26 Thomas Bartlett, 'General Humbert takes his leave' in *Cathair na Mart,* 11 (1991), p. 102.

The Prime Informant

1 Recent evaluations of the United Irishmen and the threat they posed at home and abroad can be found in Nancy Curtin, *The United Irishmen in Ulster and Dublin* (Oxford, 1994), D. Keogh and N. Furlong (ed.), *The Mighty Wave: the 1798 Rebellion in Wexford* (Dublin, 1994), P. Weber, *On the Road to Rebellion: the United Irishmen and Hamburg* (Dublin, 1996). Marianne Elliott, *Partners in Revolution: The United Irishmen and France, 1793–1815* (New Haven, 1982) is indispensable.

2 R. R. Madden, *The United Irishmen, their Lives and Times,* First series (London, 1842), i, p. 147.

3 W. J. Fitzpatrick, *Secret Service under Pitt* (Dublin, 1892), pp. vi–vii.

4 [Henry MacDougall], *Sketches of Irish Political Characters* (London, 1799), p. 180.

5 I have with some reluctance followed the information set out by Fitzpatrick, *Sham Squire,* pp. 4–15 in this account of Higgins' early life.

6 Based on legal papers published by Fitzpatrick, *Sham Squire,* pp. 9–10.

7 Brian Inglis, *The Freedom of the Press in Ireland, 1784–1841* (Dublin, 1954), pp. 54–55.

8 Mary Lyons (ed.), *The Memoirs of Mrs Leeson, Madam, 1727–97* (Dublin, 1995), p. 239: Higgins was intimate with Richard 'Dasher' Daly, the theatre manager and duellist – he fought 19 duels in two years (Constantia Maxwell, *Dublin under the Georges* (London/Dublin, 1946), p. 88)); Thomas 'Buck Whalley, a notorious bravado and gambler who, for a bet, walked to Jerusalem in 1787 (Sir E. Sullivan (ed.), *Buck Whalley's Memoirs* (London, 1906)); Colonel O'Kelly, the race-horse owner (W. J. Fitzpatrick, *Ireland before the Union with extracts from the unpublished diary of John Scott, Earl of Clonmell* (Dublin, 1867)), pp. 78–9; John Scott, Earl of Clonmell, a notoriously corrupt judge (see Fitzpatrick, *Ireland before the Union*); Henry Lawes Luttrell, Earl of Carhampton, who narrowly escaped conviction for the abduction and rape of a child (Fitzpatrick, *Ireland before the Union*, pp. 129–130).

9 R. Hill, *From Patriots to Unionists: Dublin City Politics and Irish Protestant Patriotism, 1660–1840* (Oxford, 1997), pp. 228, 249–50.

10 [MacDougall], *Sketches*, p. 183.

11 Northington to ____, 23 March 1783 in Historical Manuscripts Commission, *Dropmore* (London, 1892), i, p. 203; see also for the history of the *Freeman* at this time, Inglis, *Freedom of the Press*, pp. 35–7.

12 National Archives, Dublin, Rebellion Papers, 620/18/14, Higgins to Alexander Marsden, 18 May 1801. The file 620/18/14 contains the large majority of Higgins' letters but they are not separately listed.

13 Kent Record Office, U840/0143/1, Pratt papers, Higgins to Sackville Hamilton, 29 March 1795.

14 See N.A. 620/18/14: Higgins to Cooke, 3 February 1797.

15 N.A. 620/18/14, Higgins to Alexander Marsden, 18 May 1801.

16 N.A. 620/18/14: Higgins to Cooke, 17 December 1797.

17 Kent Archives, U840/0143/1, 29 March 1795.

18 I am preparing an edition of these letters for publication. There are two collections of Higgins letters – a small number in the Pratt papers in Kent County Archives and much larger bundles in the Rebellion papers, National Archives, Dublin. There are large gaps in the latter collection – almost no letter for the whole of 1799, for example – and these may indicate that some letters were destroyed.

19 N.A. 620/18/14: Higgins to Cooke, 28 December 1796; *ibid.,* 1 September 1797.

20 N.A. 620/18/14: Higgins to Cooke, 29 December 1797.

21 N.A. 620/18/14: Higgins to Cooke, 7 March 1798.

22 N.A. 620/18/14: Higgins to Cooke, 15 August 1796.

23 N.A. 620/18/14: Higgins to Cooke, 24 September 1797.

24 N.A. 620/18/14: Higgins to Cooke, 2 December 1798.

25 See Higgins' reports on MacNally in N.A. 620/18/14: Higgins to Cooke, 11 October 1796, and 26 November 1797. For MacNally's career as a castle informer see Fitzpatrick, *Secret Service,* pp. 174–210.

26 N.A. 620/18/14: Higgins to Cooke, 23 April 1797.

27 Kent Archives Office, U840/0143/4, Higgins to Hamilton,

28 N.A. 620/18/14: Higgins to Cooke, 28 February 1798.

29 N.A. 620/18/14: Higgins to Cooke, 18 May 1801: Higgins claimed to be out of pocket some £500 on wages, dinners, and presents for his informers.

30 N.A. 620/18/14: Higgins to Cooke, 26 May 1797

31 N.A. 620/18/14: Higgins to Cooke, 12 January 1798, 19 September 1800; Higgins to Marsden, 12 September 1800.

32 N.A. 620/18/14: Higgins to Cooke, 10, 14 March 1798.

33 N.A. 620/18/14: Higgins to Cooke, 2 November 1796; 25 May 1797.

34 N.A. 620/18/14: Higgins to Cooke, 18 March 1801: Higgins wanted Cooke to intervene with Archbishop Troy to have Moran promoted.

35 N.A. 620/18/14: Higgins to Cooke, 24 October 1796.

36 N.A. 620/18/14: Higgins to Cooke, 9 April 1797.

37 N.A. 620/49/137: Cooke to Marsden, 1 November 1801.

38 For Francis Magan, see Fitzpatrick, *The Sham Squire*, pp. 127–30.

39 N.A. 620/18/14: Higgins to Cooke, 14 March 1797.

40 N.A. 620/18/14: Higgins to Cooke, 22 December 1797.

41 N.A. 620/18/14: Higgins to Cooke, 3 May 1797.

42 N.A. 620/18/14: Higgins to Cooke, 12 January 1798.

43 N.A. 620/18/14: Higgins to Cooke, 20 May 1798.

44 N.A. 620/18/14: Higgins to Cooke, 18 May 1798.

45 N.A. 620/18/14: Higgins to Cooke, 15 May 1798.

46 N.A. 620/18/14: Higgins to Cooke, 18 May 1798.

47 There is a useful account of the capture of Lord Edward in Stella Tillyard, *Citizen Lord: Edward Fitzgerald, 1763–98* (London, 1997), pp. 268–73.

48 N.A. 620/18/14: Higgins to Cooke, 31 May 1798.

49 Fitzpatrick, *Sham Squire*, p. 130.

50 See for example his very long letter of 18 May 1801 to Alexander Marsden: N.A. 620/18/14.

51 N.A. 620/18/14: Higgins to Cooke, 4 March, 13 June 1801.

52 N.A. 620/47/154 Magan to Cooke, c August. 1799; 620/10/118/6, Magan to Cooke, 8 February 1801; N.A. State of the Country Papers, Second Series, no. 3837, Magan to William Elliott, 26 November 1806.

53 Higgins' will is noticed in a bound volume in the National Archives, Dublin, entitled Charitable Bequests: Prerogative, Consistorial and Diocesan returns, January 1801–December 1813, volume 1: There is discussion of the will in Fitzpatrick, *Ireland before the Union*, pp. 94–103

SCOUNDRELS ALL – PRIESTS AND PRELATES IN '98

1   R. Musgrave, *Memoirs of the Irish Rebellion of 1798,* 4th edition (Indiana, 1995), p. 453.

2   E. Hay, *History of the Insurrection in the County of Wexford, A.D. 1798* (Dublin, 1803); T. Cloney, *A personal narrative of those transactions in the County of Wexford in which the author was engaged at the awful period of 1798* (Dublin, 1832).

3   J. Caulfield to J. Troy, 10 September 1799, DDA..

4   J. Caulfield to J. Troy, 9 June 1798, DDA.

5   [James Caulfield], *A Vindication of the Roman Catholic Clergy of the town of Wexford during the late Unhappy Rebellion* (Dublin, 1799), p. 18.

6   M. Byrne, *Memoirs* (Paris, 1863), I, pp 54–7.

7   P. Kavanagh, *A Popular History of 1798* (Dublin, 1870).

8   L. M. Cullen, 'The politics of Clerical Radicalism in the 1790s' in L. Swords (ed.), *Protestant, Catholic and Dissenter; the clergy and 1798* (Dublin, 1997), p. 274.

9   I. R. McBride, *Scripture Politics* (Oxford, 1998).

10 N. Curtin, *The United Irishmen: Popular Politics in Ulster and Dublin, 1791–98* (Oxford, 1994), p. 134; W. MacMillan, 'Presbyterian Ministers and the Ulster

Rising' in L. Swords, *op. cit*, pp 81–118

11 D. Miller 'Irish Christianity and Revolution' (a paper delivered at 1798 Rebellion Conference, Notre Dame, March 1998; R. R. Madden, *Lives of the United Irishmen* (Dublin, 1842–6), 7 vols.

12 P. Comerford, 'Church of Ireland Clergy in 1798' in L. Swords, *op. cit*., pp. 219–53.

13 L. M. Cullen, *ibid*, p. 274.

14 Howell, State Trials, XXV, pp. 833–45: M. Elliott, *Partners in Revolution; the United Irishmen and France* (New Haven, 1982), pp. 62–8; T. Bartlett (ed.), *Life of Theobald Wolfe Tone* (Dublin, 1998), pp. 96–102.

15 G. Taylor, *A history of the rise, progress and suppression of the rebellion in the county of Wexford in the year 1798* (Dublin, 1800), p. 99: J. Stock, *A narrative of what passed at Killala ... during the French invasion* (Dublin, 1800).

16 P. O'Donoghue, 'The Catholic Church in the age of imperialism and rebellion, 1782–1803' (Ph.D., University College, Dublin, 1975); Dáire Keogh, *The French Disease; the Catholic Church and Irish Radicalism, 1790–1800* (Dublin, 1993).

17 Thomas Hussey to Richard Burke, 28 August 1790, *Burke Correspondence*, iv, p. 134.

18 Cox, *Irish Magazine*, March 1815; Duigenan, cited in J. D'Alton, *The Memoirs of the Archbishops of Dublin* (Dublin, 1838), p. 486.

19 P. Duigenan, *A fair representation of the present state of the Church of Ireland* (London, 1799), p. 18.

20 J. Troy to J. Carroll, Baltimore, 13 August 1796, Baltimore Diocesan Archives.

21 T. Hussey, *A pastoral letter to the Catholics of the united dioceses of Waterford and Lismore* (Waterford, 1797)

22 T. Hussey to J. Carroll, 29 September 1799, Baltimore Diocesan Archives.

23 J. Carroll, Baltimore, to J. Troy, 12 November 1798, Dublin Diocesan Archives: J. Troy to Thomas Bray, 15 April 1997, Cashel Diocesan Archives.

24 J. Troy to T. Bray, 8 December 18792, Cashel Diocesan Archives.

25 Musgrave, *Memoirs*, p. 67; Byrne, *Memoirs*, i, p. 54.

26 K. Whelan, 'The role of the Catholic priest in the 1798 rebellion in county Wexford' in K. Whelan (ed.), *Wexford History and Society* (Dublin, 1987), pp 296–315; K. Whelan, 'The Wexford priests in 1798' in L. Swords (ed.), *Protestant, Catholic and Dissenter,* pp 165–85.

27 D. Keogh (ed), *The Life of the Rev James Coigly ... as written by himself during his confinement in Maidstone Gaol* (Cork, 1998).

28 Coigly, *Life*, pp. 14–18.

29 T. Bartlett (ed.), *Life of Tone*, p. 860.

30 D. Keogh, 'The Most dangerous villain in society; Fr John Martin's mission to the United Irishmen of Wicklow in 1798' in *Eighteenth Century Ireland*, vii (1992), pp. 115–35.

31 *Ibid.*

32 W. Gahan, *Youth Instructed in the grounds of Christian religion with remarks on the writings of Voltaire, Rosseau, T. Paine, etc.*(Dublin, 1798), p. 149.

33 W. Cox, *Irish Magazine*, 1808.

34 W. Farrell, *Carlow in '98*, p. 224.

35 J. T. Gilbert (ed.), *Documents relating to Ireland, 1795–1804* (Dublin, 1893), p. 73.

36 Petition of Revd M. Barry, 15 November 1799, National Archives, Rebellion Papers, 620/56/49.

PARTNERS IN THE STRUGGLE: THE WOMEN OF 1798

1   P. J. Jupp, 'The roles of royal and aristocratic women in British politics 1782–1832' in Mary O'Dowd and Sabine Wichert (eds), *Chattel, servant or citizen; women's status in church, state and society* (Belfast 1995), p. 105–6.

2   Stella Tillyard, *Aristocrats: Caroline, Emily, Louisa and Sarah Lennox 1740–1832* (London 1994), p. 69.

    Ibid., p. 71.

4   *Ibid.*, p. 395.

5   David Dickson, 'Paine and Ireland' in D. Dickson, D. Keogh and K. Whelan (eds), *The United Irishmen: republicanism, radicalism and rebellion* (Dublin 1993), p. 140.

6   Mary McNeill, *The life and times of Mary Ann McCracken 1770–1866: a Belfast panorama* (Belfast: Blackstaff, 1988; facsimile of first edition 1960).

7   Nancy Curtin, 'Women and eighteenth-century Irish republicanism' in Margaret MacCurtain and Mary O'Dowd (eds), *Women in early modern Ireland* (Dublin 1991), pp. 140.

8   John Gray, 'Mary Anne McCracken: Belfast revolutionary and pioneer of feminism', in Dáire Keogh and Nicholas Furlong (eds), *The women of 1798* (Dublin 1998), pp. 47–63.

9   Dáire Keogh, 'The women of 1798: representations and realities', in Mary Cullen (ed.), *1798; 200 years of resonance* (Dublin, 1998), p. 65.

10 Anna Kinsella, 'Nineteenth-century perspectives: the women of 1798 in folk memory and ballads', in Keogh and Furlong, *The women of 1798*, p. 196.

11 Kevin O'Neill, 'Mary Shackleton Leadbeater: Peaceful Rebel', *ibid.*, p. 142.

12 *Ibid.*, p.162.

13 McNeill, *Mary Ann McCracken*, pp. 126–8.

14 O'Neill, 'Mary Leadbeater', pp. 150–3.

15 *Journals and memoirs of Thomas Russell 1791–5*, edited by C. J. Woods (Dublin, 1991), p. 86.

16 Nancy Curtin, 'Matilda Tone and virtuous republican femininity', in Keogh and Furlong, *The women of 1798*, pp. 26–46.

17 Curtin, 'Women and republicanism', p. 134.

18 Helena Concannon, *Women of 'ninety eight* (Dublin, 2nd edition, 1920) p. xiii; McNeill, *Mary Ann McCracken*, p. 129.

19 Kinsella, 'Women in folk memory', p. 188.

20 Concannon, *Women of 'ninety-eight*, pp. 299–300.

21 Curtin, 'Women and republicanism', pp. 134–5.

22 Quoted in Concannon, *Women of 'ninety eight*, p. xii.

23 Mary Helen Thuente, 'Liberty, Hibernia and Mary Le More: United Irish images of women', in Keogh and Furlong, *The women of 1798*, pp. 9–25.

24 Concannon, *Women of 'ninety-eight*, pp. 297–8.

25 R. R. Madden, *Antrim and Down in '98,* (Glasgow, n.d.), p. 244.

26 Kinsella, pp. 192–3.

27 Daniel Gahan, *The people's rising: Wexford, 1798* (Dublin, 1995), p. 132.

28 Peadar MacSuibhne, *Kildare in 1798* (Naas, 1978), p. 61.

29 Nicholas Furlong, *Fr John Murphy of Boolavogue 1753–1798* (Dublin, 1991), p. 133.

30 *Ibid.*, pp. 53 –4.

31 Kinsella, 'Women in folk memory', p. 191.

32 *Ibid.*, p. 192.

33 John Beatty, 'Protestant women of county Wexford and their narratives of the

rebellion of 1798', in Keogh and Furlong, *The women of 1798,* pp. 113–36.

34   *Ibid.,* p. 120.
35   *Ibid.,* p. 118.
36   R. R. Madden, *The United Irishmen; their lives and times,* 3rd series, iii (Dublin, 1846), p. 182.
37   *Ibid.*
38   *Ibid.,* p. 187.

1798 AND THE BALLADMAKERS

1   Irish language songs do not fit into the street ballad genre and as such are outside the scope of this paper.

2   Georges-Denis Zimmermann, *Songs of Irish Rebellion: Political Street Ballads and Rebel Songs, 1780–1900* (Dublin, 1967), p. 39.

3   Pádraig Mac Gréine, 'Traditions of 1798' *Béaloideas: The Journal of the Folklore of Ireland Society,* Vol. IV, part IV (Dublin, December 1934), pp. 393–5.

4   J. Collingswood Bruce and John Stokoe, *Northumbrian Minstrelsy* (Newcastle-upon-Tyne, 1882. Rpr. Hatboro, Pennsylvania, 1965), pp. 71–3.

5   Séamus Mac Mathúna, *Traditional Songs and Singers,* (Dublin, 1977), pp. 28–9.

6   Zimmermann, pp. 161–165.

7   'Dunlavin Green', Colm Ó Lochlainn, *Irish Street Ballads* (Dublin, 1939, rpr. 1967), pp. 106–7.

8   'Text given to me by Donal O'Sullivan, who had it from Francis-Joseph Bigger, the noted Belfast antiquary. I have never seen any printed version of it, either on broadsides or otherwise.' Zimmermann, p. 158.

9   Zimmermann, p. 158.

10   'The Battle of Granard' in Seán Ó Brádaigh, *Songs of 1798: The Year of the French* (Dublin, 1982), pp. 29–31. *Cf.* IFC1901: pp. 259–262. The style suggests mid nineteenth century. IFC refers to texts in the Main Manuscript Collection in the archive of the Department of Irish Folklore, University College, Dublin. My thanks to the Head of the Department for permission to use these sources.

11   IFC1517: pp. 149.

12   IFC1858: pp. 41–2.

13   IFC481: pp. 142–7. See note 41.

14   Ó Lochlainn, pp. 54–5, 207.

15   Zimmermann, 156–7. *Cf.* Ó Lochlainn, pp. 130–1.

16   'Derry Gaol' sung by Sarah Makem, Keady, Co. Armagh. LP record, *The Folk Songs of Britain, vol. 7.* (12T195 Topic Records, London, 1970). See Eleanor R. Long, 'Derry Gaol' From Formula to Narrative Theme in International Popular Tradition', *Jahrbuch für Volksliedforschung* (Berlin, 1975), pp. 62–85, n.b. pp. 74–5 and the same author's *'The Maid' and 'The Hangman': Myth and Tradition in a Popular Ballad.* (Berkeley, 1971).

17   Alfred Preceval Graves, 'Little Jimmy Murphy' *Journal of the Irish Folk Song Society,* Vol. XIII, (London, June 1913), pp. 22–3, and the LP by Frank Harte, *And Listen To My Song* (Ram Records, Dublin, RMLP 1013).

18   IFC1440: pp. 146–150, IFC1902: pp. 206–9, IFC1879: pp. 223–3 and Seán Ó Brádaigh, *op. cit.,* p. 24.

19   IFC1119: pp. 293–4. See also 'Shaun Crossa at Dungiven', *Old Come=All=Ye's (Derry Journal,* n.d. [*ca.* 1920?]), p. 59.

20   IFC250: pp. 644–9.

21 IFC78: pp. 249–258, IFC559: pp. 232.

22 IFC465: pp. 212–7.

23 IFC194: pp. 290–5. See also IFC521: pp. 272–7.

24 IFC1137: pp. 167–170.

25 IFC57: pp. 130–144.

26 Patrick Galvin, *Irish Songs of Resistance* (New York, 1962), p. 7.

27 Zimmermann, p. 80.

28 *Ibid.,* p. 226.

29 Martin MacDermott, *Songs and Ballads of Young Ireland* (London, 1896), pp. 253–4.

30 *Ibid,* 365, also Zimmermann, pp. 228–9.

31 Zimmermann, pp. 228–9.

32 *Henry V,* Act IV, Scene 4.

33 Breandán Breathnach, *Folk Music and Dances of Ireland* (Cork, Revised Edition, 1979), pp. 17–19.

34 For a detailed analysis of this episode see Zack Bowen, *Musical Allusions in the Works of James Joyce* (Dublin, 1975), pp. 194–201.

35 Ó Brádaigh, pp. 41–2.

36 *Ibid*., p. 60.

37 Tom Munnelly, 'The Manuscript Songbook of John McCall (1822–1902)' in *Lares* (Giá Bulletino della Societá di Etnografia Italiana, Firenze, Ottobre–Dicembre 1985), pp. 454–477.

38 *Selected Ballads and Poems of P. J. McCall* (Wexford, 1955), p. 23 and p. 24.

39 Thomas Packenham, *The Year of Liberty* (London, 1969), pp. 198–9. Also, Sir Richard Musgrave, *Memoirs of the Rebellions in Ireland* (London, 1801. Third ed. 1802) Vol. 1, pp. 525–6 plus affidavits, App. XX. Nos. 5–12.

40 Paddy Berry, *Wexford Ballads* (Wexford, 1982), pp. 29–30.

41 Tom Dunne, '1798: Memory, History, Commemoration', *Journal of the Wexford Historical Society* 16 (Wexford, 1996–7), p. 23.

42 Benjamin Pemberton Binns, 'Lines on the Burning of Scullabogue Barn' in Richard Robert Madden, *Literary Remains of the United Irishmen,* (Dublin, 1887), pp. 107–109. My thanks to Terry Moylan for drawing my attention to the above references.

43 Gearóid Ó Broin, 'A Study of the Ballad Lore of Wexford' *Journal of the Wexford Historical Society* 16 (Wexford, 1996–7), p. 160.

44 William Rooney, 'Ninety-Eight: A Centenary Ode', in Stephen J. Brown, *Poetry of Irish History,* (Dublin, 1927), pp. 250–2.

45 IFC1851: pp. 133–4.

46 IFC339: pp. 290–2.

THE CONTRIBUTORS

Cathal Póirtéir is a graduate of University College Dublin. He is a Senior Radio Producer in RTÉ where he works on current affairs and features programmes. His published works include *Famine Echoes, Gnéithe den Ghorta, Glórtha ón Ghorta* and *The Great Irish Famine*.

David Dickson is head of the Department of Modern History Trinity College Dublin. He has published extensively on eighteenth-century Irish history in the areas of demography, urban and regional development. Recent publications include *The United Irishmen: Radicalism, Republicanism, Rebellion* (co-edited with Kevin Whelan and Dáire Keogh) and *Arctic Ireland*, a study of the 1740–41 famine.

Kevin Whelan is Michael J. Smurfit Director of the Notre Dame–Keugh Studies Centre, Dublin. His most recent book is *Fellowship of Freedom. The United Irishmen and the 1798 Rebellion* (1998).

Hugh Gough is Associate Professor of Modern History at University College Dublin, author of *The Newspaper Press in the French Revolution* (Routledge, 1988) and *The Terror in the French Revolution* (Macmillan, 1998).

Marianne Elliott is Professor of Modern History and Director of the Institute of Irish Studies at Liverpool University. She is author of *Wolfe Tone. Prophet of Irish Independence* (Yale University Press, 1989 and 1998), *Partners in Revolution. The United Irishmen and France* (Yale University Press, 1982 and 1998), and is currently completing *A History of the Catholics of Ulster*.

Tommy Graham is completing a PhD on Dublin's United Irishmen at Trinity College Dublin. He is joint editor of *History Ireland* and secretary of the Dublin 1798 Commemoration Committee.

A. T. Q. Stewart, formerly Reader in Irish history in Queen's University, Belfast, author of *A Deeper Silence* (Faber, 1993) and *The Summer Soldiers* (Blackstaff, 1995).

Breandán Mac Suibhne is a graduate of University College, Dublin and Carnegie Mellon University, Pittsburgh. His research interests include the social history of eighteenth and nineteenth-century Ireland, historical demography and identity politics. He is currently lecturing in the Department of Modern History, UCD.

Brian Cleary hails from Oulart in County Wexford. He has lectured widely at home and abroad on 1798. He works as a translator in the Houses of the Oireachtas.

Harman Murtagh is a lecturer at Athlone Institute of Technology and editor of *The Irish Sword,* the journal of the Military History Society of Ireland of which he is a vice-president.

Thomas Bartlett is Professor of Modern Irish History at University College Dublin. He has recently edited the *Life of Teobald Wolfe Tone* (Lilliput, 1998).

Dáire Keogh lectures in the Department of History, St Patrick's College, Dublin City University. He is the editor of *A Patriot Priest: the Life of Revd James Coigly 1761–1798* (Cork University Press, 1998).

Mary Cullen is an Academic Associate at NUI, Maynooth, and a Research Associate at the Centre for Women's Studies, Trinity College, Dublin.

Tom Munnelly is a full time collector with the Department of Irish Folklore in University College, Dublin. He has a particular interest in folk song and has been based in County Clare for more than twenty years.

More Interesting Books

THE GREAT IRISH FAMINE

EDITED BY CATHAL PÓIRTÉIR

This is the most wide-ranging series of essays ever published on the Great Irish Famine and will prove of lasting interest to the general reader. Leading historians, economists, geographers – from Ireland, Britain and the United States – have assembled the most up-to-date research from a wide spectrum of disciplines, including medicine, folklore and literature, to give the fullest account yet of the background and consequences of the Famine.

THE FRENCH ARE IN THE BAY
THE EXPEDITION TO BANTRY BAY 1796

EDITED BY JOHN A. MURPHY

Revolutionary ferment was in the air in the Ireland of the 1790s. The United Irishmen aspired to put an end to traditional sectarian antagonism, to establish a brotherhood of all Irishmen based on equality and the Rights of Man, and to 'break the connection with England'. Their inspiration was the French Revolution, 'the morning star of liberty' in Ireland, as Wolfe Tone described it.

The French, yielding to Tone's solicitations, decided to strike at Britain by invading Ireland. The fleet that set sail from Brest on 15 December 1796 was a formidable one but blizzards and gales made a landing in Bantry Bay impossible and scattered the fleet so badly that by the end of the month what was left of the great armada was limping home to France. If the French had landed in 1796, a successful nationwide rebellion might well have ensued.

The French in the Bay comprehensively examines the dramatic events of December 1796. Scholars from various disciplines, leading experts in their fields, explore the many facets of the expedition – the French strategy; the role of Wolfe Tone; the military and naval contexts in Britain and Ireland; popular beliefs and expectations; the perspective of political balladry; the Bantry dimension; the wider social and political frameworks; and, not least, the role of the weather in political destiny. After all, the Bantry Bay expedition could have changed the history of these islands, weather permitting!

EYEWITNESS TO 1798

EDITED BY TERENCE FOLLEY

In 1798, Ireland, that 'most distressful country', was the cockpit of three separate rebellions: the people's rising in Wexford, the revolt of the United Irishmen in Ulster and the invasion of the French in the west. Although influenced by American radicalism and French Jacobinism, the bloody and terrible events of that year were unique in Europe and never repeated on the same scale in Irish history. This is a collection of various eyewitness accounts of the rising, assembled for the first time. Some may be familiar to the readers, others are obscure and unknown. They give an unmatchable flavour of what it was like to live through or participate in the events of 1798. It is a history of real people, written by themselves.

THE COURSE OF IRISH HISTORY

EDITED BY T. W. MOODY AND F. X. MARTIN

Though many specialist books on Irish history have appeared in the past fifty years, there have been few general works broadly narrating and interpreting the course of Irish history as a whole, in the light of new research. That is what this book set out to do; and it is a measure of its success that it is still in demand.

The first of its kind in its field, the book provides a rapid short survey, with geographical introduction, of the whole course of Ireland's history. Based on the series of television programmes first transmitted by Radio Telefís Éireann from January to June 1966, it is designed to be both popular and authoritative, concise but comprehensive, highly selective but balanced and fair-minded, critical but constructive and sympathetic. A distinctive feature is its wealth of illustrations.

The present edition is a revised and enlarged version of the original book. New material has been added, bringing the narrative to the IRA ceasefire of 31 August 1994; the bibliography, chronology and index have been augmented accordingly.

MICHAEL COLLINS AND THE MAKING OF THE IRISH STATE

EDITED BY GABRIEL DOHERTY AND DERMOT KEOGH

Michael Collins was one of the most important leaders of his or any other age in Irish history. His contribution to the founding of the Irish state was immense even by the standards of a talented generation which included politicians of the calibre of Eamon de Valera, Arthur Griffith, Willam T. Cosgrave, Richard Mulcahy, Kevin O'Higgins, Patrick McGilligan, Harry Boland, Seán Lemass, Frank Aiken and Seán MacEntee.

Collins has generally been portrayed in writing and film as a revoloutionary man of action, a guerrilla leader, a military tactician and a figure of great personal charm, courage and ingenuity. He was in fact a man of many parts. These essays illustrate the multifaceted and complex character that was Michael Collins.

This book is a professional evaluation of Michael Collins and his contribution to the making of the Irish state. With contributions from many of the leading historians working in the field, and written in an accessible style, the essays make full use of archival material and provide new findings and insights into the life and times of Michael Collins.

The contributors examine Collins as Minister for Finance, his role in intelligence, his policy towards the north, his career as Commander-in-Chief, the origins of the Civil War, his relationship with De Valera and how academics view his place in Irish history.

The collection also includes two personal memoirs by Fr Gearóid O'Sullivan and Margot Gearty on Collins and the Kiernans of Granard, County Longford. Both shed new light on Kitty and on her remarkable sisters.